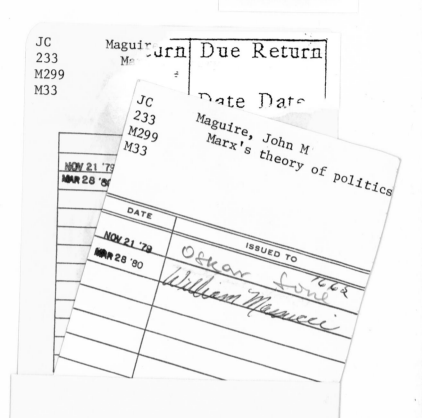

Marx's Theory of Politics

Marx's Theory of Politics

JOHN M. MAGUIRE

CAMBRIDGE UNIVERSITY PRESS

CAMBRIDGE

LONDON · NEW YORK · MELBOURNE

Published by the Syndics of the Cambridge University Press
The Pitt Building, Trumpington Street, Cambridge CB2 1RP
Bentley House, 200 Euston Road, London NW1 2DB
32 East 57th Street, New York, NY 10022, USA
296 Beaconsfield Parade, Middle Park, Melbourne 3206, Australia

First published 1978

Printed in Great Britain
at the University Press, Cambridge

Library of Congress Cataloguing in Publication Data
Maguire, John M.
Marx's theory of politics.
Bibliography: p.
Includes index.
1. Marx, Karl, 1818–1883 – Political science.
i. Title.
JC233.M299M33   320.5'32   77-90214
ISBN 0 521 21955 8

Thanks are due to Burt Franklin and Co. for permission
to include in chapter 1 part of J. M. Maguire, 'Marx,
Engels and Totalitarianism', *Reviews in European
History*, II, 4 (December 1976), 671–2; and to Reidel
Publishing Co. for permission to include in chapter 6
part of J. M. Maguire, 'Marx on Ideology, Power and
Force', *Theory and Design*, 7, 315–29.

Contents

Acknowledgements   vii

Introduction   1

1 The early theory of politics   6

2 Perspectives on revolution: Marx's position on the eve
   of 1848   28

3 Germany: revolution and counterrevolution   48

4 Reflections on the reaction in France   77

5 Problems of political action   113

6 Politics in the mature economic theory   138

7 The later political writings   171

8 Aspects of the general theory   205

   Conclusion   240

   Bibliography   243

   Index   249

for Aveen

Acknowledgements

I have made great demands on a vast number of people in preparing this book, and I have not been denied. I received help of various kinds from Brian Barry, Pierre Birnbaum, Jerry Cohen, Michael Evans, John Goldthorpe, Max Hartwell, Colin Lucas, Steven Lukes, David McLellan, Tim Mason, Zbigniew Pelczynski and Alessandro Pizzorno. I single out only three of my academic creditors. Alan Ryan, who was my supervisor during my doctoral research at Oxford, has helped more than anyone else with the content of the book. He mixes encouragement, rigorous criticism and a grasp of the point of such enterprises in a quite unique blend, and I am extremely grateful to him. Leszek Kolakowski, who replaced him for a time, gave me both insights and encouragement at a vital stage in the research. Philip Pettit has read the complete draft and helped by his comments and his enthusiasm. My wife Aveen has made it possible for me to devote the necessary time to this project over the last five years. She has provided all kinds of help, from encouragement to criticism of both style and content. Her support has been invaluable. I am grateful to University College, Dublin, for leave of absence while at Oxford, and to Nuffield College, Oxford, for electing me to a Research Fellowship during which I did the bulk of my research in highly conducive circumstances.

Department of Ethics and Politics   JOHN M. MAGUIRE
University College Dublin
Ireland
August 1977

Introduction

This is a study of how Marx treats politics. It is set in the context of his materialist theory of society and history, which has aroused such interest and controversy, but is not a study of that theory as such. This is not because I think the interest misplaced, or the controversy fruitless, but because I believe that an important contribution is to be made by looking thoroughly at how Marx operates in a specific area. Not only is politics the specific area which interested him most; it is also the one where he was most keenly aware of not having achieved a comprehensive and definitive viewpoint. Marx has of course received much attention as a social and political thinker in the broad sense, in works from which I have derived much help. I, however, have concentrated on his specific treatment of politics and, within that, on the positive rather than the normative aspects of his approach. As well as being a major part of Marx's 'unfinished business', the area which I have chosen is crucial to Marxist thought, posing the question of how political structures, and political conflict, can be integrated in an economically based theory of society and history.

It might be said that such a study cannot be conducted, for want of material and of indications of Marx's basic approach. As we shall see, there is no lack of material. As for his basic approach, I have found that it is possible to reconstruct the theory behind his empirical assertions at the various stages of his career. There are obvious dangers. The material is by no means of a uniform weight, being written in quite different circumstances for quite different reasons. A careful decision has to be made as to the emphasis to put on each work. Moreover, we must beware of foisting on Marx bits of 'theory' which he would rightly disown. On the other hand, he does claim to have interesting things to say about politics because of having a scientific theory of it. We are entitled, perhaps obliged, to probe the presuppositions, consistency and validity of what he says. I have not done this in any negative spirit, although I have frequently been critical. My belief is that Marx's achievement can be best served by trying to subject it to the rigorous criteria by which he wished to succeed.

Although no historian, I frequently discuss Marx's views in the light of what historians think of the topics in question. The most rewarding way to grapple with Marx's thought is to see him trying to make sense of the events of his time, and attempt to measure his successes and failures. I hope that there is not too much 'amateur history' for the professional historian. While I have consulted everything he wrote, in my presentation I have concentrated on those areas where he is applying some (explicit or implicit) theory. I am sure that the political scientist will want to elaborate certain lines of interpretation beyond the point where I leave them; I hope that I have indicated the right direction. This holds also for the broader question of elaborating a distinctive and solid contemporary Marxist science of politics; I hope that that enterprise will benefit from a clear statement of the content and merits of Marx's own treatment.

Chapter 1 explores some of the basic positions which Marx held in his early writings. These are informed by the unifying theme of all his treatment of politics: the correlation between capitalist industrialisation and bourgeois political power. Most of the time Marx claims quite straightforwardly in these writings that as their economic power increases, the bourgeoisie will gain increasing political sway. The chapter argues however that, although Marx ignored or was unaware of the fact, his theory even at this early stage contains intimations of the way in which, because of their conflicts with the lower orders, the bourgeoisie's political power can turn into a two-edged sword.

Chapter 2 begins with a discussion of Marx's concept of the bourgeoisie as a class, and looks at what he thought of the first French revolution. This discussion does not attempt either 'a Marxist account of the revolution' or to set out what Marx would have said had he written the work on the subject which, characteristically, remained but a project. It does however set what we can glean of his views on it against contemporary criticisms of the 'Marxist stereotype'. As well as arguing that on a number of points Marx would appear to escape their strictures, this discussion also, and chiefly, sets the scene for our investigation of the topics on which he did write in detail. The rest of the chapter looks at his expectations for the coming revolutions in France and Germany, as set out in the *Communist Manifesto*. We note that the particular alignment of forces which Marx expects – with the lower orders supporting the bourgeoisie until the latter's crucial battles are won – is but one out of a range of possibilities, others of which would prove disastrous for Marx's hopes.

Chapters 3 and 4 show that in fact the disastrous alignments prevailed. The German bourgeoisie, keenly aware of the threat posed to it by the demands of peasants and artisans, relied on the support of the old state forces and thus made possible a restoration of the authoritarian monarchy. Where the German bourgeoisie failed to win power, the French bourgeoisie failed to keep it. In their conflict with the lower orders they were con-strained so to depend on the President, Louis-Napoleon Bonaparte, that he was enabled to stage a successful coup. As well as expounding the broad lines of Marx's account, these two chapters explore the notions about revolutionary crisis and the process of its resolution which Marx is employing here.

Chapter 5 examines a topic raised by the preceding two chap-ters: how Marx explains the political actions of individuals and groups. From a careful analysis of his usage, it emerges that he does not claim that 'all motivation is economic', although he does think that in crises people will act so as to protect their economic rather than any other, conflicting interests. It is shown that by 'necessity' Marx understands not some overarching metaphysical predetermination, but rather the kind of cumulative process whereby people, who could in principle have decided otherwise, involve themselves in irreversible consequences of the decisions which they do take. The chapter also documents the shift in Marx's perspectives away from expecting that the bourgeoisie hold the key to the immediate future, to belief that the proletariat is the only class still capable of really revolutionary action.

Chapter 6 begins by showing how Marx treats politics within the conception of the economic structure of capitalism in his mature economic works. It shows how the role of force in chang-ing social structures is to be distinguished from the roles of power and ideology within social structure, and goes on to discuss Marx's approach to proletarian revolution. It discusses the kind of necessity which Marx believes holds of this revolution, and looks at the main lines of his thought on revolutionary strategy, by contrast with the strategic views of Bakunin, Lassalle and others whom he opposed.

Chapter 7 deals with how Marx treated the politics of Britain, France and Germany in the decades after the 1848 revolutions. It discusses Marx's expectation that the bourgeoisie would come to the helm politically as industry developed, and concludes that Marx's success in this claim, while not negligible, was far from total. It concludes by looking at how coherent a theory of the state Marx comes up with in his latest pronouncements, and argues that while it is profound and provocative, it is far from consistent and comprehensive.

Chapter 8 looks more directly at general theoretical issues than do the other chapters. It begins by briefly presenting the nature of Marx's materialism – both 'methodological' and 'sociological' – and the central contention of his materialist conception of history. This puts the preceding investigation in its broader context, and serves as an introduction to the discussion of Marx's general conception of the nature, emergence and abolition of politics. An account is given of Marx's attitude to early communal societies, and his depiction of their disintegration under the impact of private property. His views on the chances of survival of the Russian rural commune, and on the possibility that Russia can arrive at communism without an intervening capitalist stage, are discussed, and their significance for his general attitudes considered. The chapter goes on to discuss how Marx conceives of the relation between politics and class society. A point from chapter 1 is put in wider context here: there is in Marx, besides the relatively simple correlation between politics and class, the basis of a more complex view which situates class itself within a wider concept of the division of labour. This more complex account can better handle some of the cases which the simpler account has to regard as exceptions, although this is achieved by relaxing some of the stringency of the latter. Marx's distinction between *government* (to be found in all societies) and *politics* (the species of government peculiar to class societies) is discussed. While the distinction leaves some problems unsolved, it is a plausible one. Marx's belief that government in communist society will be nonpolitical is less naive than is often allowed, but here again there are problems about the sheer size and complexity of modern society – even without capitalism – which Marx does not satisfactorily resolve, and which raise the possibility of a survival or re-emergence of politics in some form.

The conclusion suggests that we are left, after our examination of Marx, with a number of useful 'tools' for the Marxist analysis of politics: a basic assertion about the role of the economy in society, which can be applied in the area of politics; notions about how classes will act in political struggle, about revolutionary crises and their resolution, and about the nature of political 'foundedness'; an understanding of the place of politics in the Marxist conception of social structure; the broad lines of a revolutionary strategy based on Marx's mature economic theory; an interpretation of the nature of his claims about the political structure of industrial society, and general notions about the nature of politics, the conditions of its emergence and the possibility of its abolition.

1. The early theory of politics

This chapter will examine Marx's ideas about the relation between modern society and politics, as these emerge in his writings prior to the *Communist Manifesto*. As well as establishing the main lines of his thought on this subject – and thus also the main lines of our inquiry – it will argue that there are implicit in the notions which Marx employs at this time certain tensions of which he was not fully aware but which would force themselves on him as concrete history made realities of them.

Theory of the state in embryo

A famous Irish novelist once answered the claim that the Irish people were priest-ridden with the rejoinder that the priests were people-ridden. If we take the priests as analogy for the state (an analogy never far from his mind) we find much the same paradox in Marx's treatment of the relations between state and civil society. Nowhere does this emerge more sharply than in the 1843 *Critique of Hegel's Philosophy of Right*, which swings alarmingly between the thesis that society is state-ridden (i.e. that the state tyrannises over society) and the thesis that the state is society-ridden (i.e. that it is a mere reflection of social conditions). Sometimes Marx seems to be arguing that if only society were freed from the trammels of bureaucracy, it could develop naturally along the right lines. No sooner have we decided that this is the plot, than he implies that what is really wrong is that the state, the would-be sphere of freedom and community, is bound too closely to the evil reality of civil society. Neither argument on its own can make sense of the whole work: there is here a 'built-in tension' between two views of the state–society relation.

In Hegel's theory, Marx tells us, the state is the sphere which as it were 'tops off' a fundamentally sound civil society. It is the sphere in which the struggle of individuality and competition is integrated with community. But Marx claims that Hegel's institutional provisions have

underhandedly evolved into a guarantee against the electors, against their self-confidence...In order to achieve political significance and efficacy [civil society, that is, the 'unofficial class'] must rather renounce itself as what it is, as unofficial class. Only through this does it acquire its political significance and efficacy. (*CHPR*, pp. 125, 77)

Here we see the state arrogating to itself the power of society, forcing society to undergo a 'transsubstantiation' before it will recognise it (p. 77). The summit of this arrogance is achieved by the bureaucracy, which is the state's tyranny crystallised in a specific institution. In the perfected organism of a true human community there would be no divorce between society itself and its organising power; in our imperfect world, the bureaucracy exists independently, as the 'organising power' abstracted from the rest of society. To that extent it is a mere 'formalism'. But insofar as it 'constitutes itself as a real power and becomes itself its own material content' this formalism, this mere 'illusion', becomes a very 'practical illusion', becomes the vehicle of the individual careers and power-lust of the bureaucrats: in short, their 'property' (pp. 46–7). The bureaucracy expresses the fact that the state structures, rather than serving society, achieve power over it.

Alongside this view of the state epitomised in the bureaucracy, we have the quite opposite view of it as the mere *instrument* or *servant* of civil society, reflecting, even in its most essentially *political* heart, the social conditions which it is supposed to rule:

Independent private property, or actual private property is then not only the support of the constitution but the constitution itself. And isn't the support of the constitution nothing other than the constitution of constitutions, the primary, the actual constitution?...

What then is the power of the political state over private property? Private property's own power, its essence brought to existence. What remains to the political sphere in opposition to this essence? The illusion that it determines when it is rather determined. (*CHPR*, pp. 107–8, 100)

Here we have not only the direct antithesis of the 'dominant' state but also a striking hint, for this early stage in his development, of Marx's 'economically-based' theory of politics. Despite its own delusions of grandeur, we are told, this servile state is merely the roundabout device through which private property regulates its own affairs.

We may now turn to consider some other early works subsequent to the *Critique*. Much has been made of the accuracy of Marx's alleged attribution to Hegel of the remark that history repeats itself, first as tragedy and then as farce. It should be noted that Marx attributes to Hegel only the claim that history repeats itself, and then says: 'He forgot to add: the first time as tragedy, the second as farce' (*EBLB*, p. 146). Marx is here quoting an authority weightier even than Hegel: namely himself! In a letter to Ruge in March 1843, he says of Frederick William IV of Prussia that 'The comedy of despotism in which we are being forced to act is as dangerous for him as tragedy was once for the Stuarts and the Bourbons' (*EW*, p. 200). In an article of the following year he says that it is good for the other nations 'to see the *ancien régime*, which in their countries has experienced its *tragedy*, play its *comic* role as a German phantom' (*CCHPRI*, p. 247).

The 'tragedy' for Marx, of course, was that Frederick William's 'comedy' was to have a far longer run than he expected, as we shall see in chapters 3 and 7 below. For the moment, what interests us is that these passages have more than a literary significance. They show the falsity of a tempting misconception about Marx's reaction to Louis-Napoleon Bonaparte's coup d'état in France in 1851. The misconception is that Marx, having held exclusively to the 'servile state' view, was rudely awakened by Bonaparte's coming to power, and for the first time forced to acknowledge that the modern state's role could not naively be reduced to that of serving the economically dominant class. The truth is that Marx's reflections on the 1851 coup are a return, not only in imagery but also in topic, to earlier phases of this thought. Far from seeing the Jacobins of the First French Revolution as tragic figures for the first time in 1851, in response to Bonaparte's coup, he has already analysed their tragedy in 1844–6. When he gives the name 'Bonapartism' to the new French regime he has already, in 1844, specified the nature and significance of the 'Bonapartism' of the first Napoleon.

: In his 'Draft Plan for a Work on the Modern State' of 1845 (never, characteristically, carried out), Marx refers to the 'self-conceit' of the modern state (*DP*, p. 669) [*Selbstüberhebung*

(*MEW* III, p. 537)]. By this term Marx indicates the tendency for the state to believe that it really is at the centre of things, the sun around which society revolves. He calls this a 'confusion' [*Verwechslung*] with the ancient state of Greece or Rome. He had already sketched this theme before, in his contribution to *The Holy Family*, written with Engels in September–November 1844. There he reflected on the irony that men like Robespierre and Saint-Just, in reality inaugurating a new society freed from state control, tried nevertheless 'to model the political head of the society after the fashion of the ancients' (*HF*, p. 164; see also *JQ*, p. 17).

Their pretension is to make the state, which must be the means, the servant of society, into an end in itself. Marx reflects that it is not surprising that 'the relationship is set upon its head in the minds of the political liberators' (*JQ*, pp. 231–2), if we grasp that what happens in events like the French Revolution is that political life, previously stifled and restricted, the preserve of the clique of rulers, at last emerges into its own space. 'It unleashed the political spirit which had, as it were, been dissolved, dissected and dispersed in the various cul-de-sacs of feudal society' (p. 233). The political liberators were deceived, they 'got the relation inverted', because they saw only this, the *liberating* aspect of the political revolution.

Robespierre, Saint-Just and their party fell because they confused the ancient, realistic and democratic republic based on *real* slavery with the modern spiritualist democratic representative state which is based on emancipated slavery, on bourgeois society. What a terrible irony it is to have to recognise and sanction in the Rights of Man modern bourgeois society, the society of industry, of universal competition, of private interest freely following its aims, of anarchy, of the self-alienated natural and spiritual individuality, and yet subsequently to annul the manifestations of the life of that society...[The Rights of Man] proclaimed the right of a man who cannot be the man of the ancient republic any more than his *economic* and *industrial* relations are those of the ancient times. (*HF*, pp. 164–5; translation slightly amended from *MEW* II, p. 129)

'The Jewish Question' gives us what we might call the structural basis of the tragedy of the Jacobins. The very state which they tried to erect into a real community in fact *presupposes* its own divorce and abstraction from social reality; 'far from abolishing these *factual* distinctions, the state presupposes them in order to exist, it only experiences itself as *political state* and asserts its *universality* in opposition to these elements' (*JQ*, p. 219). This is why 'the political drama necessarily ends up with the restoration of religion, private property and all the elements of civil society, just as war ends with peace' (p. 222).

As well as Frederick William IV and the Jacobins, Marx also pays attention to a third case of a state dominating, or attempting to dominate, civil society. This is the state of Napoleon I:

Napoleon was the last act in revolutionary terror's struggle against bourgeois society, which had been equally claimed by the revolution, and against its polity. Granted, Napoleon already discerned the essence of the modern state: he understood that it is based on the unhampered development of bourgeois society, on the free movement of private interest etc. He decided to recognise and protect that basis. He was no terrorist with his head in the clouds. Yet at the same time he still regarded the state as an end in itself, and civil life as a treasurer and as his subordinate which must have no will of its own. He perfected the Terror by substituting permanent war for permanent revolution. He fed the ego of French nationalism to complete satiety but demanded the sacrifice of bourgeois business, delights, wealth etc. as often as it was expedient to the political aim of conquest. If he despotically oppressed the liberalism of bourgeois society – the political idealism of its daily practice – he showed no more pity for its essential material interests, trade and industry, whenever they conflicted with his political interests. (*HF*, pp. 166–7; see also *IISH*, B17, p. 11)

Marx's attitude to these topics is very important to the question whether, at least at this stage in his career, he was a Jacobin. This has been argued most strongly and notably by Lichtheim (Lichtheim 1961, pp. 55 and 87ff; see also Levine, ch. 4). I believe that this argument is false and importantly so. Of course Marx *is* a Jacobin if by that name we mean one who is committed to the values of liberty, fraternity and equality proclaimed by the French Revolution, one who wishes to realise them in a refractory civil society. But the crucial distinction between the Jacobins and Marx is his realisation, and their inability or refusal to grasp, that within the structure of the bourgeois world this project is tragically impossible. Even in the 1843 *Critique* he says that modern political life is 'the scholasticism of popular life', an estrangement whose fullest expression is monarchy. He sees the republic as 'the negation of this estrangement *within its own sphere*' (*CHPR*, p. 32; emphasis added). This conveys his grasp that no overcoming of political estrangement can be complete while there are still two distinct spheres, one 'social' and the other 'political'. Even at this early stage, he is as critic to the tragic political drama in which the Jacobins were actors.

Having dwelt on these instances of would-be dominant states we must finally consider the argument of a recent commentator who goes so far as to claim that we find in Marx, before the collaboration with Engels, only such a theory and no mention of the state's being *servile* to social forces (See Hunt, esp. pp. 124–31). He argues from the fact that it is Engels who first clearly formulates the notion of the servile state to the false conclusion that we find in Marx, prior to the *German Ideology* of 1845–6, *only* a quite distinct and 'incompatible' theory of the state as dominant over society. Hunt makes two assertions, each of which is false. The first is that in Marx's pre-*German Ideology* writings we do not have the *generic* conception of the state as servile to social forces; the second is that we do not find there the *specific* conception of the state as servile to the bourgeoisie.

The first assertion in its turn rests on two arguments. The first of these is that where Marx *does* represent the state as a 'product' or 'reflection', it is as a product 'simply of the general egoism of civil society' (Hunt, p. 126), rather than of any social group or groups. If we look, however, at just one of Marx's *Rheinische Zeitung* articles, that on 'Debates on the Law on Thefts of Wood', written in 1842 before the *Critique*, it becomes quite clear that Marx is not very interested in 'egoism' in the individualist sense. What he attacks is the 'egoism' of particular group interests, such as the knightly, the peasant or the urban estate, which leads them to judge questions not objectively and universalistically, but in accordance with their material property-based interest, *which is shared by all the members of the estate* (see *MECW* I, e.g. pp. 138, 145, 168–70, 242). Hunt makes the second claim that where we do encounter phrases in the *Critique* suggesting that the state is a 'reflection' of private property, a careful reading shows that all that is meant is that 'the ruler and his servants own the state as their private property' (Hunt, p. 66). It is true and interesting that many of the *Critique*'s assertions are to be so interpreted, although there are other substantial assertions in it which strain Hunt's interpretation beyond breaking-point. Marx's discussion of primogeniture as Hegel's guarantee that the landed interest will participate in politics seems to me clearly to assert – whatever else it also asserts – that such arrangements give an exaggerated political weight to particular and minority property interests (see *CHPR*, e.g., pp. 98–100, 107, 109). But we do not need a lengthy interpretation of the *Critique*: the *Rheinische Zeitung* article which I have already cited clearly employs the conception of a servile state. The 'selfishness' of the forest-owning interest (*MECW* I, p. 242) demands vengeance on the poor who exercise their customary right to gather wood. This logic,

which turns the servant of the forest owner into a state authority, *turns the authority of the state into a servant of the forest owner*...All the organs of the state become ears, eyes, arms, legs, by means of which the interest of the forest owner hears, observes, appraises, protects, reaches out, and runs. (*MECW* I, p. 245)

Not only this: Marx goes on to add that the forest owner's logic would mean that he would be guaranteed large material gains while paying nothing to 'his business manager, the state' (p. 251). Hunt briefly mentions one of these passages, but dismisses the proposed inference on the grounds that the whole argument is conditional and that Marx 'was well aware that the diet had no genuine control over legislation' or over the royal despotism (p. 39). But this is anyway to admit that Marx *had* the conception of the state as servile and of how a social interest could reduce the state to such a posture, however hypothetical or anticipatory the actual argument might have been.

As regards Hunt's second major assertion, he rightly and help-fully begins by emphasising the importance of England to Engels's early experience, and how this experience led him to formulate the conception of the servile state. Hunt then tells us that Marx on the other hand wrote largely on Germany in his early years, and that one will look in vain for a 'bourgeois state' or bourgeois dominance in his *Critique*. But insofar as Marx is writing about Germany and is minimally intelligent, that is exactly what we should expect, especially from the editor of the much-persecuted *Rheinische Zeitung*. Where we would expect Marx to develop intimations of the notion of the state serving the bourgeoisie is in his studies on France, and that is just where we find them. Hunt selectively quotes Marx's argument in the *Holy Family* (quoted in full on p. 10 above) on this point. He thus presents Napoleon as 'the parasite state *par excellence*' (p. 127) rather than as reflect-ing the ambiguity between servility and dominance which Marx intends to convey. He dismisses Marx's arguments as relating to 'specific moments in French history' – *some moments!* The point is more than a matter of record. Marx on the state is quite complicated enough without raising false discontinuities. The absence of servility *to the bourgeoisie* in Marx's writings on Germany leads Hunt falsely to conclude to a total absence of any conception of servility. This would make the tensions of the Marxian conception of the state a product of the collaboration with Engels, whereas they lie much deeper in Marx's own theory, whatever emphasis Engels added to them.

A note on terminology

In our discussion so far, we have encountered states with three different relations to modern society. To be more precise, we could say that the state has three possible relations to the class which is socially dominant in modern society, namely the bourgeoisie. In the first place, it can be *servile*, in that it serves the bourgeoisie's interests. In the second place it can be *dominant*, in that it imposes its will on society (including the bourgeoisie). In the third place, in a situation where it cannot in fact be dominant, because of the power held by the bourgeoisie, it can nevertheless refuse to be meekly servile, and try to be dominant: in that case, it is *pretentious*.

It might be objected that this terminology does no more than redescribe what commentators have been aware of for a long time: the variety of state postures contained in Marx's works. But it does more than that, in that it assigns stable and fixed terms, which we can use to analyse and interpret the variety. In themselves they are not a theory, but they allow us to put Marx's theory into a clear form, and moreover to show up the tensions in that theory and to chart its development. It might also be objected that they are my terms, and do not reflect Marx's usage. This is not quite the case, since there are instances of Marx's using such terminology himself.[1] But the terminology is indeed explicitly and avowedly *interpretative*: it is designed to enable us to understand and analyse Marx's thinking, rather than just to record it. The

[1] For 'servile' and its cognates see, e.g., *IIQ*, p. 154, *R1848*, p. 179 (*MEW* VI, p. 8), *EBLB*, p. 187 (*MEW* VIII, p. 151), *CWF Drafts*, p. 151; see also p. 75 below. For 'pretentious' and its cognates, see *G*, p. 884 (*Grundrisse*, p. 844), *CSF*, p. 139 (*MEW* VII, pp. 104–5), *CWF Drafts*, pp. 148–50.

usefulness of the terms in question will emerge in the course of our study.

The structure of bourgeois society

Our topic in this study is Marx's theory of politics, as he applies it to society; it is not his social theory as such. But we cannot grasp the significance of the theory of politics if we do not understand its social context, at least in broad outline. In this section I want to give some features of that context, the discussion of which will be more fully resumed in chapter 6. The later discussion will be based almost entirely on *Capital*; the present discussion is based almost entirely on the *German Ideology*, which is the '*Capital*' of the early writings.

The relationship of modern society to its politics is a peculiar one. We have already seen that the Jacobins could grasp only the politically positive side of this relation, namely the *liberation of politics* from previous restrictions. They could not grasp that at the same time there occurred a *liberation of civil society* from political restrictions.

But the perfection of the idealism of the state was at the same time the perfection of the materialism of civil society . . . Political emancipation was at the same time the emancipation of civil society from politics, from even the *appearance* of a universal content. (*JQ*, p. 233)

Marx tells us that the very term 'civil society' properly emerged only in the eighteenth century, 'when property relations had already extricated themselves from the ancient and medieval communal society' (*GI*, p. 49). This image of modern property *extricating* itself is of the essence. It is central to Marx's analysis of modern economic conditions that they could not have developed to their own finality within the human (albeit an exploitative human) scale imposed by feudalism. If the productive capacity of capitalism is to be realised, then men must serve as means to this end. Their fate must become accidental, what happens to which individual being an unplanned *resultant* of the market. Edward Heimann neatly pinpoints the peculiarity of this state of affairs:

The situation prevailing in such an economic system is most paradoxical. For a free economy is, after all, an economy, and as such, according to our definition, it presupposes the establishment of a hierarchy of needs

and of a method for the proportional allocation of means to their satis-
faction. Yet all this is accomplished without a central authority in charge
of operations!. . . economics is confronted with the problem of explaining
this paradox and of opposing to the time-honored notion of order through
authority the conception of order through liberty. This has been the
problem and the program of economics ever since the days of Quesnay
and Adam Smith, its founders. (Heimann, pp. 9–10)

It is, of course, the 'problem and program' of Marx also. He does
not reject the account which Adam Smith gives of the matter, in
which individual strivings interact with one another to achieve a
social pattern of consumption and production. But what in Adam
Smith is described as the 'invisible hand', and becomes in Hegel
the 'cunning of reason' which achieves men's ends unbeknownst
to them, Marx puts in critical historical perspective by calling it
a system of *alienated human activity*. Our aim here is to understand briefly what Marx means by this claim, and particularly
what it means for his concept of social class.

Marx's account, surprisingly to those who read his critics rather
than his texts, is a profoundly *individualist* one. He begins by
stating his basic position:

The premises from which we begin are not arbitrary ones, not dogmas,
but real premises from which abstraction can only be made in the
imagination. They are the real individuals, their activity and the material
conditions under which they live, both those which they find already
existing and those produced by their activity. (*GI*, p. 31)

So much does Marx insist on making sense of social processes
in terms of actual men's activity that he rejects any account of
society as having 'its laws apart, which have nothing to do with
the persons of which society is composed, and its "own intelligence", which is not the intelligence of common men' (*PP*, p.
91). In this rejection, indeed, Marx lets himself go farther than he
normally is, or ought to be, prepared to go. His system does allow
in a sense of an 'intelligence' not that of common men, namely
the economic coherence which establishes itself over against men
in pre-communist society. The passage however is of importance
because it shows us Marx's very deep commitment, while talking
of alienation, to showing its roots in real human activity rather
than in any transcendent and inexplicable forces. He strikes a
better balance of these two objectives when he tells us that while
'individuals have always built on themselves', they have had to
build on themselves as they actually are, 'on themselves within

their given historical conditions and relationships, not on the "pure" individual in the sense of the ideologists' (*GI*, pp. 94–5). The modern social system, for example, is certainly the product of men's action rather than of some mysterious superhuman force; but, given that men are not in a position to choose their situation or even the kinds of men they shall be, there is no guarantee that the results of their actions will not crystallise into conditions dominating them. 'The social history of men is never anything but the history of their individual development, whether they are conscious of it or not' (Marx to Annenkov, in *PP*, p. 181). Quite so; however, when they are not conscious of it, that is not because of some oversight on their part, but because we have not reached the stage in history – communist society – where men are in a position clearsightedly to determine the course of their social interaction. Even when men are not in this situation, it still remains true that the social conditions under which they act continue to have validity as social conditions only because men continue to accept them as such and, in so accepting them, to reproduce them as conditions for a further cycle of action. 'The conditions under which individuals have intercourse with each other...are thus the conditions of their self-activity and are produced by this self-activity' (*GI*, p. 89; see also pp. 83–4).

The central feature of these conditions in pre-communist systems is the emergence of a *class structure*. There are many complexities and nuances, not to say unclarities, in Marx's concept of class; these will emerge where relevant in their proper places throughout our study. For the moment we are considering its broadest features and its place in Marx's social theory. Nowhere, paradoxically, does his individualism emerge more clearly than here. He goes to some lengths to emphasise that the real concrete experience of a given individual cannot simply be regarded as identical with the conditions of his or her class:

It follows from all we have been saying up till now that the communal relationship into which the individuals of a class entered...was always a community to which those individuals belonged only as average individuals, only in so far as they lived within the conditions of existence of their class – a relationship in which they participated not as individuals but as members of a class. (*GI*, p. 93; see also *PP*, p. 100)

Marx upbraids Stirner for arguing 'that "well-being" *as rentier* is inherent in the individuals who are at present rentiers, that it is inseparable from their individuality' (*GI*, pp. 238–9; see also p. 95). He later meets the anticipated charge from the bourgeoisie that communists wish to abolish individuality by saying that 'by "individual" you mean no other person than the bourgeois, than the middle-class owner of property' (*CM*, p. 82).

Not only does Marx present class relations in this way as merely alienated individual activity; he also argues that they emerged historically from interregnum periods in which individual activity achieved a temporary, transitional freedom from class conditions. He gives an historical instance in his account of the flight of the serfs from the feudal countryside, when the mere 'anarchy' of individual biographies was replaced by structure as a result of certain individuals' having acquired economic resources without which others could not work. 'The gradually accumulated small capital of individual craftsmen and their stable numbers, as against the growing population, evolved the relation of journeyman and apprentice, which brought into being in the towns a hierarchy similar to that in the country.' (*GI*, p. 36) The existence of such accounts (for further material see pp. 147–49 below) and their incorporation in general terms into the theory are very important, since they help us answer the very difficult question of how 'real' classes are. This concerns the dispute between 'realist' and 'nominalist' accounts. On the realist account, when we speak of a class as acting, reacting, dying, reviving and so forth we are speaking of a real entity which need not be translated or 'reduced' into stories about particular individuals. On the nominalist account, 'class X' is merely a *name*, merely a word, which unites for a particular analytical purpose a group of individuals, who are the sole reality. Marx's polemic against Stirner is instructive here. Whilst Stirner's extreme 'egoism' leads Marx to put his stylistic emphasis on the *terminus ad quem*, his argument makes it clear that in his view the *terminus a quo* of the emergence of classes is an interregnum of unstructured, individual activity: 'personal relationships necessarily and inevitably develop into class relationships and become fixed as such' (*GI*, pp. 492–3). Even if we returned to the interregnum we could not undo the necessity of the emerging structure:

competition certainly begins as a 'competition of persons' possessing 'personal means'. The liberation of the feudal serfs, the first condition of competition, and the first accumulation of 'things' were purely 'personal acts'. If, therefore, [Stirner] wished to put the competition of persons in the place of competition of things, it means that he wishes to return to the beginning of competition, imagining in doing so that by his good will and extraordinary egoistical consciousness he can give a different direction to the development of competition. (*GI*, p. 420)

So Marx agrees with the 'nominalist' account in denying the ultimate reality of classes: both 'structurally' and 'chronologic-ally' he claims that they are alienations of individual activity. But he agrees with the 'realist' account in the very important sense that, once an interregnum is over, individuals are born into already-crystallised class relationships, so that it is actually necessary to speak of the class as being prior to the actions of the individuals composing it:

> the class in its turn achieves an independent existence over against the individuals, so that the latter find their conditions of existence predes-tined, and hence have their position in life and their personal development assigned to them by their class, become subsumed under it. (*GI*, pp. 69–70)

We may thus characterise Marx's conception of class as an 'emergent realist' one, where classes are shown both theoretically and historically to have no more ultimate reality than that of an alienation of human activity, but are very real in their effects on their members in all pre-communist societies. We now turn to a closer consideration of Marx's ideas on the role of politics in the particular class system of bourgeois society.

'The modern state' – a complex concept

Having seen some main features of the bourgeois social order, we may commence this section by looking at Marx's reasons for his claim that the normal posture of the state in this social order will be one of servility to the bourgeoisie. The bourgeoisie are dominant within their mode of production, and, as this mode of production becomes dominant within society, they can establish control over the political order and even mould it to their liking. In short, they buy out the state and take it over. As early as 1844, Marx claimed that the 'games played with state loans show to what extent it has become a toy in the hands of businessmen, etc'(*NM*, p. 265). This theme frequently recurs in the following few years. As the bourgeoisie come to control the wealth previously controlled by nobles, 'the state has to beg from the bourgeoisie and is finally bought up by the latter' (*GI*, p. 404).

To this modern property corresponds the modern state, which, purchased gradually by the owners of property by means of taxation, has fallen entirely into their hands through the national debt, and its existence has become wholly dependent on the commercial credit which the owners of property, the bourgeois, extend to it, as reflected in the rise and fall of state funds on the stock exchange. (*GI*, p. 79)

Marx notes that as early as the eighteenth century, the French government was able to raise a loan from Dutch merchants only on condition that 'a private individual should stand security for the state' (*GI*, p. 401). It was this power of bourgeois money which ended the pretensions of the first Napoleon, when the Paris exchange-brokers, by delaying funds for the Russian campaign, forced Napoleon to start it dangerously close to the winter.

Just as the liberal bourgeoisie was opposed once more by revolutionary terror in the person of Napoleon, so it was opposed once more by counterrevolution in the person of the Bourbons. Finally, in 1830 the bourgeoisie put into effect the wish it had had since 1789, with the only difference that its political enlightenment was now accomplished and that it no longer considered the constitutional representative state the ideal of the state and no longer intended to fight for the salvation of the world and for universal human aims but, on the contrary, considered it as the official expression of its own *exclusive* power and the *political* recognition of its own particular interests. (*HF*, p. 167)

The upshot of all this argument is Marx's famous claim that 'the executive of the modern state is but a committee for managing the common affairs of the whole bourgeoisie' (*CM*, p. 69). This sentence sums up the claim about modern politics which we shall be examining throughout this study, and we shall explore its precise meaning at various points in the process. For the moment we are interested in how it summarises what we might call Marx's early 'ideal picture' of bourgeois rule. This is a situation where everyone – that is, in our model so far, bourgeois and proletarians – accepts the legitimacy of the bourgeois relations of production and the roles which these impose. In this situation the state can be seen by everyone as a pure instrumentality which serves the 'common good', by settling questions which have to be settled at a general social level, and by preserving the conditions for the market mechanism to reconcile individual and social benefit. In operating this way the state is in fact maintaining and servicing the bourgeois social order, and is thus really serving the bourgeoisie; but since everyone regards that order as natural and proper, and thus accepts their place within it, everyone can see the state, in working this way, as 'representing' them, that is, as acting on their behalf.

An essential feature of Marx's thinking, even in his earlier writings, which emerges in this ideal picture is his tendency to downgrade and even at times dismiss politics. While dedicated to surpassing bourgeois society, he has a keen appreciation of its rationality and its self-regulating powers; so much so, indeed, that he often dismisses the appeals to 'ideas' made by romantic, utopian and other enemies of the bourgeoisie. A number of times he stresses that men in modern civil society are held together by their relations in civil society, and not by religious or political 'nonsense' (see *GI*, p. 41 and *HF*, p. 163). This tendency in Marx raises an interesting question for us. There has been much controversy, polemical and scholarly, over the validity of Marx's belief that the state could 'wither away' after the workers' revolution, that it could be transformed into simply the way in which the whole society settled its own business (see pp. 229ff. below). But a more relevant question, since there was no successful workers' revolution in his lifetime, is why politics did not wither away after the *bourgeois* revolution. If bourgeois civil society is as self-regulating as Marx claims, why did it need the superadding of politics at all? In the answer to this question lie buried the central tensions of Marx's theory of politics and the state.

To begin with, nothing gives the lie to the notion that politics is dead in bourgeois society more surely than does Marx's own activity. His whole effort was directed towards making the workers aware that the conditions of bourgeois property were neither natural nor legitimate, and that they could be overturned. In so acting he may have been the foremost, but he certainly was not alone, and he symbolised the fact, of which the bourgeoisie could not remain long unaware, that their order of things was open to radical questioning. There is a passage in the *German Ideology* which casts a more dubious light on the ideal picture of untroubled bourgeois rule which we have just considered. Having given an account of the way in which men's actions establish alien forces over against them, which crystallise into an order of things that men have made but not chosen, Marx continues:

out of this very contradiction between the interest of the individual and that of the community, the latter takes on an independent form as the *State*, divorced from the real interests of individual and community, and at the same time as an illusory communal life, always based however, on the real ties existing in every family and tribal conglomeration... and especially, as we shall enlarge upon later, on the classes, already determined by the division of labour, which in every such mass of men separate out, and of which one dominates all the others. (*GI*, p. 45)

Marx does not believe that the bourgeois social order which this state serves is unreal; it is very much a reality, and is even a real general interest of people *seen within their roles in bourgeois society*. But from the point of view of the genuine community of communist society, it is a merely *illusory* communal interest. The modern state, when it 'represents' everybody in this society, is in fact representing the workers only in an illusory manner – representing, as it were, their ideological misconception of themselves. It represents the bourgeoisie in a real sense, in that representation at the political level is the safeguard of their interests at the economic one. This ambiguity of political representation leads Marx to revise his claims that political values and institutions are *merely* illusory by saying that: 'In the previous [i.e., precommunist] substitutes for the community, in the state, etc., personal freedom has existed only for the individuals who developed within the relationships of the ruling class, and only insofar as they were individuals of this class' (*GI*, p. 93).

It thus emerges that even in the 'ideal picture' which we drew above, bourgeois civil society is self-maintaining only while people's conception of their real position is distorted by the ideology with which the state complements it. If conditions in civil society were seen in the raw for any length of time by a large number of workers, they would reject and destroy it, or at least try to do so. It is only when they have a sphere in which they see themselves as equal, free and fraternal along with their 'fellow-citizens', the bosses, that they can make an acceptable totality of their experience, and see any unacceptable features of daily life in the 'right' perspective. Thus even the 'apolitical' functioning of 'self-maintaining' civil society requires the aid of politics, in what we might call its 'suppressed ideological' function. But if the 'general interest' of bourgeois society cannot be upheld in this manner, if the workers begin to reject the ideology and contest the society, then the state is needed in a much more direct manner:

> Bourgeois society, which is based on competition, and its bourgeois state, owing to their whole material basis, cannot permit any struggle among the citizens except the struggle of competition, and are bound to intervene not as 'spirit' but with bayonets if people 'seize each other by the throat'. (*GI*, p. 403)

Thus if the suppressed *ideological* function of the state is rejected, it has to fall back on a (previously suspended) *repressive* one. This reliance on politics does not of course falsify Marx's claim that the bourgeoisie will dominate society. Nor does the reliance on *repressive* politics falsify his claim that politics will be a servile instrument of the bourgeoisie. But the situation contains dangers for them.

The move to repression means that the bourgeoisie are allowing the state to operate without the checks enforced on it by representative institutions. It might be retorted that the bourgeoisie are now in a stronger position, because they have dropped the pretence of a real representation of everybody. They are however encouraging the state to operate in an authoritarian, even despotic, manner, while on the other hand the increasingly clear class nature of their rule is fuelling the original hostility of the workers. They are relying on the state to discriminate between those whom it is to *repress*, and those whom it is to continue to *represent repressively*. The conceptually neat distinction involved here is less apparent to a state which, previously accustomed to '*representing*' everybody, has now to stop short of *repressing* everybody. It might again be retorted that in this situation the bourgeoisie are really repressing the workers directly themselves, and will not be repressed by *their own* state personnel. However, the situation is encouraging to any pretensions harboured by established politicians, and there is the even more serious danger of a coup. If the working class are not strong enough to win the struggle with the state, there is an ideal opening for an adventurist pretender who can combine the attractions of politically defeating the hated bourgeoisie with a specious appeal to the ideology fostered and then abandoned by them. There is thus a danger of a pretentious state which can emerge from the servile state's role.

As well as the suppressed ideological and the suspended

coercive roles of the modern bourgeois state, there is a third one which is perhaps less important, but which needs mention. Even if they were the only human inhabitants of a world of profit-producing machines, the bourgeoisie would need a state in order to regulate their own affairs. Just because it is 'a *class* and no longer an *estate*, the bourgeoisie is forced to organise itself no longer locally, but nationally, and to give a general form to its mean average interest' (*GI*, p. 79). The reason is that the bourgeois way of life is an essentially *competitive* one, where people's success is neither fore-ordained nor quite outside their control, and there is thus the constant temptation to go a bit farther than the rules allow:

The attitude of the bourgeois to the institutions of his regime is like that of the Jew to the law; he evades them insofar as it is practicable to do so in each individual case, but he wants everyone else to observe them. (*GI*, p. 195)

This fact that bourgeois conditions are themselves a relatively unplanned resultant, rather than conditions which individuals unreservedly accept as exactly what they wish, means that the state has to enforce *his own class conditions* on the reluctant bourgeois. Marx graphically captures the state's 'ruling-class cohesion' function – as well as its suspended repressive one – some years later, when he describes the state as 'no more than a reciprocal assurance of the bourgeoisie against its individual members and against the exploited class' (*MEW* VII, p. 288). He quite rightly rejects the inference from this power of the bourgeois state over the individual bourgeois to the conclusion that that state has power over the bourgeois *class*: 'The fact that the ruling class constitutes its joint domination as public power, as the state, [Stirner] interprets and distorts...as meaning that the "state" is constituted as a third force against this ruling class and absorbs all power in relation to it' (*GI*, p. 397). But given the other circumstances outlined already, the fact that the state is already accustomed, in its most servile posture, to repressing individual members of the bourgeois class can aid the shift from servility to pretension.

Two 'overviews' on the state

We have isolated three terms as sets of 'intellectual pincers' to grasp the variety of Marx's thinking on the state. We can speak in terms of them of the 'servile', 'dominant' and 'pretentious' postures of the state. I have said that these terms in themselves do not constitute a theory, but that they can clarify the theory which Marx proposes. The theory will put forward some argument as to the relations between these three postures. I shall refer to the posited relation between postures as an 'overview' on their relation to one another. This term is necessary because we shall have to encounter not one but in fact two 'overviews' on the role of the state. One is the overview which will be familiar to anyone with even slight knowledge of Marxism. It is what I call the '*chronological succession*' overview. It asserts that the normal posture of the state in modern society is one of servility to the bourgeoisie. It allows that there can be a pretentious, even perhaps a dominant, state in certain historical conjunctures, but only in the 'interregnum' between established social formations, where the bourgeoisie is not yet firmly established as the dominant force in society. It claims that as the bourgeoisie becomes socially established, a dominant state will be rendered impossible and any pretensions thereto will receive short shrift. We shall examine the succession overview in some detail in this section; it is the overview which Marx explicitly held, and asserted in his writings. But if we reflect on what we have encountered in the previous section, we will see that, although Marx is unaware or chooses to appear unaware of it, there is a second overview which can be inferred from his overall theory. This is the overview which asserts that the possibility of a pretentious state is contained in the state's servile posture even within the bourgeois social formation: I call it the '*structural contradiction*' overview, to indicate the tension between the two postures in it.

The succession overview is already implicit in the argument about the first Napoleon which we have quoted, and it is put in more general terms in an article which Marx wrote against the views of Karl Heinzen, an anti-communist republican, in October 1847. Heinzen says that the unjust social conditions of which socialists complain are maintained by the traditional rule of the princes, who are thus the real enemy. Marx draws on the distinction, which we have already discussed, between economic and political power, to argue that this state of affairs is but transitional:

The economists call capital, for example, 'the command over other labour'. We are thus confronted with two kinds of power. On the one hand, the power of property, that is, of the property-owner; on the other hand, the political power, the state power. 'Force also dominates property' means that property has not yet got the political power in its hands, but is rather vexed by it, for example, by arbitrary taxes, by confiscation, by privileges, by the disturbing interference of the bureaucracy in industry and trade and the like. In other words: the bourgeoisie is not yet politically constituted as a class. The state power is not yet its own power. In countries where the bourgeoisie has already conquered political power, and where political rule is nothing less than the rule, not of the individual bourgeois over the workers, but of the bourgeois class over the whole of society, Mr. Heinzen's dictum has lost its meaning. (*MCCM*, pp. 134–5; amended translation from *MEW* IV, p. 337)

Marx goes on to make a point which occurs not only in this article, but quite frequently in other pre-1848 works (see, e.g., *JQ*, p. 239 and *HF*, p. 153). This is the argument that civil society makes the state, rather than *vice versa*. When Heinzen speaks of politics dominating society, he means

the princes on top of the social structure in Germany. He does not doubt for a moment that they have made and are daily renewing their social foundation...[His common sense refuses to see] that the apple did not make the apple tree. (pp. 147–8)

This analogy is a little too crude for the precise theoretical point which Marx wants to make. The central issue is that politics has a derivative rather than a fundamental status in society; in other words, people remain in political power because they have a certain relation to the social, i.e., economic, structure. Marx thus argues that the 'powerful reactionary role' of the princes which so impresses Heinzen 'only proves that in the pores of the old society a new society has evolved, which feels the political husk – the appropriate covering of the old society – to be an unnatural fetter which it must burst' (p. 151). This argument does not depend on the kind of temporal priority which the apple tree has over the apple. For example, as we shall see in the case of conquest in chapter 8 (pp. 207–10 below), the centrality of the need for regular reproduction does not mean that social and political conditions inimical to the needs of production cannot survive for a period before succumbing, or even that it is impossible that someone should attempt *de novo* to impose such conditions. Social structure emerges not because forces of production necessarily change first followed by everything else; rather, what decides whether any new or old institution will endure and become a solid part of the structure will be its suitability to promoting production. The order in question is basically one of functional importance, not of chonological sequence.

Given this derivative status of politics, the *succession* overview follows naturally. Any independence of politics from the economy will be a feature merely of the interregnum, of a situation where no new dominant class has succeeded one whose power is smashed or on the wane:

> The independence of the state is only found nowadays in those countries where the estates have not yet completely developed into classes, where the estates, done away with in more advanced countries, still have a part to play, and where there exists a mixture; countries, that is to say, in which no section of the population can achieve domination over the others. This is the case particularly in Germany. (*GI*, p. 79)

While the succession overview attributes any instances of state pretensions to delayed succession, the contradiction one argues, as we have argued in the preceding section, that even after the bourgeoisie have established themselves as the political rulers of bourgeois society, the possibility of a pretentious state's emergence is inherent in the state's functions of serving the bourgeoisie. The crucial passage about the state as representative of the illusory communal interest in modern society, which we have already analysed, is preceded directly by one of Marx's most graphic images of alienation:

> This fixation of social activity, this consolidation of what we ourselves produce into an objective power above us, growing out of our control, thwarting our expectations, bringing to nought our calculations, is one of the chief factors in historical development up till now. (*GI*, p. 45)

What the *contradiction* overview asserts is that the bourgeoisie themselves are victims of this system of alienated forces. Marx makes this point in the *Holy Family*, where he says that both proletariat and bourgeoisie represent human self-alienation, although the bourgeoisie represent its positive and not its negative face (*HF*, p. 51). This clearly means, not that the bourgeoisie occasionally feel unhappy or culturally deprived, but that they as well as the workers participate in a structure which they maintain by their activity but over which neither they nor anyone else have untroubled control. For that very reason their political domination of the society called after them cannot be taken for granted. In calling this the 'contradiction' overview I have in mind the Hegelian notion, where a contradiction is revealed in reality as an instability between two states of affairs each of which implies the other and neither of which can establish itself definitively.

Conclusion

In this chapter, we have looked at various features of Marx's early theory of politics. We have looked at the tensions in his very early writings, between what we have called chiefly the 'servile' and the 'pretentious' postures of the state. We have examined the structure of modern, that is bourgeois society, in Marx's theory of it, and stressed the fact that it is a structure made but not controlled by men – a system of alienation. We have seen the argument by which Marx claims that the state in this system will normally serve the interests of the bourgeoisie. We have argued that there is one account which, while denying that a pretentious state is a standing, 'structural' possibility in modern society, allows that a pretentious state might hold on to power for a time before the bourgeoisie first conquer it. We have however also argued that there are possibilities of the emergence of a pretentious state even in an established bourgeois polity (the contradiction overview of the state's postures). It must be stressed that both the 'pretentious state' and the 'contradiction overview' are possibilities which I have diagnosed as lurking within Marx's account of the matter. They are implied in what he says, but most of the time he is unaware of these implications, or at least ignores them. The two overviews differ, in that the contradiction one is based on the very *concept* of the modern state, while the succession one refers more to the historical conditions for its emergence. We now turn to consider the latter.

2. Perspectives on revolution: Marx's position on the eve of 1848

Introduction

The purpose of this chapter is to reproduce the theoretical perspectives with which Marx entered actively into the 'year of revolutions' in his native Germany. It begins by analysing his notion of who the bourgeoisie are, and how they rose to power in the French Revolution. It concludes by examining the details of his perspectives for bourgeois revolution in Germany, and shows some potential weaknesses and tensions in those perspectives. A similar point is made for the different case of France, where the bourgeoisie are already in political power.

Origins and rise of the Bourgeoisie

Our topic, as has already emerged, is not Marx's 'sociology' as such, although this is the context for his theory of politics. While we have already examined some of what we might call the 'formal properties' of his concept of class (see Giddens 1973, pp. 100–6), we must complement this discussion by a brief account of what he understood by the specific class-name 'bourgeoisie', and how he understood their rise to power. It will emerge in our study that the crucial claims of his which were to be tested in his lifetime are those about the nature and activity of that class. As in the previous chapter, we proceed mainly from the chief work of 'social theory' in the early period, the *German Ideology* (see especially *GI*, pp. 65–78).

The best way of identifying the bourgeoisie in Marx's theory is as the 'descendants' of the burghers, the *Bürgertum* or *Bürgerstand* of the medieval and renaissance periods. These, as their name implies, were town-dwellers. But not all town-dwellers were burghers; a burgher was at least a man of some standing in town, so that journeymen and the rabble of day-labourers would not qualify. But, crucially, not even every man of standing was a 'burgher' in the central sense. This is because Marx uses the term precisely to designate the new kind of economic agent who posed a threat to the guilds, the 'feudal organisation of trades' (*GI*, p. 35). The vanguard of this emergent group is the *merchant*, enabled by slowly improving communications to establish trade between his and other towns in goods still being produced under unchanged guild conditions. Their activities set up a 'reciprocal action between production and commerce' (*GI*, p. 68). Not all merchants were for long content simply to circulate what others produced, and they sought ways of controlling production themselves. Where they could not defeat the guild structures in the towns, they sought out lines which could be produced outside their technological and institutional restrictions. 'Weaving was, therefore, carried on mostly in villages and market-centres without guild organisation, which gradually became towns, and indeed the most flourishing towns in each land' (*GI*, p. 71). The name 'burgher' stands for the merchants and merchant-manufacturers who were dominant in these new towns, and whose activities in the old towns were increasingly corroding the guilds. Marx tells us that, over a long period and because of their increasing communication of a common interest, these isolated 'burgher corporations' evolved into a 'burgher class' (*GI*, p. 69). ['*Bürgerschaften...Bürger-klasse*' (*MEW* III, p. 53).] These were the rich and influential merchants, increasingly involved in the actual production of the commodities in which they traded. The discovery of new trade routes gave a great impetus to manufacture along the new lines, that is by propertyless workers under a capitalist rather than by journeymen under a master. It is important to note that among the 'big bourgeoisie' (*GI*, p. 73) ['*grosse Bourgeoisie*' (*MEW* III, p. 57)] produced by trade and manufacture, we have a division between the merchant – whether manufacturer as well or not – and the manufacturer who was not a merchant. Marx tells us that during the great era of trade and navigation, stretching from the middle of the seventeenth almost to the end of the eighteenth century, 'the manufacturers...all the time were inferior in political importance to the merchants' (*GI*, p. 75).

To determine the historical validity of this account would carry us far beyond our topic, to an historical inquiry into feudal society and what Marx said about its passing. But we may fill out our picture of the bourgeoisie, and thus equip ourselves for the later analysis, by noting a number of respects in which the account is innocent of that unclarity of social definition which is often alleged against Marx.

In the first place, we have the question of the *non-economic bourgeoisie*. These are lawyers, '*officiers*', and other professional people who are not nobles but equally are not involved in trade and manufacture. Two problems arise: how, given the centrality of trade and manufacture to the notion of the bourgeoisie, we can apply the term to such people; and, assuming that we can do so, how we establish their solidarity of interest and action with the economic bourgeoisie. Here we see the importance of Marx's tracing the historical development of the bourgeoisie from their location in the new towns, and those sectors of the old towns, which were in tension with the feudal economy. The lawyers, professors, civil servants and others making up the non-economic bourgeoisie were the non-economic groups who developed in these expanding commercial enclaves. Their life-experience was of this milieu, their intellectual and political struggle was with the restrictions which it met. Once more I stress that I am not assessing the historical accuracy of Marx's account. What I am concerned to point out here is that Marx's notion of a non-economic bourgeoisie as the political and intellectual 'wing' of the rising burghers is reconcilable with the centrality of economic activity to the definition of the bourgeois class.

Another important point concerns the divisions within the economic bourgeoisie itself. It is tempting to read Marx as defining the bourgeoisie in terms of modern (i.e. nineteenth-century) capitalist industry, so that the 'real bourgeois' is the capitalist running a large factory; other groups such as financiers, ranching landowners and so on would then be located as more or less 'bourgeois' or related to the 'real bourgeoisie'. This temptation is fuelled by the *Communist Manifesto* itself, largely because it is one of that work's chief intentions to depict the bourgeoisie as succumbing to the march of a modern industry which they *necessarily* promote. From the preceding account it emerges, however, that it is at least as faithful to Marx's theory to see the connection of modern industry with the bourgeoisie as a contingent (though also fundamental) one, rather than as a definitional truth. In fairness to the *Manifesto*, even there we find that there is an evolution from an initial situation of manufacture to the later one of modern machine industry; this evolution is a major theme in *Capital* (see *CM*, p.

69, and *Capital* 1, chs 14 and 15). In the same way as the *Manifesto* and *Capital* see 'industry' evolving from manufacture to machine industry, we may also see the whole economic bourgeoisie as evolving from a pre-industrial to an industrial complexion. Thus, within Marx's conception of the economic bourgeoisie, we may distinguish an early phase when the majority, and certainly the most influential, of its members are in commerce, banking and such occupations, from a period when industry is central. Moreover, even within the latter period, we can allow of the existence, and sometimes the crucial importance, of the financial and commercial bourgeoisie. We shall see later that Marx sometimes includes large landowners within the 'bourgeoisie' (see p. 174 below).

The first French Revolution

When we turn to the rise of the bourgeoisie to political power, it is difficult to escape the all-pervading influence of the French Revolution of 1789 on Marx's thinking. This will emerge clearly in subsequent chapters. The narrowmindedness and lack of élan of the German bourgeoisie is compared with the famous night of 4 August 1789; Bonaparte's coup d'état of 1851 is treated as the farcical re-enactment of the coup of his more illustrious uncle; at every step we find contemporary events compared, often sharply contrasted, with relevant stages of the historical process of 1789–1815. Marx's early notebooks show evidence of keen interest, and much reading, in this area (see *IISH*, Series B 14–18). At one point, Marx planned to write a history of the Convention (see McLellan 1973, p. 105). The brief *Draft Plan* of 1845, already referred to on p. 8 above, begins with a section entitled 'Genetic History of the Modern State *or* The French Revolution' (*DP*, p. 669). Surprisingly, none of these projects came to fruition, and Marx never wrote a work on the French Revolution. Speculation as to why is as difficult here as with any other of his many unfulfilled projects. It may however be relevant that, while always fascinated by history, especially European history, he almost always confined himself in what he actually wrote to the elaboration and contemporary application of his theories, using history at most for illustration. In this he differs from Engels, who produced far more strictly 'historical' work. We are at a considerable loss in the absence of what would have been at worst a provocative masterpiece, since nothing is more controversial than the 'Marxist' version of the French Revolution! The controversy has raged over a stereotype which is generally agreed to date from Jaurès in the early years of this century, although as we shall see, Marx bears some responsibility for it. We cannot ignore the Revolution, since it so influences Marx's actual writings, and sets the scene for many of the events which we must discuss. Equally, however, it is dangerous to work out what Marx *might* have or *ought to* have said, and measure that against the criticisms of historians; it is, in any case, an equation with too many unknowns. The following brief discussion will look at what appear to be the reasonable criticisms by contemporary historians of the 'Marxist' stereotype, and then see to what extent Marx would appear to differ from that stereotype in the references which we do find in his works. I must stress that this should not and will not be a 'reconstruction' of the work which Marx did not write; it will, however, introduce some of the main themes of our inquiry.

Marx's responsibility for the later emergence of the 'Marxist' stereotype arises mainly from the *Manifesto*. As we shall see in chapter 8, it is both possible and necessary to distinguish between Marx's notion of how a social formation hangs together when formed and his notion of how it historically comes together in the first place (see pp. 205–10 below). Not only does Marx not draw this distinction in the *Manifesto*, however: he even talks as though he himself had confused a structural model with the movement of history. We get an image of all the elements of the bourgeois social formation appearing suddenly together at a point, and cruising serenely forward:

At a certain stage in the development of these means of production and exchange, the conditions under which feudal society produced and exchanged...became no longer compatible with the already developed productive forces; they restricted production, instead of promoting it; they became so many fetters. They had to be burst asunder; they were burst asunder. Into their place stepped free competition, accompanied by a social and political constitution adapted to it, and by the economical and political sway of the bourgeois class. (*CM*, p. 72; omission restored from *MEW* iv, p. 467)

The thing is almost magical, and Shapiro is justified in calling it 'a simple (or simple-minded) view of both the French Revolution and revolutions in general' (Shapiro, p. 503). In his critique of Proudhon, Marx asks how can the 'single logical formula of movement' explain the structure of society 'in which all relations coexist simultaneously and support one another?'(*PP*, pp. 110–11). We might well ask of Marx's argument here, how the conception of all the relations coexisting and supporting one another squares up to the facts of a historical transformation such, for example, as the French Revolution. We may take the stereotype to consist of the following elements: a *feudal* social order is attacked by a *bourgeoisie distinct from the nobles*, who are a *product of capitalist industrial growth*, who use their power to create the *conditions for further capitalist development*; which in fact *ensues*; the movements of the *peasantry represent a similar polarity*, larger peasants supporting and smaller opposing the bourgeois aims. The most comprehensive attack on the stereotype has been made by Professor Cobban, in his *The Social Interpretation of the French Revolution* (Cambridge, 1964). In the discussion that follows I draw on that work even where I do not directly quote it.

Recent research has thrown much doubt on the notion of a bourgeoisie antagonistic to the nobility as a result of being economically and socially distinct from them. The major work here has been done by Taylor, who argues that both successful bourgeois and nobility partook in what he calls 'proprietory' rather than capitalist wealth, the crucial distinction being that in the former, what is sought is an assured return and status, rather than the 'Accumulate! Accumulate!' which Marx regards as the watchword of the capitalist (Taylor, G. V., pp. 471–82; see p. 142 below). He shows that even the bourgeois who were economically distinct from the nobility – those in trade and commerce – regarded themselves as for that reason inferior, and used their success to transfer from commercial to proprietorial status. Not only this, but it is very difficult to present *anything* that happened in the French Revolution as a product of industrial capitalism, since it had not properly got going by the time: 'industrial capitalism as distinct from artisan organisation or from merchant or landowning capitalism did not yet exist at the end of the eighteenth century' (Palmade, p. 49). This leads Cobban to stress that the bourgeoisie which *did* make the revolution was one of 'landowners, *rentiers* and officials' (Cobban 1964, p. 173). At the other pole of the alleged social conflict, Cobban claims, we must also accept qualifications: he doubts whether there was much left in eighteenth-century France that could meaningfully be called 'feudal'. The bulk of the feudal restrictions on internal commerce, he argues, had been removed before the Revolution, and by bureaucratic reformers rather than bourgeois revolutionaries. He concludes that 'if "feudalism" in 1789 did not mean seignorial rights, it meant nothing' (p. 35) – and of course, these seignorial rights were bought up by many successful bourgeois as their ticket of entry to proprietary status.

On this basis, Cobban attacks the stereotype's account of the *policy* of the revolutionary bourgeoisie. He denies that they attacked these seignorial privileges, which they did not even mention in their *cahiers* of grievances, because, he says, they valued them, and in large number already owned them. He points out also that, on industrial policy, they failed to fulfil the 'Marxist' vocation, voting, even when the *Montagne* or radical party dominated the Convention, in favour of Navigation Laws and other obstacles to free trade (1964, pp. 68–72). Not only the bourgeoisie, but also the economy, failed to play its role: capitalist industry probably suffered during the Revolution (see p. 75), and it certainly did not become dominant or even develop significantly for decades to come. Finally, Cobban attacks the stereotype for its account of the peasant movements. In order to keep alive the idea of a solid anti-feudal phalanx, he alleges, the Marxists manufacture a rural bourgeoisie of well-to-do peasants, who allegedly clamoured for division of common lands so as to increase their property. They are opposed, in the stereotype, by a 'rural proletariat' anxious to maintain their rights to the common lands on which they depend, and from whose division *they* cannot hope to gain. Cobban points out that this whole picture runs counter to the fact that 'as the revolution moves to the left, instead of diminishing, the pressure for dividing up the common lands increases' (p. 112). This pressure, he points out, came from the landless poor peasants, rather than from a would-be rural 'bourgeoisie'. Moore supports this claim, noting that 'the poor peasants had no generalised attachment to the village community', and that 'the rich peasants were often the only ones to use the common lands for pasture' (Moore, p. 71; see also pp. 80–1, note 105).

I have already said, and must unreservedly repeat, that the

general approach of the *Manifesto* to all these processes is quite idealistic and implausible. In fairness, we must note that it contains some arguments which go against this general approach, while some of the other works are infected by it (see, e.g., *GI*, pp. 76–8). I am concerned with the work's general import. One can understand how it can spawn wild claims like Soboul's that 'in the capitalist society born of the Revolution, industry was destined to dominate commerce' (Soboul, pp. 260–1). But it is permissible to ask what indications there are in Marx's pre-1848 writings that he need not have stuck to such unrealistic assertions, while maintaining the essentials of his theory; we now proceed to this question. There is at least one central point on which other works of the period contradict the stereotype. Where it presents the 'simple-minded' picture of the bourgeois order springing full-blown to life overnight, Marx elsewhere emphasises that the development of capitalism involves several profoundly different and protracted stages (see, e.g., *GI*, pp. 74–6).

In another work of the period he recognises that 'modern industry and competition were not yet well developed under the Constituent Assembly and under the Empire' (*PP*, p. 170). Where he is not succumbing to idealist fantasies, Marx tends to regard the bourgeois political revolution not as the product of mature bourgeois big industry, but rather as the point where the bourgeoisie become strong enough to gain political power, which must be *used* to establish the hold of industry over society, and even to settle internal tensions between the industrial and other economic bourgeoisie. Stressing this aspect of his thought allows us to take the onus off the 'capitalist forces of production' in explaining the Revolution, although we shall see that we thereby raise problems about its contribution in turn to the development of those forces.

If we interpret Marx in this way, then an interesting use can be made of some qualifications to the Cobban–Taylor line made by recent historians. Their comments do not reject what Cobban and Taylor claim to have established, but they show that it needs to be put into a complex context. One of the chief points missing from the Cobban–Taylor accounts is the fact that we cannot take as a static given the 'nobility' to whom the bourgeoisie were becoming so strangely assimilated. Lucas tells us that 'the nature of the nobility had been undergoing tremendous change since the

end of the fifteenth century' (p. 97). He proposes three major
causes: the nobility's financial difficulties, the absolute monarchy's pressure against their independence, and the monarchy's
need to resort to the crass marketing of offices to replenish its
treasury. Barrington Moore says that in the sixteenth century
when the increase in precious metals drove up prices 'there are
indications of something approaching a crisis in seigneurial
incomes' (p. 42). He refers to 'capitalist influences radiating out
from the towns' (p. 56). This would be absurd if we understood
it to mean 'the pressure of big industry', but Moore is more
cautious than that (see p. 69). If by 'capitalist' we understand
commercial capital, used by merchants putting money to make
money, then the point is valid, and we must modify the picture
of bourgeois incorporation in 'the nobility' by noting the way in
which the old nobility was itself affected by commercial, i.e.
bourgeois, conditions. There is little doubt that, unlike what
happened in England (which will be discussed briefly in chapter
7 below), the fusion of bourgeoisie and nobility in France moved
in the direction of the nobility rather than vice versa (see Moore,
p. 109). But it must be noted that even if the bourgeoisie chose
to ape the nobility, and sometimes to abandon trade altogether
once their fortune was made (see Taylor, G. V., p. 485), it was
increasingly only through trade and commerce, the despised
activities, that anyone could gain either wealth *or* status in
French society (see Lucas, pp. 109–12).

Having said this, we must also note an inherent danger in the
Cobban–Taylor line of criticism: that, by remorselessly criticising
the exaggerations of the Revolution, we may lose sight of what
was being exaggerated in the first place, the real Revolution which
did happen (see Shapiro, pp. 510–11). Neither Cobban nor Taylor,
be it said, denies that there was a revolution. While criticising
Cobban's attempt to fill the void with 'a new class struggle
interpretation' (p. 490), Taylor certainly agrees with the thesis
that there was a major *political* Revolution. Having denied
that the distinction between bourgeoisie and nobility was economic, he allows that there was a *juridical* discrimination (p. 488),
and that the Revolution abolished this (p. 490). But in the light
of the social background as portrayed by Lucas and Barrington
Moore, this political change becomes socially extremely significant:

The Revolution mortally wounded the whole interlocking complex of aristocratic privilege: monarchy, landed aristocracy and seigneurial rights, a complex that constituted the essence of the *ancien régime*. It did so in the name of private property and equality before the law. (Moore, p. 105)

[The elite was redefined] in such a way that it could never be divided again by artificial distinctions within it. The characteristic of elite status was recognised to be the control of landed property...The revolutionary crisis did result in the emergence of an elite defined in terms of landholding and function, with the hereditary element confined to the simple passage of wealth and its advantages from one generation to another in a family. The Revolution did therefore provide a social framework within which the acquisition of nobility was to be increasingly irrelevant and which allowed elite status to develop into the attribute of men of wealth however acquired and however expressed. (Lucas, pp. 125–6)

In the light of these points, we may accept Cobban's cautions about 'feudalism', but see a different significance in them. Marx himself, indeed, sees 'feudalism' as declining over a very long period in his *German Ideology* account, and dates to long before the prominence of bourgeois *industry* the process whereby 'the power of the aristocrats passed in the form of money into the pockets of the bourgeoisie' (*GI*, p. 241). We have much less reason for surprise, then, when we see the bourgeoisie fail to attack the seignorial privileges, in which they themselves participate, on the eve of revolution. Cobban himself makes this all the more explicable in that he shows the extent to which the real barriers to internal trade had already been knocked down; all the more reason for the bourgeoisie, enabled to make their money in the first place, to desire to spend it on what was universally regarded as the acme of status. Nor would Marx have any problem with the point made by Cobban, that the revolutionary bourgeoisie voted *for* barriers to foreign trade. Marx's theory postulates an earlier period in which the bourgeoisie seek internal freedom and external protection, followed by a more adventurous later approach to the world market. It is interesting that what Marx sees the English and French bourgeois revolutions as conquering is 'free competition inside the nation itself' (*GI*, p. 76). What Cobban presents as a paradox – that the votes in question were 'in response to addresses and petitions from the commercial cities' (p. 69) – then becomes an indication of the extent to which the economic bourgeoisie, though not politically in the lead (see

Cobban 1968, p. 285 and Lucas, p. 96), were able to make their voice heard, and that along lines which Marx would have expected. Once more we find one of Cobban's points telling much more against the Marxist stereotype of writers such as Soboul (and the Marx of the *Manifesto*) than against Marx's own historical analysis.

Before making our final assessment, we must note the remaining criticism which Cobban makes: that of the attempt to discover a rural 'bourgeoisie' and 'proletariat' to mirror the conflict at higher levels of society. It is interesting that on a number of occasions Marx specifically opposes the premature 'proletarianisation' of rural movements. He sees the sub-division of landed monopolies as a necessary stage through which land tenure has to go (*EPM*, pp. 321–2), and argues that the peasants will see the need for collectivisation only after the experience of parcellation (*GI*, pp. 395–6). He attacks Kriege, a German 'True Socialist' in the U.S., not for allying himself with the agitation for land but for treating it as though it were a genuine communist movement: Kriege, Marx says, fails to realise that 'communist tendencies in America had originally to emerge in [the] apparently quite anti-communist agrarian form' of agitation for parcellation (*ZK*, pp. 9–10).

At the beginning of this assessment of how Marx fares against the Cobban–Taylor criticisms, we 'prised apart' the bourgeois revolution and the development of bourgeois industry. Having done that, we found that there was a pretty good case to be made for the view of the Revolution as the outcome of the impact of commercial influences on a 'feudal' structure, with a number of rather complex qualifications. All of this, it seems to me, is compatible with what Marx needs to maintain in the historical application of his structural conception. But we must now return to the relations between the Revolution and bourgeois industry, this time looking forward. Cobban's argument that the revolutionary years were actually bad for industry may well be correct, but it is irrelevant, since no one expects the economy to do well during prolonged political crisis. More worrying for Marx would be the claim that the Revolution actually *retarded* capitalist development. Palmade does point out that the Revolution, by destroying large amounts of liquid capital, probably did put an end to the development of a certain *kind* of capitalist development in France. But as he comments fairly that 'the close dependence on overseas links constituted the weakness of such an economy' (p. 44), we are justified in seeing the Revolution, to this extent, as actually jerking the economy out of an attractive dead-end. But we face problems as to the direction in which it did start travelling, if 'travelling' is an apt image for the rather stagnant, land and money-oriented economy which lasted until 1848. Here we find the sting in the tail of the French pattern of noble–bourgeois fusion. Barrington Moore notes that rather than transforming the structure of agriculture by driving out peasants and enclosing vast estates for commercial improvements, 'those nobles who represented the leading edge of commercial advance in the French countryside tried to extract more from the peasants' (Moore, p. 52; see also pp. 55 and 109). While this kind of fusion does not falsify the notion of a bourgeois revolution along the lines which we have followed here, it was to prove a powerful and tenacious foe of the emergence of capitalist industry to economic predominance, as we shall see in chapters 4 and 7 below.

Thus we may conclude this account of the rise of the bourgeoisie, as exemplified in the French Revolution, as follows. There is a basis in Marx's own writings for 'decomposing' the structure as presented in his more idealist moments, and when we do this we can make fair sense of the Revolution within his theory. The pattern into which the elements of the structure crystallised in the Revolution constitutes a serious problem for the central claim which cannot be taken out of Marx's theory, namely that the bourgeois revolution will contribute without major setbacks to the development of capitalist industry and to its conquest of the economy. We may allow him the perspective of 'the Revolution' as a complex and protracted process of transformation in which the establishment of the July monarchy, overthrowing the restored Bourbon or 'Legitimist' one, was a crucial victory for the bourgeoisie (see *CM*, p. 88). We may also grant him that

The history of the French Revolution, which started in 1789, did not end in 1830 with the victory of one of its components enriched by the consciousness of its own social importance. (*HF*, p. 167)

But in subsequent chapters we shall encounter some of the vicissitudes of his predictions about the political developments involved in the further realisation of that revolution.

Perspectives of the *Manifesto*

We have already noted that the *Manifesto* gives an account of the rise of the bourgeoisie. It sees them developing through stages of social advance, each parallelled by a corresponding political advance, until:

the bourgeoisie has at last, since the establishment of modern industry and of the world market, conquered for itself, in the modern representative state, exclusive political sway. The executive of the modern state is but a committee for managing the common affairs of the whole bourgeoisie. (*CM*, p. 69)

The next major theme is that of their inevitable downfall. The reason has already been elaborated in the *Holy Family*: the very nature of bourgeois progress involves the numerical increase of the proletariat, and involves also their maturing into an alternative capable of taking control of industrial society (see *HF*, pp. 51–3). Unlike earlier social formations, capitalism cannot simply stand still forever: it is of its essence to grow. But this necessary mobility brings about a movement similar to the bourgeois supersession of feudalism:

The productive forces at the disposal of society no longer tend to further the development of the conditions of bourgeois property...The conditions of bourgeois society are too narrow to comprise the wealth created by them...But not only has the bourgeoisie forged the weapons that bring death to itself; it has also called into existence the men who are to wield those weapons – the *proletarians*. (*CM*, p. 73)

A major feature of capitalist development, on Marx's theory, is its *simplification*. This is in essence a résumé of the economic model contained in the *EPM* (see *EPM*, pp. 282–321 and Maguire 1972, chapter 3). In that model a two-sector economy of land and industry becomes capitalised; within this one sector, there emerge two great classes, capitalists and workers. In the *Manifesto* this analysis is put in sociological and political context. 'Society as a whole is more and more splitting up into two great hostile camps, into two great classes directly facing each other: bourgeoisie and proletariat' (*CM*, p. 68). This simplification raises two issues. The first is the historical question of the fate of what I call *transitional intermediate groups*, namely, those destined to be wiped out by the rise of the bourgeoisie to prominence. The second is the question of the fate of *structural intermediate groups*, namely

those thrown up within bourgeois society who are neither bourgeois nor proletarian. (Those groups are not always the 'middle'
layers of their own social formation. I call them 'intermediate'
because they are in one way or another 'caught in the middle' of
the great Marxian drama between bourgeoisie and proletariat.)

In discussing these two questions, we cannot avoid the vexed
question of Marx's usage of such words as 'middle-class', on which
in its own right a lengthy article could be written. Sometimes Marx
speaks of the bourgeoisie as a 'middle-class' between the feudal
ruling class and the masses; in this sense he speaks of the 'manufacturing middle class' replacing the feudal masters (*CM*, p. 69).
[Moore has here inaccurately translated '*Mittelstand*' (*MEW* IV,
p. 463), which should read 'middle estate'; throughout the rest of
this study, I shall make such a correction where necessary,
without drawing attention to it on each occasion.] We may take
it as a safe rule of thumb that Marx, although sloppy in his usage,
tends to use '*Stand*' ('estate') rather than '*Klasse*' ('class') when
he is speaking of (a) the position of groups in feudal, i.e. estate-
based, society, or (b) the position of groups in bourgeois society
who are neither bourgeois nor proletarian, that is, who are not
fundamental economic classes. Our account of the rise of the
bourgeoisie in the first section of this chapter traces their development from subordinate to dominant status, which Marx
sums up by saying that 'it is a *class* and no longer an *estate*'
(*GI*, p. 79). For this reason, we may take 'middle estates' here
to refer to the transitional and structural non-bourgeois groups
indicated.

Marx has quite a lot to say about the fate of the transitional
middle estates. 'The hitherto existing middle estates' he tells us,
'the small manufacturers, merchants and rentiers, the handicraftsmen and the peasants, all of these classes fall into the proletariat' (*CM*, p. 75). Some of them decline because their capital
is insufficient to compete with the big bourgeoisie; others, because
their skill is overtaken by new methods. I take it that the former
are the small manufacturers, merchants and rentiers, while the
latter are the handicraftsmen and peasants. It also seems fair to
call the former 'petty bourgeois', since it seems to be they whom
Marx has in mind when he says that 'In Germany the petty-
bourgeois class, a relic of the sixteenth century, and since then
constantly cropping up again under various forms, is the real social

basis of the existing state of things' (*CM*, p. 92). To return for the moment to our earlier discussion of the rise of the bourgeoisie, we may now include the guild-masters in this group, despite our earlier exclusion of them from the category of 'burgher', since in the course of the bourgeois development they become dominated by bourgeois conditions and reduced to the status of small property-owners, that is, petty bourgeois. They end up, as it were, in but not of the bourgeois world, which is the characteristic of all petty bourgeois groups: 'in the guilds was concentrated the petty bourgeoisie, which no longer was dominant in the towns as formerly, but had to bow to the might of the great merchants and manufacturers' (*GI*, p. 73).

At this point we must advert to the central paradox of the *Manifesto*. Beginning with an account of the rise and inevitable decline of the bourgeoisie, and even delineating the subsequent workers' regime, it was nevertheless written for a country which its authors believed to be on the eve of its *bourgeois* revolution (see *CM*, p. 98). Hunt points out that the *Manifesto* was commissioned by the Communist League, a German artisan group formerly called the League of the Just. He says that the work is a compromise between Marx's 'scientific' stance of support for the bourgeoisie and the artisanal ideal of immediate egalitarian revolution (see especially Hunt, pp. 187–91). That Marx was trying to steer artisan thinking towards his more scientific line of thought is certainly true, but we should not overstate this point. It is not as though Marx had always simply and straightforwardly been a 'scientific' supporter of the bourgeois revolution as a necessary next step in Germany, who reluctantly had to incorporate utterly foreign strands into his thinking in 1847–8. He had had an equivocal attitude to the bourgeoisie – particularly the German one – for years, as witness his assertion in 1844 that the already-present proletarian threat had deprived them of revolutionary energy (see *CCHPRI*, pp. 255–6 and *MECW* IV, p. 265). As late as September 1847, in a speech not delivered until January 1848, Marx had written that he supported the bourgeoisie *only* in the 'revolutionary sense' that 'the free trade system hastens the social revolution' (*SFT*, p. 224). I believe that we are justified in taking the *Manifesto*'s attitude to the bourgeoisie as a revolutionary force as broadly Marx's own, and not just a compromise with the artisans for whom it was written.

It is, Marx claims, easy for the proletarians to decide their attitude to the bourgeois revolution:

[They do not] ask what the bourgeois merely *want*, but rather what they *must do*. They ask whether the present political order, the rule of the bureaucracy, or the order which the liberals are striving for, the rule of the bourgeoisie, serves as a better means of achieving their own proper aims. For this they need only compare the political situation of the proletariat in Germany with that in England, France and America, to see that the rule of the bourgeoisie not only hands the proletariat entirely new weapons for the struggle *against* the bourgeoisie, but also creates for it an entirely new political situation, as a recognised political party. (*KRB*, p. 193)

In his polemic against Heinzen, Marx allows that the workers' movement 'can only be accelerated through the revolutionary movement of the bourgeoisie against the feudal orders and the absolute monarchy', but redresses the balance by saying that, unlike Heinzen, they regard it only as a 'condition preliminary' to what they seek, and never 'as their objective' (*MCCM*, pp. 160–1).

Marx, however, cannot have been unaware that very few of the 'workers' whom he addressed – and *none* of his immediate audience – in the *Manifesto* could be called 'proletarian' in the modern sense. If he had any doubts on the score, they would have been resolved for him by some neat precision in Engels's *Principles of Communism*, a draft employed in writing the *Manifesto*. There Engels makes it clear that while there have always been poor workers, there have not always been proletarians 'any more than there has always been unbridled competition' (*PC*, p. 5).

The manufacturing worker of the sixteenth to the eighteenth centuries still had, with but few exceptions, an instrument of production in his own possession – his loom, the family spinning wheel, a little plot of land which he cultivated in his spare time. The proletarian has none of these things. (p. 8)

These artisans, with something to lose by the victory of the bourgeoisie, are then likely to resist their fate. Marx does not overlook this fact in the *Manifesto*:

the small manufacturer, the shopkeeper, the artisan, the peasant, all these fight against the bourgeoisie, to save from extinction their existence as middle estates. They are therefore not revolutionary, but conservative. Nay more, they are reactionary, for they try to roll back the wheel of history. (*CM*, p. 77)

Nor indeed does he write them off as irretrievably reactionary, since he allows that they might well move in a different direction. If so, however, it is 'only in view of their impending transfer into the proletariat', and they 'defend not their present, but their future interests, they desert their own standpoint to place themselves at that of the proletariat' (*CM*, p. 77). The problem for Marx, however, as will emerge in the next chapter, is that he did not sufficiently grasp the sheer absolute or relative size of the group of people whom this analysis covers, or indeed the unlikelihood of the 'revolutionary' decision which he here allows of their making. If Rawlsian decisions are unrealistic because we cannot know the concrete circumstances in which we might land, the bargain offered the middle estates here is far more bizarre. Marx is asking them to become prisoners because paradise can be reached only through a life-sentence.

In the light of these problems with transitional groups we may set the scene for the next chapter by considering Marx's analysis of what is required for a successful revolutionary class.

No class of civil society can play this role without awakening a moment of enthusiasm in itself and in the masses; a moment in which this class fraternizes and fuses with society in general, becomes identified with it and is experienced and acknowledged as its *universal representative*; a moment in which its claims and rights are truly the rights and claims of society itself and in which it is in reality the heart and head of society. Only in the name of the universal rights of society can a particular class lay claim to universal domination. Revolutionary energy and spiritual self-confidence are not enough to storm this position of liberator and to ensure thereby the political exploitation of all the other spheres of society in the interests of one's own sphere. If the *revolution of a people* and the *emancipation of a particular class* [*Klasse*] of civil society are to coincide, if *one* class is to stand for the whole of society, then all the deficiencies of society must be concentrated in another class [*Stand*], one particular class must be the class which gives universal offence, the embodiment of a general limitation; one particular sphere of society must appear as the *notorious crime* of the whole of society, so that the liberation of this sphere appears as universal self-liberation. If one class [*Stand*] is to be the class of liberation *par excellence*, then another class must be the class of overt oppression. The negative general significance of the French nobility and the French clergy determined the positive general significance of the class which stood nearest to and opposed to them – the *bourgeoisie*. (*CCHPRI*, p. 254. See also *GI*, pp. 62–3)

I have quoted this passage at length, because it sets the groundlines for our whole discussion of German developments, both in the next chapter and even in chapter 7. It is interesting and important that Marx clearly puts a 'psychological' factor – the moment of 'enthusiasm' ['*Enthusiasmus*' (*MEW* I, p. 388)] – at the centre of the process. How people see things is crucial, even to such an 'economically based' theory of revolution. For Marx, of course, the rise of bourgeois society is not a progress in itself, but only insofar as it makes possible the workers' revolution. Insofar as people see it as a progress in itself, they are falling prey to an illusion, although an illusion which is necessary to the bourgeoisie's success. One of our central topics will prove to be the 'life-expectancy' of such revolutionary enthusiasms.

We have so far ignored the intermediate groups encountered within bourgeois society itself. These are chiefly two. The first are what I call the *structural petty bourgeoisie*, to distinguish them from the transitional one already discussed. Although Marx does claim in the *Manifesto* that bourgeois society becomes simplified, he also allows that:

In countries where modern civilisation has become fully developed, a new class of petty bourgeois ['*eine neue Kleinbürgerschaft*'] has been formed, fluctuating between proletariat and bourgeoisie and ever renewing itself as a supplementary part of bourgeois society. (*CM*, p. 89, from *MEW* IV, p. 484)

These are the mass of small property-owners who are not proletarian workers and yet are not really part of the bourgeoisie: 'cafe and restaurant proprietors, *marchands de vins*, small traders, shopkeepers, craftsmen, etc.' (*CSF*, p. 65; see Engels, *PMQ*, pp. 134–5 for a very similar account). The other main intermediate group are the peasants. These are not the peasants of pre-revolutionary times whom we encountered in the previous section: they are the people working the landed sector of the bourgeois economy. Marx does not study their situation in depth before 1848, and is therefore forced to do so in 1852, when he analyses the events in France, in which they were a major, perhaps even the main, influence. Insofar as the tendency for the whole of agriculture to be capitalised is operative, we are faced with a real rural proletariat: a mass of propertyless workers who happen to work for landed rather than factory capital (see *RIPP*, p. 953). But insofar as things do not work out quite this way, we can find ourselves faced with a peasantry who are neither the serfs of pre-revolutionary times nor such a proletariat, and are in fact *peasant proprietors.* As we have seen, Marx the economist in *EPM* recognises this dual possibility; but Marx the political analyst has not yet sufficiently taken into account the implications for the bourgeoisie of a large mass of rural propertyholders who no longer can be bought off by the destruction of large landholdings. The tension between peasant property and the capital which exploits it is explosive, especially when it erupts at the same time as the bourgeoisie's conflicts with the petty bourgeoisie and the proletariat.

It is possible to criticise Marx's whole approach to social analysis, for example as it is presented in the *Communist Manifesto*. Such a criticism would say, in brief, that Marx got things quite wrong by distorting what he talked about or by leaving out some of the most important things. The line which I have taken in this section is different. It is, to suggest that even on the assumption that Marx has correctly categorised the main groups and left none out, he overlooks the fact that those groups are capable, in future situations, of producing quite different constellations, with quite different outcomes, than he predicts. In Germany, for example, the size and strength of the bourgeoisie's *transitional* enemies, allied with those *structural* enemies whom they have already made for themselves, may be sufficient to prevent the bourgeoisie from pressing forward against the old order. In France, where the bourgeoisie hold political power, the strength of their structural intermediate enemies, allied with that of the proletariat, might be sufficient to endanger their hold on power. These are, broadly, the problems which the theory had to face in those two countries, as we shall see in the next two chapters.

Conclusion

We have traced the development of the bourgeois class, noting that the presence of non-economic bourgeois and of non-industrial economic bourgeois is compatible with Marx's notion. We have looked at the controversy over the French Revolution, and said that Marx's views insofar as we can know them can be put in a form compatible with modern research, although at the cost of weakening the role of industry as a *cause* of the bourgeois revolution. The Revolution's *effects* on industry remain a problem in the case of France, as will frequently emerge in the following pages. Finally, we looked at the perspectives of the *Communist Manifesto*, and argued that the various transitional and structural groups which Marx mentions alongside the bourgeoisie and proletariat might interfere with his predictions both for countries where the bourgeoisie are in power and for those where the bourgeois revolution is 'on the agenda'.

3. Germany: revolution and counterrevolution

This chapter deals with Marx's writings in the *Neue Rheinische Zeitung*, the paper which he edited in Cologne from June 1848 to May 1849. My aim is not to give a full account of the historical events of that year in Germany, or even to expound every point made by Marx. It is to give the broad outlines of Marx's interpretation of the course and the failure of the German revolution. As always, our interest is centrally in the theory of politics (implicit or explicit) informing Marx's interpretation. The main features which will emerge are ideas about political and social revolution, constitutional crisis and coalition. Chapter 4 will discuss the writings on France 1848–51. Chapter 5 will deal with further and deeper questions about presuppositions contained in these notions. It would be a mistake to see this and the next chapter as concerned with 'exposition', and chapter 5 with 'theory'. Rather, some basic variables and presuppositions are discussed in chapter 5, assuming the analysis of Marx's theory already carried out in the two chapters preceding it.

Prelude to revolution

All the tensions inherent in the condition of Germany came to a head with the economic crisis of 1847. Frederick William IV of Prussia responded to the discontent in his kingdom by convening the United Diet in that year. It was far from being the representative parliament demanded by the liberal opposition, being composed of representatives of the provinces, the United Estates, heads of noble families, and elected representatives of the minor nobility, the towns and the peasants. It was in essence an attempt to force opposition to the established regime to articulate itself through structures reflecting all that was traditional and 'feudal' in Germany. It even embodied a separate upper house for the nobles, only finance being discussed by all together. It was, however, on this issue that the manoeuvre foundered. After an unrepentantly paternalistic opening speech in which the king appealed to 'the people', and made clear how irrelevant he considered parliament, David Hansemann, a wool-merchant who was one of the liberal opposition, declared, in a phrase often and gleefully recalled by Marx, that 'in money questions, there is an end to sentiment' (quoted by Hamerow, p. 91). The Diet voted against the appropriations for the *Ostbahn* railway to link Berlin and Königsberg; on June 26 1847 Frederick William reverted to personal rule, and the Diet came to an end. It had however given practical schooling to Hansemann and the other liberals, and aggravated the air of tension exemplified by a food riot in April of that year.

There things might have remained, however, as far as Germany's own political initiative was concerned. Marx had put his finger on the dependence of German revolution on an external stimulus when in 1844 he declared that 'when all the inner conditions are met, the *day of the German resurrection* will be heralded by the *crowing of the Gallic cock*' (*CCHPRI*, p. 257). So it happened. A wave of revolutions started in Italy in January 1848 and spread to France in February. The news of the continental risings, especially the French one, led to demonstrations organised by the liberals and supported by peasants, artisans and other workers, which brought the liberal opposition to power in Baden-Württemberg, Bavaria, Darmstadt, Nassau, Kessel, Saxony and Hanover. In all these states roughly the same demands were granted, roughly the same people gained power, with roughly the same lack of resistance from the authorities (see Mann, pp. 92–3). German liberals, rejoicing at their easy victory, decided to meet centrally at Frankfurt. But further development required that the major German powers, Austria and Prussia, cede to the liberals with the same good grace. On 13 March Metternich, Chancellor of Austria and architect of the restoration of 1815, quietly slipped away and all was granted in Austria. In Berlin, on the other hand, several hundred people were killed by the troops before the king, a virtual prisoner of his subjects, gave in and withdrew the army, even stooping both literally and symbolically to do homage to the martyrs' corpses. Camphausen, a wealthy businessman and liberal politician, was called on to form a government, a move sanctioned by the second United Diet, called by Frederick William on 2 April 1848, at its last meeting on 19 April. To understand the composition and fate of the 'coalition' which he represented, we must look at the state of the German economy and society of the time.

Golo Mann points out that even though her political structures were already anachronistic in 1848, Germany was still fundamentally a pre-industrial country (p. 64). Hamerow estimates that in the middle of the century, only one third of her population lived outside the countryside, and that fewer than one third of non-agricultural workers were in factory rather than traditional employment. He also notes, however, that 'through efficient organisation and mechanical power the mill was able to produce a disproportionately high percentage of the total manufacturing output of Central Europe' (p. 18). The condition of Germany at this time is described by Kuczynski as 'semi-feudal'. He gives as the main reason her slow transition from feudal agriculture, which left the majority of lords and princes 'in possession of their land and also of their positions in the state administration and the army, in accordance with feudal custom' (p. 206). The three chief groups in the revolutionary coalition of March 1848 were the peasants, the workers and the liberal bourgeoisie. We shall briefly situate them in turn.

We may roughly divide German land-tenure systems between the East, where the landowners stayed on their estates, increased and centralised by enclosure, and the West, where a landholding peasantry developed, subject to a largely absentee landowning class. In the eastern latifundia, the peasants were oppressed by the exactions of the owner, who in many cases was himself a victim of economic pressures: in Prussia one third of the Junker estates passed into the hands of bourgeois before 1848. 'When the great landowner could not resist the destructive effects of a capitalistic organisation of the agrarian economy, what was the peasant to do?' (Hamerow, p. 51). In the West, where the pattern of peasant landholding and absentee landlordism developed, 'the new financial obligations proved onerous and spoiled the joy over any newly gained freedom' (Holborn, p. 6). Everywhere, rural solidarity was weakened, the many unsuccessful peasants sinking into what Hamerow calls a 'rural proletariat', recruited in the East from landless labourers, and in the West from 'peasants whose holdings were too small to be farmed efficiently' (p. 53). Thus there was crushing rural misery in all parts of Germany, which the governments – more attentive to the voice of the landowner than that of the peasant – seemed unconcerned to remedy. At the same time, however unenthusiastic for liberal principles the peasants might be (indeed however little they cared about the political issues involved), there was a liberal opposition attacking the hated governments: 'The peasantry, deserted by those on whom it called for help, bewildered by its new rights and duties, finally turned to revolution in order to cope with the perplexing questions which the nineteenth century had thrust upon it' (Hamerow, p. 55).

When we turn to the German workers, the position is much more complex. If we take as our ideal of a proletarian working class the masses of propertyless workers in factories which character-ised contemporary England, Kuczynski suggests that we find things quite different in Germany. Quite apart from the numerical inferiority of such a group, due to Germany's much lower level of industrialisation, there is the fact that certain sectors which in England would indubitably be 'working-class', such as the miners, must be excluded for Germany because of the depth of feudal attitudes and organisation (such as near-military discipline and corporate consciousness) characterising their place and style of work. Not only this, but the 'working class', exclusive of these 'missing' groups, began its development 'two generations later than in England and one generation later than in France, since important feudal ties did not fall away until much later, between 1805 and 1810' (Kuczynski, p. 213). Indeed, most of the urban masses who made the revolution in March 1848 were not at all such a modern 'working class', but were rather artisans, fighting against the disappearance of their way of life: 'Artisans, above all journeymen, were responsible for the March Days' (Noyes, p. 70). One reason for their common cause with the liberals lies in a paradox noted by Joseph Görres at the time: to the extent that there *had* been progress in ideas and ways of working in Germany under the restoration, it had been introduced under the aegis not of 'Jacobin revolutionaries' but of the 'supporters of despotism' (quoted in Mann, p. 58). The rulers of Germany's more than thirty states, while maintaining a repressive polity along the lines laid down by Metternich, were prepared, even keen, to reap the fruits of the new industrial efficiency pioneered in England. So long as none of industrialism's dangerous democratic trappings were involved, 'the rulers of Central Europe were increasingly ready to sacrifice the guild system for the economic advantages of industrialism' (Hamerow, p. 33). The apparent unconcern of the various governments about their plight explains the artisans' momentary turning to the opponents of the governments: 'And so the artisans, having exhausted all peaceful means of influencing the course of government policy, driven to despair by the prospect of economic annihilation, broke at last with established political authority and sought salvation in a new political order' (Hamerow, p. 37).

Ironically, however, this meant that they were supporting the liberals *against* the growth of bourgeois society (see Noyes, p. 70). We shall explore some of the theoretical implications of the artisan movements in this chapter and the next, but for the moment a few historical points are in order. Where the *Manifesto* envisaged a large modern industrial proletariat, with a 'tail' of declining artisans, the reality was in numerical terms quite the reverse. Insofar as he envisages full-scale industrialisation as only following after the bourgeois political revolution, Marx can accept the smallness of the proletariat. This is especially so as there are clear signs that the artisans, though numerous, were undergoing a process of 'proletarianisation' in the Germany of the time. There were nearly as many journeymen and apprentices as masters (Noyes, p. 24). Moreover, more and more artisans were experiencing, or fearing, the dreaded fall into the uncharted social space of the 'proletariat'(see Noyes, e.g., p. 74, and especially pp. 242–3). Marx's real troubles begin where the artisans resist this 'proletarianisation' tooth and nail. There were admittedly serious cleavages within the 'artisan movement', between masters and the rest, and also between those keen on an absolute restoration of the guilds and those willing to tolerate industrialisation if structured by guild regulations (not to mention the gulf between the artisans and the small and almost unrepresented proletariat). But even the most 'pro-industrial' of the artisans were demanding of the liberals restrictions on capitalist industrialism quite at odds with the latters' programme of economic freedom. This opposition of artisan and liberal was to prove disastrous for the 'coalition'.

Finally, we have the 'leaders' of the coalition, the liberal opposition. These people represented the bourgeoisie, who had almost no say in the politics of the time. From Hamerow's account there emerges the interesting fact that, whatever weaknesses there are in the idea of the French bourgeoisie in 1789 as representatives of capitalist industry, there is more sense to it for Germany sixty years later. It is interesting that it was in the course of his experience of Germany in the 1840s – particularly the political repression of liberalism – that Marx formulated the notion of social change as resulting from an imbalance between forces and relations of production. It accounts for the fact that in many of his more graphic presentations of that notion he uses the image of the forces straining forward against relations which restrict them: this was certainly how things looked to liberals and indus-trialists at the time. The wealth of documentary evidence which Hamerow gives in his chapter on 'Ideological Conflict' makes clear firstly that many of the leading liberal politicians – such as Hansemann and Camphausen – were themselves businessmen, and secondly that even the non-economic bourgeoisie in politics clearly and forcefully argued for the liberation of business from outworn restrictions as the only way to prosperity (Hamerow, chapter 4). While the bourgeoisie saw this necessity, it is also true that long before March 1848 they were keenly aware of the great danger posed to their whole project by the lower orders, and saw the limits which must be set on such general ideals as liberty, equality and fraternity. Hamerow aptly characterises their prog-ramme as 'cautious constitutionalism and unrestricted industria-lism' (p. 64). At times during the *Neue Rheinische Zeitung* writings[1] Marx pours scorn on the bourgeoisie, for failing to live up to their revolutionary vocation and become politically radical. But at other times he allows that political caution was enjoined by circumstances different from those of France in 1789. This raises the extremely difficult question of what was in the bour-geoisie's interest, of what they *might have* or *ought to have* done, which will be discussed in chapter 5. Here we take their political caution as a datum, and look at its consequences.

At one point, Marx seems to imply that the bourgeoisie might have won power on their own. He depicts the financial distress of the regime in 1847, and its inability to do without bourgeois finance. He describes the opposition as 'well on the way to success...when the *storm of February* burst forth' (December 1848; *R1848*, p. 190). But in an article in the same series (entitled

---

[1] References to the *Neue Rheinische Zeitung* in the text are to Marx's writings in it as a whole, rather than just to the collection abbreviated as *NRZ*.

'The Bourgeoisie and the Counter-revolution'), he makes it clear that this is not so. He ridicules the bourgeoisie's concern for 'the legal foundation', saying that it means nothing more than that 'the bourgeoisie wished to negotiate with the Crown on the same footing *after* March as *before* March, as if no revolution had taken place and the United Diet would have achieved its goal without the revolution' (December 1848; *R1848*, p. 198). This reluctance to recognise the revolution sprang from the bourgeoisie's realisation that 'it had to represent not its own interests but the people's interests, i.e., it had to act against itself, for a *popular movement* had cleared the way for it' (p. 191). In this dilemma, the bourgeoisie opted for order, at the cost of repressing the masses, which meant that they were left defenceless against reaction: 'the *people* remained *indifferent* at the decisive moment' (December 1848; *R1848*, p. 211), when the Berlin Assembly was dispersed, humiliated and persecuted. It would be true but incomplete to say simply that the bourgeoisie lost power because they lost the people. They lost power because they alienated the people, and because this alienation of the people involved the bourgeois governments in a policy of 'consolidation' which necessarily strengthened the forces of reaction. In other words, it is not the case that the bourgeoisie alienated the people and coincidentally fell prey to the forces of reaction. The option against one constituency and policy was to commit them, even before they realised the fact, to the reconsolidation of the old polity. The remainder of the chapter will examine Marx's structural explanation of this process. We may close this section by bringing out the bourgeoisie's reasons for fearing and repressing its March allies.

It is important, in reading Marx's *Neue Rheinische Zeitung* articles, to recall that he did not arrive in Germany until April, and that the *Neue Rheinische Zeitung* first appeared more than three months after the outbreak of revolution. This is why even his earliest articles are already bewailing the liberal bourgeoisie's errors and treacheries. In one of these articles, which shows his reliance on the first French revolution as a model, he allows that the Berlin Assembly has begun to recover some of its revolutionary energy, but declares (in bold type) that 'the Bastille has still not been stormed' (June 1848; *R1848*, p. 125).

The comparison with 1789 is brought out again when Marx

attacks the bourgeoisie's failure to meet the demands of their rural allies.

The French bourgeoisie of 1789 did not leave its allies the peasants in the lurch for one moment. It knew that the basis of its rule was the destruction of feudalism on the land and the establishment of a class of free peasant landowners. (July 1848; *R1848*, p. 143)

The occasion of this attack was the bill allegedly abolishing feudal burdens introduced into the Berlin Assembly. Marx savagely dissects this measure, showing that its distinction between old-fashioned burdens which may be abolished and others whose abolition would strike at property itself finishes by sanctioning the retention of all but a minute fraction of the peasants' grievances. Marx quotes Gierke who said during the debate that landed property was the basis of national prosperity and then argued, in a passage more revealing of his real motivations, that abolishing the burdens would be

an attack on the legal validity of contracts, an attack on the most indubitable contractual relationships, and would result in the destruction of all confidence in the stability of the civil law and therefore endanger the whole of commercial intercourse in the most threatening way. (Quoted July 1848; *R1848*, p. 142)

That Gierke was not alone in his fears is borne out by the large amount of textual evidence assembled by Hamerow, the high point of which is surely the statement by a liberal in the Württemberg parliament that the destruction of ledgers and registers of landed property is but a step from that of mortgage records and promissory notes, which in turn is only a step away from 'the division of property or a common ownership of goods' (quoted in Hamerow, p. 163). In other words, the bourgeois liberals were quite openly so worried about their kind of property that they feared to threaten property 'as such' by attacking the feudal form. The rift caused by this stance is made clear by the fact that, as Hamerow puts it, what happened in 1848 was the greatest German peasant movement since the Peasant War in the sixteenth century. The liberals' position involved abandoning what was an active, militant attack on landed property, and sometimes involved registering their opposition by armed repression in the interests of the landowners.

There was a similar pattern to the alienation of mass urban support. The artisans waged a violent eight-week campaign against factories and machines, which was suppressed by military force acting in the name of the new bourgeois governments. After this the artisans concentrated on a highly organised and vocal campaign of demands on the liberal assemblies, expressing their grievances in a series of congresses, the most notable of which met in Frankfurt in July 1848 and parallelled the Frankfurt Assembly with a 'Workers' Parliament'. Their addresses warned the liberals against a repetition of the economic liberalism of the first French Revolution, which, they said, had resulted in the ruination of the small man, the artisan with his handicraft skill. They proposed a code involving a fundamentally guild-oriented or corporate system, with the state regulating the economy and guaranteeing the workers' welfare. Factories would be tolerated, but on a short leash. The movement won some concessions from liberals needing their support, but a motion against economic freedom could not even find the required number of seconders in the Berlin Assembly. The publication in February 1849 of a report of the Frankfurt Assembly on preparing an economic code broke 'the last links in the great coalition of social classes forged in the March days' (Hamerow, p. 155). The liberals had finally lost the support of the artisans, but in fact they had been losing it for many months before (see Noyes, chapter 9).

The political structure: revolution and constitution

In this section we shall be considering the process which resulted from the breakdown of the revolutionary coalition. Rather than recounting the events, we shall analyse the notions which Marx employs in analysing them. One of the central notions which he employs is that of 'constitution' or 'foundedness'. We are familiar with the notion of a 'constitution' as a written document, setting out the relations between the various political institutions. Although Marx is concerned with 'constitution' in that sense, he is more concerned to analyse a deeper process, of which the appearance or disappearance of written constitutions is a mere symptom. That is the process whereby a polity becomes *founded* or established. This is a very dynamic, and often a bloody and violent process, in which contenders for political rule fight each other and only one emerges victorious. Marx is concerned to show us that it is impossible to make sense of such a process in the formal, institutional language which is used to describe established constitutions. Concepts like 'the sovereign', 'the basis of law' and such like become themselves contested concepts, and it is only by adverting to the real, extra-constitutional struggle of the parties involved that we will grasp the significance of the contending meanings or the manner in which one comes to predominate. The change of constitutions, in other words, requires reference to politics in the sense of revolutionary struggle rather than in the sense of untroubled administration and minor conflict. When Marx speaks, as we have seen him speak, of the emergence of the bourgeois world with its corresponding 'social and political constitution' (*CM*, p. 72) he has in mind this deeper kind of 'foundedness', of which written constitutions are but the symbol.

Revolutionary crisis

Marx is constantly concerned, throughout his *Neue Rheinische Zeitung* writings, with the *significance* of events and situations. He argues that what matters is the real position in which the National Assembly found itself, rather than its members' opinions of their position. This does not invoke some 'reality' (for example, an economic one) hovering above or below what people take to be real. What it means is that the result which people's and groups' actions will have is not straightforwardly a function of their idea of themselves and of their situation. Marx's theory about social and political revolution and constitution is designed to show what actual significance attaches to the actions of persons and groups in situations of crisis. To anticipate the upshot of his analysis, we might say that the decision of the bourgeoisie to consolidate and protect their initial gains, even against their erstwhile allies, betrayed a lack of understanding of the significance of their situation. Marx frequently indicates that significance:

Let us make no mistake...it was not a matter of an ordinary conflict between a ministry and a parliamentary opposition...This was not a case of a political conflict between two parties standing on the ground of *one* society, it was a *conflict between two societies*, a *social* conflict which had taken on a political form, *it was the struggle of modern bourgeois society with the old feudal-bureaucratic society*, the struggle between the society of *free competition* and the society of *guild organisation*, between the society of industry and the society of landownership, between the society of knowledge and the society of belief. (February 1849; *R1848*, pp. 258–9)

If we understand the significance which Marx sees in such a confrontation, and the failure of the bourgeoisie to grasp that significance, then we have come near to the core of his explanation of their defeat.

One possible misunderstanding must be dispelled. Marx's phrase suggests that a social conflict might or might not (at its own whim, as it were) 'take on a political form'. In fact this is not what he believes. In an article written around the same time as the above argument, he tells us that the social advance of a potentially dominant class reaches a point where 'it must either secure an appropriate political form or perish' (January 1849; *NRZ*, p. 223). A defeated class is unlikely literally to perish, but Marx's aphorism makes it clear that he regards a phase of political struggle, of struggle for state power, as an inescapable moment in the social advance of a class. Even in his deep gloom after the Paris June days (see p. 87 below), he resists the temptation to conclude 'that struggles over the form of the state are without content, illusory, null and void' (June 1848; *R1848*, p. 133).

It is, on reflection, strange that Marx should accuse the German bourgeoisie of not recognising the revolutionary situation in which they found themselves. Surely, it might be said, they recognised precisely the danger of the revolution, and the fact that if not checked it might go too far. But what he accuses them of mis-understanding is not the fact of the revolutionary energy of the masses. Their error, he tells us, lay in thinking that they had already established stable bourgeois political power once they had the nominal power of government.

The Prussian bourgeoisie was *nominally* in possession of power, and it did not doubt for a moment that the forces of the old state had placed themselves unreservedly at its disposal and become transformed into devoted servants of its own omnipotence. (December 1848; *R1848*, p. 195)

It is by no means necessary to Marx's argument to assert that the bourgeoisie particularly *liked* the forces with whom they implicitly allied themselves in order to suppress urban and rural insurgency. The point is that there were no other forces to hand. To go on meant to smash the old state apparatus; to stop meant to use that apparatus against the former revolutionary allies. We may examine firstly the significance of the decision, and then its consequences.

As we have seen, the bourgeoisie failed to grasp the situation of violent struggle between the old and the new societies. Keen as they might have been for total political control in the abstract, in the concrete it would have meant an unacceptable reliance on workers and peasants; they thus settled for governmental power, and turned to 'consolidating the situation' against further attacks on property and order. 'We agreed that the passage from the existing constitution to the new constitution should take place through the legal means provided by the former, and without cutting off the bond which links the old to the new' (Camphausen, quoted June 1848, *R1848*, p. 116). Marx's argument is not just that the bourgeoisie *should not* have taken power in this way; it is rather that they *could not* do so. The notions underlying this argument appear in part in the 1843 *Critique of Hegel's Philosophy of Right* (*CHPR*), and they clearly derive from Marx's reading about the first French revolution in his notebooks of the early 1840s (*IISH*, B 14–18). In the *CHPR*, Marx attacks Hegel's formulation by which in theory the constitution is presupposed to all political life whereas in practice it is recognised that the legislature changes the constitution. 'The legislature is only legislature within the constitution, and the constitution would stand *hors de loi* if it stood outside the legislature. *Voilà la collision!*' (*CHPR*, p. 55) It is not possible to read from Marx's 1843 arguments directly to his 1848 conclusions, especially as, in the former, critique of Hegel's formulations and of concrete social situations is intertwined in a complex way. What is of interest is Marx's rejection of the abstract language of constitutions, and of the inconsistencies which arise if this language is made central to an account of political change. These inconsistencies Marx sees as being resolved only if the abstraction of politics from society is overcome. It is both a normative and a factual argument.

Normatively, Marx argues that the correct political principle is to make the people themselves the foundation of the constitution; it is in this sense that the 1843 position can be called a 'radical democratic' one. But the normative argument is closely linked to a factual one, the line of which is that a truly stable constitution will be achieved only when there is no longer a 'constitution' as such; that is, when politics becomes the organising function of society itself, rather than an abstract power reflecting the defects of society (see *CHPR*, p. 57, and chapter 8 below). Since the revolution which he is urging in 1848 is not the final one which will abolish abstract politics, the factual rather than the normative element is predominant in Marx's *Neue Rheinische Zeitung* writings. It emerges in his grasp of the non-self-sufficiency of constitutions, of the need to refer to society and its movement if either the form or the change of constitutions is to be grasped. Marx attacks the attempt to present as a movement *within* a structure what is necessarily a movement *between* two structures. He is arguing that a constitutional crisis (as distinct from a conflict between elements of an established constitution) requires non-constitutional language to analyse it. This is what Camphausen is trying to deny in the speech which we have already quoted (p. 59 above). 'The unlawful "occurrence" makes Herr Camphausen a *responsible* Prime Minister, makes him a being both out of place and meaningless in the old regime, under the existing constitution' (June 1848; *R1848*, p. 117). What Camphausen and the bourgeoisie will not recognise is that they have won such power as they have, precisely through a popular uprising which is *illegal* under the old regime. Nor will they recognise that Camphausen's acting as a responsible Prime Minister rather than as a tool of the monarchy requires a whole new world in which such monarchy as survives has a totally new significance. Awestruck at the chasm opened up by the strength of their allies, they revert to the old state forces, and try to make their political revolution look like at most a constitutional evolution.

Necker did not succeed in making a quiet reform out of a revolutionary movement. The great sickness was not to be healed with attar of roses. So much the less will Herr Camphausen change the character of the movement with an artificial theory which draws a straight line between his ministry and the previous situation in the Prussian monarchy. (June 1848; *R1848*, p. 118)

We may close this sub-section by briefly looking at the alternative policy which Marx believes that the bourgeoisie should have pursued. The remarks which we have already analysed about the peasantry should make it clear that he believes that they should have been wooed by the real abolition of feudal landed property and burdens. Marx is less vocal about the 'workers'; he says less about how they could have been attracted by the spread of bourgeois industry at the expense of their artisanal livelihood. But he is not unaware of the problem, as is shown by his attempts to convince them that their real interest lies with the bourgeoisie:

we say to the workers and the petty bourgeois: it is better to suffer in the contemporary bourgeois society, whose industry creates the means for the foundation of a new society that will liberate you all, than to revert to a bygone society, which, on the pretext of saving your classes, thrusts the entire nation back into medieval barbarism. (January 1849; *NRZ*, p. 225)

The difficulties of this proposed alliance of bourgeoisie and pro-letariat or quasi-proletariat have been discussed in chapter 2. But the final aspect of the proposed alternative strategy is what interests us most here. This is the approach which, Marx argues, Camphausen should have adopted to the old political order.

Every state which finds itself in a provisional situation after a revolution requires a dictator, an energetic dictator at that. We attacked Camphausen from the beginning for failing to act dictatorially, for failing to destroy and remove the remnants of the old institutions immediately. (September 1848; *R1848*, p. 161)

Marx follows this argument by saying that Camphausen, by his 'constitutional fairy-tales' of 'agreement' between the old and new political orders, gave heart and breathing-space to the forces of the old, with the result that the defeated party 'strengthened its positions in the bureaucracy and the army' (*ibid.*). Camp-hausen's device of recognising a separation of powers left the ministry hopelessly trying to mediate between the Crown and the Assembly.

Behind the Crown lay hidden the counter-revolutionary camarilla of the nobility, the military and the bureaucracy. Behind the majority of the Assembly stood the bourgeoisie...The ministry could only avoid a conflict between the Assembly and the Crown by unilaterally recognising the principle of public safety, even at the risk of a conflict between the ministry itself and the Crown. (September 1848; *R1848*, pp. 161–2)

The next sub-section will bring out the consequences of this failure to assume supreme powers in the name of public safety (a clear reference back to the first French revolution).

Consolidation and foundations

Those consequences follow from the bourgeoisie's premature decision to *consolidate* the gains which they have made. The decision is premature because the bourgeoisie are mistaken in thinking that they are in firm political control of the situation. Given that they are not, their 'consolidation' is a consolidation of the *old* political forces which they momentarily overthrew in

March, with the result that in November 1848 the monarchy 'replied to the bourgeois semi-revolution with a complete counter-revolution' (November 1848; *R1848*, p. 179). Our aim in this sub-section is to probe the notion of 'foundations' which Marx employs in the argument.

To begin with, this is not a purely scientific term which Marx as a social scientist foists on the actors in the drama. Camphausen himself explains his '*Vereinbarung*' or 'agreement' with the Crown by rejecting the notion 'that the entire constitution of our state has been overthrown, that what we see before us has ceased to exist in law, and that all our institutions require a new legal foundation' (quoted June 1848; *R1848*, p. 116). This reference to 'the legal foundation' Marx interprets as meaning that the bourgeoisie are unwilling to recognise the revolutionary presuppositions of any real political control on their part. Let us examine these 'presuppositions', or, in other terms, what Marx regards as necessary for a regime to be politically 'founded'.

When Marx tells us that March has destroyed or 'swallowed up' the foundations of the old political order (June 1848; *R1848*, p. 117) he is not speaking literally, since his whole point is that those foundations persist, and ultimately receive back their old monarchist superstructure. It is only *implicitly*, in terms of the normative sequence of events which it initiates and requires, that March has destroyed the old foundation. The persistence of that foundation emerges in Marx's account of the situation around the time of the King's counter-coup:

The King, as the *Neue Preussische Zeitung* correctly notes, stands '*on the broad foundation*' of his '*hereditary divine*' rights...On the other side, the *National Assembly* has *no foundation whatsoever*, its purpose being to constitute, to lay the foundation. (November 1848; *NRZ*, p. 150)

What the King is here relying on are the material and psychological presuppositions of his acting as ruler. That Marx is not concerned to juxtapose to these some abstract a-historical 'right' of the new order is shown by his insistence throughout the *Neue Rheinische Zeitung* writings that legitimacy derives from victory in political struggle. He consistently refuses to invoke transcendental criteria whereby one could say that the bourgeoisie, for example, have a right to rule before they have established themselves as successful rulers. This is ethically a very problematical stance, justified only by Marx's optimism that the course of history will in fact move in the right direction. Here, however, our interest is in seeing how he refuses to grant to political language and concepts a validity over and above the results of struggle between potentially dominant ways of life.

But while Marx's theory rejects a meta-historical basis of 'right-to rule', he does not exclude the attitudes of the governed from his definition of 'foundedness'. In other words, he accepts the important distinction between a government holding down a resentful populace by force alone, and a government which is recognised by the people to have a right to govern within the accepted order of things (however ideologically conditioned this recognition may be). The presence of this element in Marx's theory is to be seen in the many references to the attitudes of the non-bourgeois groups in this chapter, and in the second section of chapter 2.

But possession of government power and recognition from the governed do not appear to exhaust Marx's notion of 'foundedness'. He also makes the point which we noted in an earlier context that there is all the world of difference between being 'the government' and having control of all the organs of state power (see p. 58 above). Under Hansemann, who succeeded Camphausen,

the old Prussian police, the state prosecutor's office, the bureaucracy in general and the army were all 'strengthened' because, in Hansemann's deluded view, since they were in the *pay* of the bourgeoisie, they were therefore at its *service*. The important thing is that they were 'strengthened'. (December 1848; *R1848*, p. 205)

He believed he was strengthening that state power which is worthy of credit, of bourgeois confidence, but he only strengthened the state power which simply insists on confidence, and, where necessary, obtains it with grape-shot because it possesses no credit. (*Ibid.*, p. 203)

Thus Marx argues that the state forces which the bourgeoisie did not dare to destroy – the army, the bureaucracy, the police and so forth – were suited to the operation of the old political order, and had a variety of motives ranging from political convictions to personal ambition (see *R1848*, pp. 259–60 and *NRZ*, p. 221) for wishing to return to that pre-revolutionary situation. The fall of the Hansemann ministry is a case in point. This was occasioned by the Assembly's insisting on execution of an order banning reactionary political intrigue in the army. The Hansemann ministry fell because it was impossible to press this policy without the radical reconstruction of state institutions, including the army, which as we have already seen the bourgeoisie were unable or unwilling to carry out. The Assembly's momentary tough-mindedness unfortunately was no more than that, so that the king was further encouraged to his counter-coup.

All these considerations yield the following tentative account of 'foundedness' as the notion is used by Marx in the *Neue Rheinische Zeitung* writings: a group's political rule is 'consti-tuted' or 'founded' when it can rule for the society on the basis of a constitution giving it the right to rule, in a framework of fundamental laws explicitating that right, where it controls not just the formal seat of government authority but also the organs of state which normally and willingly carry out its intentions and commands, and where either the significant (perhaps majority) sections of the population accept its right to govern or no alter-native ruling group is in a position plausibly to make a claim to fulfil the preceding criteria. I am aware that this is neither a limpid nor an original definition. I believe however that it is important to proffer it, since it brings out two important aspects of Marx's thinking: (a) the fact that Marx's criteria for political foundedness are not directly reducible to the criteria for a group's *social* dominance or lack thereof (a point which will be discussed later); (b) the importance of what we might call 'cultural' or 'psycho-logical' factors in Marx's theory. Rather than being quite divorced from economic and physical power, the moment of recognition points to the fact that these two sources of political power must be sanctioned by popular recognition if a situation of political crisis is to be resolved.

Marx's argument will then be that because the bourgeoisie fulfilled one of these criteria – they held government power – they thought that it was safe for them to consolidate their situation. The consequence of their not fulfilling the remaining criteria was that the forces, institutions and attitudes referred to in those criteria gradually began to crystallise into something more and more resembling the old polity on the old political foundations.

Process and structure

The preceding sub-section shows that Marx argues centrally that what the bourgeoisie saw as the consolidation of an already achieved bourgeois political structure in fact turned into the re-emergence of the 'feudal' political structure. This sub-section will look at the process whereby this occurs. The intention is to see whether Marx spells out, or at least can in principle spell out, the mechanism whereby this occurs, as distinct from simply intoning an impressive formula about 'foundations', 'half-revolutions' turning into 'complete counter-revolutions' and so on. The kind of process at work will be only briefly outlined here, since it will receive quite a lot of attention in the next chapter, and *its* presuppositions in turn will be examined in chapter 5.

The kind of thing which we have to explain is Marx's use of notions about the process whereby structure emerges, as a basis for explaining and predicting political events. He tells us that the Camphausen ministry resigned

> not because it had committed this or that blunder, but for the simple reason that it was the *first* ministry after the March revolution, it was the ministry *of* the March revolution . . . (which fact) continued to impose on it certain proprieties, certain reservations and allowances towards the sovereign people, which the bourgeoisie began to find irksome . . . The Ministry of the Deed, the *Hansemann Ministry*, followed after Camphausen because the bourgeoisie had decided to go over from the period of passive betrayal of the people to the Crown to the period of *active* subjection of the people to its own rule, as agreed on with the Crown. The Ministry of the Deed was the *second* ministry *after* the March revolution. That was its whole secret. (December 1848; *R1848*, p. 199)

It would be unnecessary and tendentious to say that there we have an explanation in terms of structure, since that would add nothing to the fact that the bourgeoisie, once it had sold out on its March allies, had to ditch the government which had incurred revolutionary debts to those allies. But Marx's explanation is that from this point on, once this decision had been taken, the bourgeoisie found themselves increasingly victims of the reconsolidation of the old political structure. And moreover a basic reason why they found themselves in this predicament is here indicated: the very necessity of having allies, of building a coalition. In a world where one's own power is insufficient to ensure one's objectives, especially a world with only a small number of (themselves often opposed) potential allies, clear and unpleasant choices have to be made, none of which is likely to look or prove totally satisfactory. I believe that this *necessity of choosing* where there is a limited choice of possible strategies and coalitions is of major importance to Marx's explanations of politics. We might say, then, that people are free to choose in situations, but that they are not free not to have to choose, nor as to the options between which they have to choose. That Marx goes beyond this position, and actually explains what choices people will make (see chapter 5 below), is beside the present point, since that is not what he is doing here. Here his concern is with the fact that the bourgeoisie had to choose one side or the other, and with the consequences of choosing the side they did.

On this point he makes a prediction which relates closely to our discussion of foundations. In discussing the Hansemann ministry's curbs on press freedom, Marx says that 'on the day when this law comes into force, the bureaucracy will be able to celebrate and rejoice; it will be more powerful, more unhindered and stronger than before March' (July 1848; *R1848*, p. 136). Even if Marx's position as an editor here leads him to exaggerate the centrality of press freedom (which is by no means certain), the interest is that as early as July he is predicting the renascence of the old state forces. Looking back on this period after the failure of the revolution, he says that the bourgeoisie's actions gave the old forces 'a breathing-space in which to recover from their terror and completely reconstitute themselves' (December 1848; *R1848*, p. 187). Marx even allows that Hansemann was sincere and liberal in his intentions: he wanted to strengthen the state power not only against his March allies, 'but also against the reaction' (December 1848; *R1848*, p. 203). Marx's point is that crushing the first enemy could not but mean, in the concrete circumstances, embracing the second one. On the basis of this analysis he made what is probably his major and best prediction in all his *Neue Rheinische Zeitung* writings. At the time of the fall of Camphausen, he argued as follows:

Some kind of temporary left-centre cabinet could perhaps follow the ministry of 30 March in a few days' time. However, its real successor will be the *ministry of the Prince of Prussia*. (June 1848; *R1848*, p. 128)

As with any scientific proposition, we may fairly distinguish the generalised claim here being made from the particular member of the relevant class in terms of which it is formulated. The Prince of Prussia did not, of course, form a ministry. But Marx's phrase indicates a *type* of ministry, a point which emerges clearly when Marx talks of 'the Princes of Prussia, the Brandenburgs, the

Wrangels' (November 1848; *R1848*, p. 182; see also pp. 157 and
159). The prediction then becomes much better, and is in fact
fulfilled by the imposition of the Brandenburg ministry as first
blow in the *coup d'état* of Frederick William IV in Berlin in late
1848. It might be argued that Marx was not very prescient in
making this prediction. But it must be noted that he makes it as
early as June 1848, when few if any other participants in the
revolution grasped the long-term significance of the bourgeoisie's
decision to consolidate. Golo Mann, no great Marx-enthusiast,
nevertheless frequently admits the 'frightening intelligence'
(Mann, p. 104) with which he perceived what others would not
or could not see.

However, another of Marx's predictions, a few months after
the June one, appears to achieve truth at the expense of testability.
In September, when the Hansemann ministry was forced to resign
over the issue of army intrigues (see p. 63 above), he said that
the ministerial crisis admitted of one of two solutions: either a
Waldeck ministry recognising the sovereignty of the people and
consolidating a real revolution, or else a Radowitz–Vincke ministry signalling the destruction of the Assembly and all the gains
of the revolution (September 1848; *R1848*, pp. 157–8). But rather
than being uselessly circular, this prediction brings out clearly
what Marx takes himself to be doing in explaining and predicting,
at least in the *Neue Rheinische Zeitung* articles. In the first place,
he sees the events involved as crucially dependent on human
action: 'which of the two sides gains the victory will depend on
the attitude of the people, and in particular on the attitude of the
democratic party. The democrats must choose' (September 1848;
R1848, pp. 159–60). In the second place, then, Marx is placing
before the various parties the implications of either choice which
they might take, which accords with the interpretation of his
explanations which we have just proposed. This does not fore-
close the distinct question of whether Marx *also* believes that he
can and should explain the choices which are made, as has
already been made clear. This issue will arise in chapter 5.

Thus we may say that Marx does provide a plausible mechanism
for the process invoked by his explanations: bourgeois power
could not rest on the bourgeois class alone, and the bourgeoisie
had to choose between realising their own political ideals more
fully than they cared to, on the foundation of a popular alliance,

and reverting to the old political foundation which eventually meant their loss of government power.

Coalitions and power

Talking about 'Marx on coalitions' calls to mind Dr Johnson's likening a woman preacher to a dog doing tricks: the point, he claimed, was not that it was done well but that it was done at all. It would be ridiculous to construct a fully fledged 'Marxian theory of coalitions' from Marx's writings, at least those in question here. I simply wish to point to the importance, in his thinking about the bourgeois revolution, of notions about coalitions and how they fail which are more commonly associated with non-Marxist approaches to politics.

We have already seen that it is a central part of Marx's theory that the bourgeoisie require popular support; as he puts it in a neat phrase, 'in order to oppose the Court, they had to pay court to the people' (*R1848*, p. 190). We have already seen the broad lines of how they alienated this support after the initial victory. On that point, Marx puts forward a counterfactual claim which suggests some interesting observations on the relative importance of numbers, opinions and force. In June 1848 he urges the Frankfurt National Assembly (see p. 49 above) that if it simply opposed the reaction resolutely 'it would have conquered a position in the public esteem impregnable to bayonets and rifle-butts' (*R1848*, p. 121). This counterfactual might be put down simply to Marx's enthusiastic role as exhorter, except that he makes a similar analysis several months later, in a more reflective and less exhortatory mood:

The power of arms was defeated everywhere in the February and March days. Why? Because it represented *nothing* but the *governments*. After the June days the power of arms has conquered everywhere, because everywhere the bourgeoisie is to be found in collusion with the governments. (November 1848; *R1848*, p. 175)

These arguments suggest a generalisation, as regards the types and degrees of power involved, to the effect that (bourgeoisie linked by esteem to people) are more powerful than (government with only force), whereas (bourgeoisie linked by esteem [or fear] to government with force) are more powerful than the people on their own opposing that bourgeois-led coalition. It would be tendentious further to formalise Marx's arguments: the intention is simply to show that such calculations have a place in his thinking about confrontations.

One further aspect of Marx's thought on coalitions is of interest also. This is, that he has what in modern terms we would call a 'trade-off' notion of how they succeed or fail. For example, he makes the point that the Camphausen ministry, afraid either openly to side with the reaction or to espouse the revolutionary role of the Assembly, 'achieved nothing apart from making itself impossible for all parties, and bringing about the very collision it wanted to prevent' (September 1848; *R1848*, p. 162). A similar argument is spelt out in somewhat greater detail about the failure of its successor, the Hansemann ministry, which:

suffered the misfortune that all its economic attacks on the feudal party took place under the aegis of the *forced loan*, and that its reforming measures in general therefore appeared to the people to be merely financial expedients to fill the coffers of the strengthened 'state power'. The result was that Hansemann reaped the hatred of one party without gaining the favour of the other. (December 1848; *R1848*, pp. 206–7; see also *ibid.* p. 208)

Nations and powers

The one major topic about 1848 in Germany which I have sys-tematically excluded so far is that of nationalism. The omission was deliberate, reflecting as it does the divorce between the theory which Marx and Engels were trying to operate and the phenomenon of nationalism which constantly thwarted their analysis and efforts. In this section we will discuss nationalism, as well as the related topic of German unification.

Nationalism

It has often and justly been observed that Marx and Engels were wildly optimistic in their proclamation in the *Communist Manifesto* that nationalism was virtually a thing of the past. But equally often people fail to distinguish between kinds of nation-alism, and between the kinds of problem which they pose for the Marxian theory. The events of Germany in 1848 in no way falsify the *Communist Manifesto* argument that nationalism will be of diminishing importance *once bourgeois society is developed*. What they do show is that Marx and Engels had failed to equip them-selves, before 1848, with a theory of the role of nationalism *in the transition to bourgeois society*. This failure meant that their reaction to nationalist phenomena in the revolution was mostly intemperate, unbalanced and even racist. It has been pointed out that Marx wrote little on the question, leaving to Engels the two topics of debates in the Frankfurt National Assembly and the national question. This is certainly so, but does not acquit Marx of the blame earned by Engels. There is no evidence of Marx's seriously dissenting from Engels's line, and McLellan notes his praise for Müller-Tellering's anti-semitic offerings from Austria (McLellan 1973, p. 214n). These two facts forbid us to acquit Marx of racism.

But our first concern here is not moral assessment. The reason why we must briefly examine Engels's 'analysis' of the question is that it will at least show us what the problem was, and what implications it has for the state of the theory. The datum to be explained is well put by Engels:

At first the year 1848 brought the most frightful confusion to Austria, by momentarily freeing all these different peoples who had hitherto been in thrall to each other through Metternich's agency. Germans, Magyars, Czechs, Poles, Moravians, Slovaks, Croats, Ruthenes, Rumanians, Illyrians and Serbs all came into conflict, whilst the individual classes within each of these nations also fought each other. But order soon came into this confusion. The disputants divided into two huge armed camps: on one side, the side of revolution, were the Germans, Poles and Magyars; on the other side, the side of counter-revolution, were the others, i.e., all the Slavs with the exception of the Poles, plus the Rumanians and the Saxons of Transylvania. (January 1849; *R1848*, pp. 216–17)

The central defect in Engels's 'analysis' is his attempt to deduce the conduct of these nations from alleged rigid dispositions explicable with a high degree of necessity from 'the whole previous history of the peoples in question' (*ibid.*, p. 217). This is further complicated by his inconsistency, in that he recasts this history as fundamentally 'revolutionary', or fundamentally the opposite, according as particular nations turn one way or the other over time.

A glaring example of both faults is his treatment of the Czechs. In June 1848 he castigates Germany for failing to liberate and support all the oppressed nations rather than endorsing 'the old oppression of Italy, Poland and now of Bohemia too, by German troops' (June 1848; *NRZ*, p. 39). The result of Germany's sins is that 'the gallant Czechs...are placed by an unhappy fate on the side of the Russians, the side of despotism opposed to the revolution' (*ibid.*, p. 40). But by February 1849 the Czechs have become one of the 'small nations, dragged along for centuries by history against their will, [which] must necessarily be counter-revolutionary' (*R1848*, p. 230). Engels withdraws his condemnation of German colonial interference in the history of the peoples 'who never had a history of their own', and says that Germany's dealings with them are: 'some of the best and most commendable of the deeds we and the Magyar people can pride ourselves on in the course of our history' (February 1849; *R1848*, p. 236). This is a direct contradiction of the argument which he proposed in June of the preceding year, when he said that the fact of the Slavs' being predominantly agricultural rather than commercial left a niche for the unsavoury ministrations of Jews and of the Germans, who demonstrated 'their vocation as the philistines of world history' (August 1848; *NRZ*, p. 84).

The circularity and unscientific nature of Engels's invocation of rigid, historically-grounded dispositions is shown by his argument, after he has declared the peoples in question to be irretrievably 'unhistorical', that:

If the Slavs had begun a *new revolutionary history* at any time within the period of their oppression, they would have proved their capacity for independent existence by that very act. The revolution would have had an interest in their liberation from that moment onwards. (February 1849; *R1848*, p. 237)

On one reading of the logic of dispositions, this flatly contradicts Engels's explanation of the Slavs' not having been revolutionary in terms of their history. On another reading, it at least requires that Engels find in their history factors grounding either disposition, which would leave open the question of which disposition would in fact become operative, thus destroying his rigid argument.

But to demonstrate the inconsistency, necessitarianism and racism of Engels's 'analysis' does not remove the problems which he so unsuccessfully confronted. To criticise Engels is not to imply that the national aspirations awakened in 1848 could all have been accommodated. To fill the gap in their theory would require a book in itself, and an inquiry into nationalism which is outside both my scope and my competence. One final point is in order, on the question of what might reasonably have been said. It is by no

means clear that Marx and Engels were wrong in the concrete
options which they made, for the nations ready to espouse the
revolution and against those opposing it. But here at least one's
reasons matter as much as one's actions, and not just on grounds
of style. To do the right thing but for a racist reason is to write
off the *future* development of the peoples concerned. Whatever
the justice of the policy options which it grounds, one can expect
little light for the future from a theory which proclaims that 'The
general war which will then break out will scatter this Slav
Sonderbund, and annihilate all these small pig-headed nations
even to their very names' (Engels, January 1849; *R1848*, p. 225).

German unity

A second, and equally important, aspect of the national question
was that of German unity. This was crucial in two respects.
Firstly, the fact that Germany was fragmented before 1848 meant
that the bourgeois liberal movement also was fragmented and thus
weak. Secondly, the revolution itself foundered on the impossibility of achieving any German unity which could not be vetoed
by either Austria or Prussia or both. As early as June 1848 Marx
stressed the consequent weakness of the Assembly at Frankfurt,
which stood not so much above as apart from the Berlin and
Vienna assemblies, in the name of 'Germany'.

Frankfurt is only an ideal centre, corresponding to the previously existing
ideal, i.e., only imagined, unity of Germany . . . Whereas the French and
the English national assemblies stood on the volcanic soil of Paris and
London, the German National Assembly was content to find a piece of
neutral ground, where it could reflect on the best possible constitution
and the best possible order of business without its peace of mind being
disturbed. (June 1848; *R1848*, p. 121)

The second half of this argument raises the complex question of
the relation between bourgeois development and national unification. Marx clearly regards German unity as vital for real bourgeois development: 'How', he asks, 'could any modern tasks be
accomplished on the basis of a land divided into thirty-nine parts?'
(June 1848; *R1848*, p. 123). It would be difficult to establish a
watertight entailment between nation and bourgeoisie, but a
developed bourgeoisie outside the nation-state context is almost
equally hard to envisage. To begin with, as we saw in chapter 2,
the bourgeoisie develop from being an estate ('*Bürgerstand*') to

being a class ('*Bourgeoisie*' – see p. 23 above). Being a class does not perhaps imply living in a nation, but it certainly implies opposing feudal princedom, whether that is already established in a nation or fragmented into many small units. It is not logically impossible for bourgeois society of a kind to develop in units smaller than the 'Germany' envisaged by Marx. But for that to happen, we would have to have a number of bourgeoisies developing within their smaller boundaries, without the stimulus of a successful national unification struggle, to the point where they could separately topple the several entrenched petty princes. At the very least, one could argue that if bourgeois society does not entail national unity, certainly national unity would be a crucial spur to the development of bourgeois society.

One of the main reasons why German unity never got off the ground during the revolution is the opposition of great powers, internal and external. The internal powers were Prussia and Austria. They deadened the impetus for unity by their successful reaction against the politics of its proponents, and when either was tempted to risk such dangerous politics, so long as the resulting Germany was firmly under its control, the other was always there to veto such plans. The external great powers, England, France and Russia, were all equally opposed to the development of a new central-European great power. The combination of their opposition with Prussia's reluctance to accept the implications of her involvement brought about the conclusion in August 1848 of the Treaty of Malmö, whereby Prussia ceded her gains in the war with Sweden over Schleswig-Holstein. Engels bitterly castigated the abandonment of 'the first *revolutionary war* waged by Germany' (September 1848; *NRZ*, p. 114). It is perhaps his frustration both with the complexities of nationalism and with the interference of the great powers which leads Marx so frequently to call for another 'revolutionary war', this one with Russia. He has in mind the wars of 1792 against European reaction which saved the French Revolution, both internally and externally, because the need for mobilisation thwarted the reactionaries. Blanqui, indeed, had tried consciously to re-enact this drama with his incursion into the French Assembly in May 1848, demanding a revolutionary war against Poland (see *CSF*, p. 58, *MPF*, p. 194, and De Luna, pp. 116–18). Marx would have been well aware of this attempt at the time, shortly after his leaving Paris for Cologne in April 1848.

Lassalle was later to argue with justification that, as the parallel war in Germany, even if it were to be successful, would not be a *popular* war, it would most likely confirm the Hohenzollern in their position rather than have the impetus within it which would drive towards revolution. If a repeat of the French wars of 1792 had been possible, then its effects could well have been as Marx envisaged, but the parallel could have been made realistic only if all the other contrasts between the two cases, already examined in this chapter, had not obtained (see Evans, pp. 124–5).

Conclusion: the prospects for reaction

The fate of the German revolution falsifies the *Manifesto*'s correlation of 'each step in the development of the bourgeoisie' with 'a corresponding political advance of that class' (*CM*, p. 69). The reason for this was that the bourgeoisie's conflict with 'feudalism' was overlaid by conflicts with other groups, of an intensity which drove the bourgeoisie to reaction. On our distinction as set out earlier (see pp. 40–1 above), the artisans are clearly a *transitional* group, resisting the destruction of their way of life by emergent bourgeois society. The situation with the peasants is less clear-cut. The abolition of serfdom under the Napoleonic occupation did not end manorial obligations, and did not lead to a full-blooded peasant proprietorship on the French model, even in the South and West where parcellation tended to occur. In the North and East we can see the beginnings of latifundia on a pattern similar to capitalist farming. The crucial point, which Hamerow makes, is that the destruction of manorialism was not complete even by 1848, a point which Marx explicitly makes several years later (see Hamerow, pp. 53–4, and *NYDT* 19 October 1858, in *MEW* XII, p. 591). Both kinds of peasants – tenants to absentee landlords in the South and West, and landless peasants on latifundia in the North and East – may be seen as suffering from the early penetration of *bourgeois* commercial pressures into 'feudal' agriculture, and it might be claimed that they are therefore a *structural* rather than a transitional group. But even insofar as in 1848 Marx did allow of small peasant proprietorship as a structural feature of the bourgeois economy, the peasants of the South and West had not yet clearly achieved that status; equally, while the ranches of the North and East are foreshadowings of capitalist exploitation, their labourers had not achieved the juridical and economic 'freedom' characteristic of the citizen of bourgeois society. It might be suggested that, if my distinction is so hard to apply, I should withdraw it. But it is important to see which of the difficulties encountered by Marx's theories arise from the kind of entity which bourgeois society is when it gets going, and which of them are due to the problems of getting it going in the first place. The difficulty in classifying the German peasants is illuminating, showing as it does the extent to which the lower orders had been adversely affected by bourgeois conditions *before* the bourgeoisie made their bid for power. We may conclude our discussion of the point by saying that the lower orders with whom the bourgeoisie came into conflict were mainly transitional rather than structural, but that the difficulty of deciding the matter reflects on the relative 'lateness' of the bourgeoisie's struggle for power.

The German events forced Marx explicitly to recognise that the state is an active element of the social formation, capable of significantly affecting it, and that its behaviour cannot be foreclosed by a neat conceptual formula. True, he still uses the phrase about the government as 'a committee to administer [the bourgeoisie's] general interests' (*R1848*, p. 261). But he now sees such a committee as something which the bourgeoisie have to 'hack out' of reality. He notes how vital it is for them 'to demote the bureaucracy and the army from the position of masters of trade and commerce', and emphasises that it must '*make* them into mere organs of bourgeois commerce' (*R1848*, p. 260). As long as this is not done, they can seriously retard the bourgeois economy:

The basic principle of the imposed Prussian constitution is to use the taxes for maintaining the state as an oppressive, independent and sacred force contraposed to industry, commerce and agriculture, instead of *degrading* it by turning it into a profane *tool* of bourgeois society. (*NRZ*, p. 224)

Marx does not, and could not plausibly, claim that such a state is *impossssible* in bourgeois conditions; he says rather that it 'is unsuitable for' ('*paßt nicht für*') such conditions (*NRZ*, p. 225, from *MEW* VI, p. 195). It is its 'unsuitability' which, he believes, will put an end to its pretensions. Marx thus does not reduce the criteria for political foundedness straightforwardly to those for social foundedness, and even accepts that the reaction can use its political power to shore up its social basis: 'It is *entirely* consistent, when it attempts to replace free competition by the guild system, mechanical spinning by the spinning-wheel and the steam-plough by the hoe' (*NRZ*, p. 225). In admitting this fact, Marx does not abandon his basic claim: the succession may be delayed, but succession there will be. The further development of the economy, bringing new social prominence to the bourgeoisie, will make the reaction increasingly unstable, so that its victory 'only concludes the first act of the drama' (*R1848*, p. 248). We shall return to the drama in chapter 7.

4. Reflections on the reaction in France

This chapter deals with Marx's analyses of events in France from 1848 to 1851. These events began with the February revolution and ended with the *coup d'état* of Louis-Napoleon Bonaparte in December 1851. The treatment will resemble that of the German events in chapter 4. There is however a difference, in that the writings on France tend to dwell more on the notion of process in the revolution and its aftermath, whereas the German ones emphasise more the notion of constitution. But both notions are present in both sets of writings, so that our study of France will complement that of Germany in theoretical terms. Since Marx's own texts on France lay such emphasis on periodisation, I shall divide this chapter according to the periods which Marx analyses rather than in the more explicitly theoretical manner adopted in the preceding chapter. This suits the exposition and analysis of Marx's notion of process which, as I have said, will be one of our central concerns.

A word about the writings involved is in order. The first is a series of articles which Marx wrote for the *Neue Rheinische Zeitung-Revue*, which he edited in London in 1850. Marx projected four articles on the French events, of which he wrote the first two. He wrote a third which differed from the originally-projected third article, but was a part of the series. He did not write the projected fourth article. In 1895, however, Engels took the three articles actually written, and added to them as a 'fourth chapter' two extracts from a review of European affairs which he and Marx had written for a later (in fact the last) number of the *Revue*. He called the whole *The Class Struggles in France: 1848 to 1850* (*CSF*), and it is this version which we are analysing. The second is a series of articles which Marx wrote in 1852, and which Joseph Weydemeyer published as a complete issue of his journal *Die Revolution* (New York 1852) under the title *The Eighteenth Brumaire of Louis Bonaparte* (*EBLB*).

Prelude to revolution

In social terms, the France which we encounter on the eve of 1848 is not radically unlike the one which we left at the aftermath of the first French Revolution. There was undoubtedly an increase in industry during the period 1815–48, and Palmade tells us that 'a new overall equilibrium of the economy tended to appear in which industrial, commercial annd financial sectors weighed as much as agriculture, the traditional source of influence' (p. 115). Palmade records the successes of the economy in this period (pp. 81–6), and Price notes the expansion in railways, engineering, metals and textiles (Price 1972, pp. 15–16). But having said all that, we must agree with both these authors that industrial development had been neither qualitatively nor quantitatively spectacular. Such 'industrialists' as there were, with the sole exception of exporters, were heavily protectionist (Palmade, pp. 102–3). Moreover, the scale of 'industry' was exceedingly small, at times being barely discernible from that of established craft production. While Palmade was correct that land was beginning to be matched in importance by other economic sectors, it must be stressed that within those sectors industry was very much the junior partner. An important reason for this was that the evolution of a rich class of '*notables*' – aristocratic and bourgeois proprietors – caused an extremely conservative attitude to investment to percolate through society from its top layers. All classes of potential investors were deflected from industrial investment by the relatively high profit to be made from financing the state debt (see Palmade, p. 78).

Politically, the July Revolution of 1830 had seen the restored Bourbon dynasty replaced by the House of Orleans under Louis Philippe. While the defining characteristic of all kinds of '*notables*' continued to be landed property, it is true that this change meant a defeat for the purely land-based fraction, and the advancement of a group who combined landed with financial wealth. Marx depicts the July Monarchy of 1830–48 as a regime dominated by all those interested in profiting from the state debt: 'bankers, stock-market barons, railway barons, owners of coal and iron mines and forests, a section of landed proprietors who had joined their ranks – the so-called *financial aristocracy*' (*CSF*, p. 36). Marx tells us in the same place that the industrial bourgeoisie were actually part of the opposition during this period. While calling it 'forced', Palmade allows that Marx's account 'had some basis in fact' (p. 105). Price says that his picture is broadly right, and that the group identified by Marx showed signs of having an influence 'seemingly not proportionate to their presence in the Chamber' (Price 1972, p. 41). He notes that Marx also appears correct 'in indicating the resentment felt by most manufacturers of government fiscal policy' (p. 43).

In 1847 there occurred a massive economic crisis, which affected particularly the lower orders: peasants, artisans and proletarians. Recovery began in mid-1847, and the revolution in fact occurred during a period of increasing prosperity, 'but that the revolution could occur in February 1848 was in large part due to the social unrest and discontent caused by the economic crisis' (Price 1972, p. 86). At the same time as the crisis, there came some of the most shattering revelations of the scandalous doings of the financial aristocracy or 'bankocracy'. The republican bourgeoisie, favoured by the industrialists because of their opposition to the dominance of financial interests, thus found themselves at the head of a revolutionary movement, when all that they had contemplated was, at the very most, a change of government and policy. It might be useful to the reader briefly to outline the chronology of the events with which we have to deal. Louis Philippe abdicated in February 1848, and shortly afterwards the republic was declared. In April a Constituent Assembly was elected, which was dominated by *notables*. The workers were placated by the creation of National Workshops, which in fact were little more than 'indoor relief'. In June, when the Government decided to close them down, there took place a massive confrontation of workers (largely artisans) and the bourgeoisie in Paris; the workers were savagely defeated. General Cavaignac, a moderate bourgeois republican, took dictatorial powers at the request of the Assembly. Under universal suffrage, proclaimed in February, Cavaignac's unpopularity resulted in his losing to Bonaparte in the December 1848 elections for President under the proposed new constitution. Bonaparte took over on 20 December, and replaced the republican government by an Orleanist one under Odilon Barrot. The Constituent Assembly disbanded in May 1849, to be replaced by a Legislative Assembly, with a majority of *notables* but a strong minority of 'reds'. The petty bourgeois social democrats tried a rising in June 1849, in protest against Bonaparte's reactionary Italian policy, but bungled it and lost many of their leaders who were imprisoned. In October 1849 Bonaparte dismissed Barrot, replacing his government by one dominated by Achille Fould, a leading 'bankocrat' and a hench-man of Bonaparte. In March 1850 the 'reds' won 20 of the 30 by-elections to fill the vacant seats of their imprisoned colleagues, and in the resultant panic the *notables*, now coalesced into the 'Party of Order', abolished universal suffrage (May 1850). Bona-parte was able to capitalise on their resulting unpopularity and their need to rely on him, and staged a successful coup d'etat in December 1851, followed by a plebiscite in which the French people massively endorsed his inauguration of the Second Empire. The conflicts which I have just outlined explain why the sequence of events in 1848–51 went as it were in the reverse direction to that of the first French revolution:

In the first French revolution the rule of the constitutionalists was followed by the rule of the Girondins, and the rule of the Girondins by the rule of the Jacobins. Each of these parties leaned on the more progressive party. As soon as it had brought the revolution to the point where it was unable to follow it any further, let alone advance ahead of it, it was pushed aside by the bolder ally standing behind it and sent to the guillotine. In this way the revolution moved in an ascending path. In the revolution of 1848 this relationship was reversed... Every party kicked out behind at the party pressing it forward and leaned on the party in front, which was pressing backward. No wonder each party lost its balance in this ridiculous posture, and collapsed in the midst of curious capers, after having made the inevitable grimaces. In this way the revo-lution moved in a descending path. Before the first February barricade had been cleared away and the first revolutionary authority constituted, the parties found themselves enmeshed in this retrogressive process. (*EBLB*, pp. 169–70)

One of our central concerns in this chapter is to elucidate the meaning of the 'retrogressive process' which Marx here invokes. He frequently speaks of, for example, various 'periods in the life-process of the republic' (*CSF*, p. 78) ('Perioden des Lebens-prozesses der Republik' (*MEW* VII, p. 49)). There is at least a fair suspicion of rigid necessitarianism about such an image, as though 'the revolution' or 'the republic' were organisms with a more or less predetermined life-process which unfolded itself without regard to the intentions or actions of men. I shall argue that Marx does indeed see structure emerging from flux in these writings, and that he sees the structure as more and more predominating over the actions of individuals and groups. But I shall argue that this is not because of a strict and absolute necessitarianism. It is rather because Marx, while allowing that individuals and groups make decisions, also believes that their possible choice of decisions is limited; taking one kind of decision commits us, with 'increasing inevitability', to making more of a similar type and lowers the probability of our retracing our steps. Chapter 5 will deal with this issue more directly; it will arise in this chapter insofar as we estimate alternative outcomes at various stages.

The life-process of the revolution

It is revealing that we must begin with a negative, namely with Marx's rejection of the democrats' conception of the French crisis. The democrats sum up the political situation throughout the whole Continent in terms of the single word: *reaction*. This, Marx grants, is an understandable impression, since in both France and Prussia, to take the two most prominent cases, strong reactionary governments are suppressing democratic freedoms with the aid of police and bureaucracy.

But this superficial appearance veils the *class struggle* and the peculiar physiognomy of this period, and it vanishes on a closer examination of the situation and the parties. (*EBLB*, p. 173)

There are two quite different ways of reading this argument, but only one is correct. The incorrect way is to read Marx as saying that political terms like 'republican', 'monarchist' and 'reaction' are a mere hallucination, a mirage which we must totally dispel if we are to penetrate to the sole reality which is the underlying class struggle. This is not merely a simplistic, but a highly misleading interpretation of Marx. Preceding chapters should have already suggested this, and the present chapter will spell it out in greater detail. But even the passage containing the argument is a sufficient case in point. Marx says that in the democrats' terms the struggle in France is

a simple struggle between republicans and royalists. However, the democrats sum up the whole course of development itself in *one* slogan: '*reaction*' – a night in which all cats are grey and which allows them to reel off their useless platitudes (*EBLB*, p. 172).

Marx is then accusing the democrats of 'summing up' a complex development in *one* slogan. He even allows that on the surface this slogan has an application. But he goes on to say that to leave it at that is to ignore all the specific questions such as what the French bourgeoisie's monarchism *means*, what the struggle between political democracy and monarchism *represents* in the quite different social contexts of, for example, France and Prussia. The democrats' error is seeing it as a *simple* struggle, to be summed up in *one* slogan. Political language is thus not *hallucinatory* (a 'seeing' of what is not there at all) but *illusory* (a partial seeing, thus a 'mis-seeing', of what is really there). Politics, then, is to be situated within, not reduced to, economic class-structure.

In specifying the context in which the French political events are to be placed, Marx draws a contrast between France's crisis and that of the same time in Germany. As we have seen, he is concerned in his *Neue Rheinische Zeitung* writings to impress on the Germans that they are faced, like it or not, with a 'life-or-death' struggle between *two forms of society*, the feudal and the bourgeois. In France on the other hand, he stresses, a similar political change – a monarchy overthrown by a coalition of bourgeoisie, petty bourgeoisie and workers – represents a merely *political* revolution on the basis of an already established bourgeois society. This emerges in the intentions and actions of the Constituent National Assembly (elected April, convened 4 May):

> The republic proclaimed by the National Assembly, the only legitimate republic, is not a revolutionary weapon against the bourgeois order but rather its political reconstitution, the political reconsolidation of bourgeois society – in a word *the bourgeois republic*. (*CSF*, p. 57)

There are two possible objections to this argument. The first is that this is exactly the intention proclaimed by the Prussian bourgeoisie as well (see p. 62 above). But Marx could and does accept the similarity of intention; his point is that the situation in France is one where the intended project is viable (ignoring for the moment its subsequent succumbing to Bonaparte), whereas in Germany it cannot but be an illusion. The second objection is that the political reconstitution of bourgeois society is anything but the aim expressed by the proletarians, artisans and by many at least of the petty bourgeois supporting the February insurrection. Again Marx would accept, even emphasise, this point. What he is arguing indeed is that the June days – the violent suppression of the workers' demands – were necessary so that the 'order of the day' should prevail over the immoderate pretensions of the bourgeoisie's lower-class allies. In Marx's view we arrive at an understanding of what is really happening not by consulting the intentions of a particular group but by an analysis of the various parties involved (covering not only their situation but also, of course, their intentions), and seeing which group, if any, has intentions which coincide with what is actually feasible (see *R1848*, p. 123).

I propose to examine the argument which Marx presents in *CSF* and *EBLB*, within the framework of the periodisation employed in the latter. Unless I draw attention to precise differences, I regard the two works as agreeing on the points covered; some important differences between their treatments (and in one case between their periodisations) will in fact emerge. It must of course be borne in mind that *CSF* does not go beyond the end of 1850, when the last of its four sections was written (see diagram, p. 101 below).

First period. From 24 February to 4 May 1848, February period. Prologue: Universal brotherhood swindle (*EBLB*, p. 233)

Marx begins *CSF* by drawing a picture of the complex and many-sectioned coalition which made the revolution and was reflected in the Provisional Government. 'It could be nothing other than a *compromise between the various classes* who together overthrew the July monarchy, but whose interests were mutually hostile' (*CSF*, p. 41). It contained representatives of the republican petty bourgeoisie, the republican bourgeoisie (called after their paper, the *National*), the dynastic (i.e., Orleanist) opposition, and only two workers' representatives, Louis Blanc and Albert. Lastly, Marx tells us, there came Lamartine, representing not a particular interest or class, but rather 'the February revolution itself, the common uprising with its illusions' (*CSF*, p. 42). Lamartine thus represented, in Marx's eyes, the essence of this first period: revolutionary enthusiasm. What he says about this phenomenon here adds little to what we have already seen in preceding chapters, except for the distinction which he draws between the strength and persistence of the 1848 enthusiam and that of the first revolution. In general, his analysis of 1848 in France consistently applies a point which he made in the *Neue Rheinische Zeitung* about the June days. Answering the Paris petty bourgeois paper *La Réforme*, which was bemoaning the collapse of revolutionary *fraternité*, he argued that such political illusions of class co-operation were illusory and misleading: 'What [in 1789] was an adequate expression of the real position, is today merely an escape from the existing situation' (*NRZ*, p. 142; for Prussia, see *MEW* VI, pp. 199–204).

This fact deserves some emphasis, since Marx is sometimes accused of exaggerating the extent of *fraternité*, that is, of the naive virtuous enthusiasm of the masses, in order to heighten the cynical viciousness of their June victors (see e.g., Price 1972, p. 111). It is true that Marx's strong pedagogical interest in teaching the proletariat the dangers of bourgeois alliances does lead him sometimes to emphasise the gullibility of the people and the extent of that gullibility; on the whole, however, the tenor of his analysis is along the lines of our *Neue Rheinische Zeitung* quote. He not only says that there is no objective basis for *fraternité*, but also shows how quickly and deeply it was challenged. The workers invaded the deliberations of the Provisional Government and forced it tardily to proclaim the republic; they also had to be fobbed off with National Workshops which earned their inmates little but the contempt and resentment of both bourgeoisie and peasants.

The proletariat had secured the republic arms in hand, and now imprinted it with its own hallmark, proclaiming it to be a *social republic*. In this way the general content of the modern revolution was indicated, but this content stood in the strangest contradiction with everything which could immediately and directly be put into practice in the given circumstances and conditions, with the material available and the level of education attained by the mass of the people. (*EBLB*, p. 153; see also *CSF*, pp. 43–4)

Unable to disavow those who had carried it to power, the Provisional Government had to go along with the idea of this radical republic. But most of its members were well aware of the threat which such ideas, backed by real popular force, held for bourgeois property and business, and they 'did everything to make it acceptable to the bourgeoisie and to the provinces' (*CSF*, pp. 47–8). Terror and political trials were disavowed, and the personnel of the July Monarchy – judiciary, army and administration – were virtually taken over unaltered. Marx also charges that, besides their fear, the *National* group in any case saw the republic as no more than 'a new evening dress for the old bourgeois society' (*CSF*, p. 48). De Luna has expended a lot of energy in rebutting this view of their ideas, showing that the government, and in many cases Cavaignac personally, had radical ambitions with regard to the democratisation of public institutions and the secularisation of education (see De Luna, chapter IX). More importantly, he characterises their attitude to the economy as neither the 'blue' nor the 'red' republicanism of the conventional polarity, but a third position, which he calls a 'moderate social or moderate interventionist point of view' (pp. 248–9). This involved ambitious plans for progressive taxation, state intervention to help certain industries and direct railway development, and a radical approach to the state's obligation to provide serious help to the unemployed and indigent (see chapters X to XII). It would however probably be fair to characterise them as the kind of reformers who want bourgeois society without its defects of whom Marx speaks on other occasions (see *CM*, p. 93). Even De Luna chronicles how in the course of the year they had to let most of their ambitions be watered down, and tells us that the 'most ardent desire' of Goud-chaux, the Finance Minister, 'was to restore the "confidence" of the affluent classes, a traditional and conservative policy but also a sensible one' (p. 274). Marx's possible ungenerosity does not amount to inaccuracy in important matters, given that a combination of fear and a basically bourgeois vision set such severe limits to the actual achievements of the *National*. When those with an interest in the persistence of the state debt, led by the 'bankocracy', started a run on the Banque de France in order to weaken the Provisional Government, the latter responded by honouring state credits *ahead* of their due date! Thus, Marx concludes, 'the February revolution directly consolidated and extended the bankocracy which it was supposed to overthrow' (*CSF*, p. 51).

Marx does allow of one factor which might have driven the revolution forward at this point. If there had been strong resistance from a determined reactionary group at home or from a foreign country, then the *National* group could have been propelled to leadership of a Committee of Public Safety, forced to resist reactionary encroachments and to grant real concessions to the masses needed for defence of the revolution. When Marx tells us that because it met no strong domestic or foreign opposition the revolution was disarmed (*CSF*, p. 48) he need not claim that such opposition would have been a sufficient condition in itself for more radical progress; it suffices that such a challenge would have gone a long way to maintaining the pure republicans' sense of mission and stilling their fear of their erstwhile revolutionary allies.

> *Second period. Period of the establishment of the republic*
> *and of the Constituent National Assembly* (*EBLB*, p. 233)

This second period covers the life-span of the Constituent National Assembly, which convened in May 1848 and disbanded in May 1849. Marx calls it the period of the 'establishment' of the republic; the original German ['*Konstituierung*' (*MEW* VIII, p. 192)] should recall the point made on pages 56ff. above: we have to do here both with the process of writing a constitutional document and with the process of establishing political rule, without which latter mere documents are meaningless. The process of constituting the bourgeois republic has three stages: firstly the active suppression of the workers; secondly the drawing up of the constitutional rules for the republic; and thirdly the gradual defeat of the *National* group once its task of 'constituting' was over.

4 May to 25 June 1848. We have already seen how threadbare was the revolutionary 'enthusiasm' of February. The tensions to which it was subject were heightened by the election of the Assembly,[1] which Marx described as an appeal from revolutionary Paris to sober France.

> It was a living protest against the pretensions of the February days and an attempt to reduce the results of the revolution to the standards of the bourgeoisie. (*EBLB*, p. 153)

This was an overwhelmingly bourgeois assembly, especially as the far from radical peasants exercised their new franchise mostly under the influence of the bourgeois *notables* of the countryside, and in any case had no love of Parisian revolutionaries (see Price 1975, pp. 28–9). Several times the Parisian workers put pressure

---

[1] France had a Constituent, followed by a Legislative, Assembly; where the context is clear, I refer to 'the Assembly'.

on the assembly, on one occasion even forcing entry; but this had little or no effect on the policy of the bourgeoisie. The workers were granted the dignity of a minister and commission of their own in the Luxembourg Palace, but the very existence of such institutions *alongside* the bourgeois ministries of Finance and Public Works emphasised rather than cured the alienation of the workers from the political and social order being consolidated by the Assembly. The National Workshops set up by the Commission were little other than thinly disguised relief agencies.

Marx certainly intends to portray the struggle which broke out in June 1848 as a confrontation between the bourgeoisie and the new rising class, the proletariat; he calls it their 'first great battle' (*CSF*, p. 58). This picture has been attacked for being too 'clear-cut' (see Price 1972, pp. 172, 188). Its chief defect is that it glosses too easily over the facts that the 'workers' involved were divided between proletarians and artisans, and that the latter were by far the larger element. It is also important to note that there was a large number of workers along with the 'proprietors, shopkeepers, clerks, intellectuals and members of the liberal professions' who suppressed the insurrection (Price 1975, p. 31). Marx is however right in stressing the broadly *class* division involved in June, as distinct from February; Price himself calls June 'a revolt of the poor in all its diversity demanding a more equitable sharing of society's wealth' (Price 1975, pp. 30–1), and also allows that Marx's account of it 'does reflect the contemporary consciousness of things' (Price 1972, p. 188). Tilly and Lees, after closely examining the evidence on participation, conclude that 'Marx's analysis of the June Days was essentially right' (Tilly and Lees, p. 201). They point out the very important fact that the large number of artisan participants 'came not from the elite artisans of the luxury trades but from crafts with mixed skill levels, sectors supplying the basic needs of an industrializing economy' (p. 202). They also note the participation of a significant number of what could be called 'factory' workers (p. 180; see also Price 1972, p. 164), and conclude that the insurrection saw the emergence of 'the trade societies, the mechanics, and the construction workers of an increasingly proletarianized labour force. Protest in France was becoming modern' (p. 202). We shall return to the significance of artisan protest at the end of this chapter (see pp. 106–07 below); here we shall study the consequences of the revolt.

I have said that we would estimate the likelihood of alternative outcomes at various stages. It would however serve little purpose to separate the first period from the first sub-period of the second, since the former covers the initial enthusiasm and the latter its breakdown. We are thus faced with a single question about both phases, as to whether the 'bourgeois definition' of the republic was really avoidable. It is difficult to think of an alternative. The bourgeoisie might have succeeded in achieving a simple change of government, or at most of the written constitution, if there had not been numerous and discontented lower orders; but such there were. Given their existence, the bourgeoisie could not avoid being carried beyond their original intentions, with the result that the basic lines of these intentions had to be forcefully restated.

25 June to 10 December 1848. The story which we have just recounted meant that, while the *National* group was now the sole governing party [Marx speaks of its 'dictatorship' (*EBLB*, p. 233) ('*Diktatur*' *MEW* VIII, p. 192)], this position had come to it in quite the opposite of the way which it had always envisaged.

It had achieved power through the grape-shot which had suppressed a rising of the proletariat against capital, not through a liberal revolt of the bourgeoisie against the throne. What it had imagined would be the *most revolutionary* event turned out to be in reality the *most counterrevolutionary*. (*EBLB*, p. 158)

The presence of the threat from the workers, which we have just discussed, meant that the pure republic had nevertheless to define itself at least in a negative respect, in that it had to defend itself from below. In so doing, its official rulers succumbed to the loftier vipers within the bosom of their own class: the Party of Order (see p. 94 below). This became the more unavoidable the more they had to alienate sections of the lower classes.

Their first confrontation came with the petty bourgeoisie of shopkeepers, small manufacturers and so on. These had fought keenly for the defence of property against the communist threat in June; but now they were quickly disabused.

The petty bourgeoisie realised with horror that by crushing the workers they had delivered themselves unresisting into the hands of their creditors. Since February their creeping bankruptcy, which they had apparently ignored, had become chronic and after June it was declared openly. Their *nominal* property had been left unchallenged as long as it had been a question of driving them to the battlefield in the *name of property*. Now that the great issue with the proletariat had been settled, the small business with the shopkeepers could be settled in turn. (*CSF*, p. 66)

It was neither vindictiveness nor stupidity which drove the *National* to alienate the petty bourgeoisie. Given their own desire to restore normalcy, overlaid by their extreme anxiety to ingratiate themselves with the bankocracy, it was rational for them to 'restore credit to a sound footing', which of course meant squeezing those whose businesses had done poorly, if they had carried on at all, in the period since February. They hesitated before the severity of petty-bourgeois reaction, but this in its turn was blunted when the workers once more became restive, demanding an amnesty for June. The proposed measures were accepted by the petty bourgeoisie, but the Pyrrhic nature of the government's victory emerged in the election of Raspail and Bonaparte as deputies for Paris in September 1848. In the same elections, the bourgeoisie of Paris voted for Fould, a famous banker from the days of the July Monarchy, thus voicing their preference for the restoration of sound business over the storms of even the *National's* modest democracy. At the same time the state's indebtedness, compounded by the costs of June, forced it to have continued and growing recourse to Fould's bankocracy for loans. The peasant, already disgruntled at the surcharge imposed on the wine tax before June, was equally disappointed in his hopes that the *National* group would bring to French life and foreign policy that '*gloire*' which he associated with the highpoint of Napoleon's Empire. The *National* were then merely tolerated with suspicion by their own class, and growing increasingly unpopular with the rest of society. 'Even at this time, when they had at their disposal a parliamentary majority and all the resources of governmental authority, power was daily slipping further from their feeble grasp' (*EBLB*, p. 162).

We might well ask, however, whether this was an inevitable process. It will already be clear that Marx is here employing the kind of 'trade-off' notion which we noted in chapter 3 (see page 69); the question then is, what allies the *National* could have enlisted to avoid their downfall. If the government had not forced the bankruptcies of the shopkeepers, it is unlikely that the petty bourgeoisie alone could have sufficed to protect them from the big bourgeoisie's ire; but to add in the weight of the workers would have meant a revocation of the June defeat, and a willingness to prosecute the revolution beyond bourgeois horizons. Even assuming that the *National*'s own horizons would have stretched this far, and that the workers bore no grudges, such an alliance would have re-opened all the questions of the February period, and alienated the *National* from their own class, who would not sacrifice their property interests to an abstract and uninterpreted principle. Looking to the right for allies, we might suggest that the government could have conciliated the big bourgeoisie by showing respect for property and order. But this is exactly what they did, and the more they did it the more power they lost! One cannot present the big bourgeoisie as a possible ally against the *National*'s fate, since the latter's task was precisely to establish bourgeois democracy (with the emphasis on the adjective). To the extent to which they fulfilled this task they destroyed what distinguished abstract political democracy from its bourgeois interpretation; in the process, their own viable identity collapsed, and they merged with their class. 'Bourgeois republicanism [,] which found expression in the life and activities of this Constituent Assembly...did not die and was not killed off, but simply decayed' (*CSF*, p. 64). But it might very properly be urged at this point that we have made Marx's explanation plausible at the expense of his fundamental theory. Where the *Communist Manifesto* has told us that bourgeois democracy is a tool innocuously employed by the bourgeoisie, here we see it as a fantasy too dangerous to be allowed. The inability of Continental bourgeoisies to achieve or retain democratic constitutions in the 1848–51 period was indeed a serious blow to the optimism expressed in the *Manifesto*, and it indeed required a re-examination of the basic theory, as we shall see below (especially pp. 199ff.). For the moment we shall simply accept that circumstances made democracy dangeous for the bourgeoisie, and follow out the consequences of this fact for the bourgeois democrats.

The constitution drawn up by the Assembly and adopted in November 1848 reflected this fact in the ambivalence of its provisions, which Marx dissected in *EBLB*. He pointed out that every article stating a right or a freedom was immediately followed by an interpretative proviso invoking 'public order' or the 'general good' or some such notion. All of these contradictions Marx sees as reflections of the basic contradiction of the whole constitution:

that it gives power to the classes whose social slavery it is intended to perpetuate: proletariat, peasants and petty bourgeoisie. And it deprives the bourgeoisie, the class whose old social power it sanctions, of the political guarantee of this power. (*CSF*, p. 71)

As regards its institutional provisions, Marx says that the constitution's 'Achilles' Heel' lies in the powers guaranteed respectively to the President and the Legislature. Paragraphs 45 to 70 mean that the Legislature can remove the President constitutionally, whereas he can remove it only by abolishing the whole constitution, that is, by a *coup d'état*. 'Here, therefore, the Constitution provokes its own forcible destruction' (*EBLB*, p. 160). This is because, although not allowing him constitutionally to overthrow the legislature, the constitution invests in the President a number of powers which clearly set him over against it as a potential challenger of its right to speak exclusively for the nation: it tries to give 'real power to the President, [and] endeavours to secure moral power to the Assembly' (p. 161). Marx explains this reliance on a strong executive as arising out of the measures which the bourgeois republic had had to take to defend itself: 'it elevated to the status of a constitutional law the extraordinary powers which the National Assembly had providently invested in its chairman in the interests of its own safety after the terror of 15 May and 25 June' (*CSF*, p. 69). De Luna points out that the decision to have a presidential executive chosen by universal suffrage was taken as early as May 1848, even before the workers' insurrection. 'The ideal of the single strong executive was widespread at that time, growing out of republican theories, the American experiences, and, negatively, dissatisfaction with the collegial revolutionary governments' (De Luna, p. 366). Thus we may see the 'authoritarian' interpretation of the presidency as in some respects antedating the 'red' threat, although this in no way contradicts Marx's argument as to why the bourgeoisie increasingly adopted that interpretation.

This reliance on a strong executive explains the decision to hold presidential elections in December 1848, before the Legislative Assembly intended as the President's counterweight came into being. The elections proved a decisive setback for Cavaignac, the *National* group's leader, who got only 1.5 million to Bonaparte's 5.5 million votes. The attitudes of the different voting groups reflect the government's failure to make a successful trade-off between the demands of the various possible constituencies offered by French society. The peasants were voting against the republic of the rich, the wine tax and the disappointing performance of the group who had promised them *gloire*. Marx sees December 10 as essentially their *coup d'état*, represented by the nephew of the adored uncle (*CSF*, p. 72). The proletariat voted for Bonaparte to avenge their June defeat, and the petty bourgeoisie did so to hit back at their merciless creditors; finally, and most ironically, the big bourgeoisie did so because the *National* was no longer tolerable 'as soon as it tried to consolidate the temporary situation as the constitutional position' (*CSF*, p. 73; amended translation from *MEW* VII, p. 45).

20 December 1848 to 28 May 1849. This sub-period runs from Bonaparte's assumption of office to the convening of the Legislative Assembly in May 1849. As soon as he acquired presidential power, especially with such an overwhelming vote behind him, Bonaparte was able to replace the *National* group with a government led by Odilon Barrot, the Orleanist who had been the last Prime Minister under the July Monarchy. Marx observes that Barrot, who had unwittingly been a vehicle of the *National*'s rise to power, was 'even more suited to function fully consciously as the stepping-stone from the bourgeois republic to the monarchy' (*CSF*, p. 75; see De Luna, p. 397). But surely Marx can hardly mean that Bonaparte, with no royal blood, wanted a royalist restoration? Indeed not; what he did seek however was the same undermining of republican democracy as such a restoration required, which explains why the two royalist bourgeois fractions, Orleanist and Bourbon, were behind him. Molé, who had already served Napoleon, the Bourbons and Louis-Philippe, declared: 'he will be our instrument, whereas Cavaignac would be our master' (Quoted by De Luna, p. 375).

The *National* group hoped that, retaining its representation in the Assembly, it could regain the ministry lost in December and thus regain control over society; but this hope proved vain. An indication of why this was so is its failure to prevent the Barrot government from restoring the salt tax which the Provisional Government had abolished. The Assembly voted clearly against the measure, waited for the government to resign, and then realised that nothing was going to happen, for behind Barrot stood

Bonaparte with his five and a half million votes. The *National* were now incapable of preventing the growing independence of the Executive. The confrontation came to a head with Bonaparte's proposal in January 1849 that the Constituent Assembly should vote to disband by a certain date, irrespective of its earlier declaration that it would do so only after it had consolidated the constitution by building in 'organic' laws guaranteeing republicanism and democracy. Marx rejects the interpretation which sees this as a constitutional crisis between parliament and executive. His argument is very similar to the one examined on pages 81ff. above:

This interpretation of January 29 confuses the language of the struggle on the platform, in the press and in the clubs, with its real content... Thus on 29 January it was not the President and the National Assembly of the *same* republic which faced each other; it was the National Assembly of the nascent republic and the President of the fully fledged republic: two powers which embodied two completely different periods in the life process of the republic. (*CSF*, p. 78)

As we have already noted on page 80 above, one might suspect here that Marx is imposing on a real historical development a conceptually neat aphorism derived from some over-arching, metaphysical notion of a 'life process'. When he tells us that 'the first day on which the Constitution came into force was the last day of the Constituent Assembly's rule' (*CSF*, p. 72), is he able to specify a plausible mechanism ensuring that this is so (given that it is not literally true, in that the Constitutional President took office in December 1848 and the Assembly lasted until May 1849)? Marx does in fact supply such a mechanism or narrative. He does not rule out the *National* group's wishing to resist the watering-down of their democratic constitution. But he points out that as soon as they voiced the slightest threat along these lines, the undesirables fell in behind them.

The moment the Constituent Assembly had called the President into question in the person of Barrot, and hence the constituted bourgeois republic and the bourgeois republic in general, all the constituent elements of the February republic ranged themselves around it – all the parties which wanted the overthrow of the existing republic and a process of violent retrogression in order to transform it into the republic of their class interests and principles. What had been done was undone; the crystallisations of the revolutionary movement became fluid again. (*CSF*, p. 80, amended in light of *MEW* VII, p. 51)

It is not inconceivable that the *National* should have led such a movement. But why would they do so in January 1849 if not after February 1848, especially when June 1848 had created an explicit break with the workers, producing fear and mistrust on both sides? The realisation of the implications of the only alliance by which it could resist Barrot and Bonaparte finally forced the *National* group to capitulate, and 'it reverted to its normal character' (*CSF*, p. 82).

Marx is, then, analysing the fall of the *National* in terms of the concrete options open to them rather than in terms of some imposed conception of a life-process in which they are absolutely helpless nodes. The fact that Marx argues in terms of the real possibilities available at any juncture rather than in terms of a uniquely predetermined process or 'path' is indicated by his obituary comment:

> They did not go under; they faded away. Their history has been played out once and for all. In the following period they figured, whether inside or outside the Assembly, merely as memories, although these memories appeared to take on new life as soon as the mere name of Republic was at issue once more, and whenever the revolutionary conflict threatened to sink down to the lowest level. (*EBLB*, p. 165)

While the *National* were making their inglorious exit, the campaign for the Legislative Assembly elections began in March 1849. There were two main parties. The first was the bourgeois Party of Order, which was in essence a coalition of the two royalist fractions, Orleanist and Legitimist (*CSF*, p. 88). Neither of these could pursue its restorationist plans without encouraging the other's, so they compromised on joint rule which would be possible only under the neutral title of 'republic'. It was a very powerful coalition, possessing vast financial resources, an already existent network of coercion and influence throughout the provinces, and an army of vassals and servants in the peasants and others dependent for their livelihood on the *notables*. In February 1849 the representatives of the petty bourgeoisie and the workers came together in the 'red' party. This was led by the petty-bourgeois *Montagne*, as Ledru-Rollin and his peers were called in derisive reference to their heroic forebears of 1789–94. The 'reds' numbered also those few peasants who had become radical. Order gained 500 of the 750 seats, and the *National* only 70. Ledru-Rollin was returned for 5 seats, more than anyone else; in all, the reds won a surprising (and, to the bourgeoisie at least, shocking) 180 seats.

*Third period. Period of the constitutional republic and the
Legislative National Assembly (EBLB, p. 233)*

This period lasts from the convening of the Legislative Assembly
right up to Bonaparte's *coup* in December 1851. Before discussing
it, we must take stock. Marx is telling the story of the 'life-process'
of the republic inaugurated in February 1848. He believes that it
could not but be a bourgeois republic, in that social conditions had
not evolved so as to make a workers' republic a viable aim. The
forceful establishment of this fact had alienated the proletariat,
and the republican bourgeois government which had done this had
gone on to alienate the peasants and petty bourgeoisie, out of
fear and conservatism. The 'big bourgeoisie' represented by the
Party of Order, not daring to be explicitly monarchist even yet
– not to mention its internal tensions on the question of 'which
monarchy?' – nevertheless had grown frightened of a party which
took the ideals of 'bourgeois democracy' a little too seriously for
safety, and which in any case was compromised by undertakings
entered into in the earlier, revolutionary phase. 'For the rest of
its brief life, the republic was to be securely in the hands of its
enemies' (De Luna, p. 399).

28 May 1849 to 13 June 1849. At this point not only were the Party
of Order in control of the new Assembly, but also the wave of
reaction was entering its final phase throughout the Continent. The
European context gave a peculiar intensity to the issue on which
the petty-bourgeois *Montagne* confronted Order and Bonaparte:
the actions of an expedition allegedly sent to liberate Italy which
in fact was assisting the suppression of the Roman revolution.
Marx sees the flaunting of this policy as a deliberate attempt to
get the *Montagne* out into the streets, where they could be
definitively crushed. One commentator observes that Marx 'probably exaggerates the deliberateness with which the bait was
offered. Nonetheless conservatives seemed anything but anxious
to avoid conflict when it became possible' (Price 1972, p. 247).
The *Montagne* however were fatally anxious to avoid conflict in
one sense: fearing the proletariat, and realising that they could not
retain leadership outside the Assembly, they tried to effect a
purely parliamentary revolution. Marx, interestingly, does not *a
priori* rule out the possibility of such a parliamentary *coup*; he

mentions the ample parallels from the Convention of the first revolution, and says that unrest among the people and the army, coupled with the newness and inexperience of the Legislative majority, seemed favourable conditions. If the parliamentary *coup* succeeded, he suggests, 'the helm of state would immediately fall into its hands' (*CSF*, p. 97). The fact that Marx goes on to discuss the failure of the *Montagne*'s hopes, without even spelling out reasons why they were dashed, suggests however that his 'estimate' of the possibilities of a parliamentary coup was largely a sardonic contrast of the 1848 *Montagne* with their heroic namesakes. He tells us that the workers were not yet sufficiently recovered from the previous June to do more than follow the *Montagne*'s lead, at most extracting from them a vague promise of action in the streets, should the parliamentary manoeuvres fail. When they did fail, the *Montagne* could put up only indignant proclamations and a street demonstration from which, Marx says, 'deep-chested notes were missing' (*CSF*, p. 99).

13 June 1849 to 31 May 1850. This period runs from the suppression of the petty bourgeois democrats to the abolition of universal suffrage in May 1850. It was dominated by the Party of Order, who acted as one with Bonaparte in declaring a state of siege, sending the democrats to a special High Court, and imposing strict rules on deputies in the Assembly. Marx says that the rump of the *Montagne* left in the Assembly owed it to their honour to walk out. When he says that if they did so the Party of Order 'was bound to disintegrate into its original component parts' (*CSF*, p. 101) without the integrative effect of an opposition, he is being optimistic. His argument does however point to the important fact that the Party of Order, in attempting to maintain their joint rule, were bedevilled by the internal tensions between their Legitimist and Orleanist sections.

Along with the repressive measures already mentioned went the disbandment of the sections of the National Guard which were disposed towards the *Montagne*. This Marx sees as beginning a process in which Order was to become increasingly enmeshed: the destruction of democratic and republican institutions so as to make democracy and republic safe for the bourgeoisie.

Thus the bourgeoisie smashed its own last weapon against the army. However, it was compelled to do so from the moment when the petty bourgeoisie ceased to stand behind it as its vassal, and instead stood before it as a rebel, just as, in general, it had to destroy all its instruments of defence against absolutism with its own hands as soon as it had itself become absolute. (*EBLB*, p. 183)

Another significant turning-point had also arrived: for the first time, republicanism was now openly associated with the *defeated* party, so that the victors could vie with one another in royalist declarations and in undermining, while professing to protect, republican institutions. Marx observes how ironic it was that the Assembly, on adjourning in August 1849, left a committee of its members 'to protect the republic'; he also observes how unwise it was to adjourn at all, leaving Bonaparte a clear stage for two crucial months (*EBLB*, p. 184).

When it reconvened in October 1849, the Legislative Assembly fell to squabbling: the rival royalist factions of Order with each other, and both with Bonaparte. Bonaparte, in his quarrels with the royalists, accused his ministers of not defending him. When he had the temerity to suggest that the royalist pretenders should leave the heaven of exile to live as mundane 'citizens of France', he was haughtily reminded that 'while the royalist coalition needed him here in France on the President's chair as a *neutral man*, the serious pretenders to the throne had to remain withdrawn from profane sight by the mists of exile' (*CSF*, pp. 107–8). Bonaparte retaliated on 1 November by sacking the Barrot ministry and replacing it by a ministry headed by Hautpoul, with Fould in the crucial ministry of finance. We might ask why Bonaparte chose Fould for the first ministry which was really his own. In the first place, they were accomplices in the speculation in government stocks which Marx so scornfully depicted (see *LNF* in *MEW* VII, pp. 296–8, and *CSF*, p. 113). But more seriously, Fould was a member of a politically crucial group: the big bankers. We have already noted the predominance of finance in the French economy of the time, and seen that it had become a directly political issue in 1848. The state finances were caught in a constant deficit position, 'a disproportion which is both the cause and the effect of the system of state loans' (*CSF*, p. 110). The only way out of this circle was either to reduce the size of the state machine – impossible, given the need for repression – or to increase taxes to replace borrowing, a burden which would fall on the *notables* of Order themselves. As neither was acceptable, the state must remain the prisoner of 'the state creditors, bankers, money-dealers and sharks of the Bourse' (*CSF*, p. 111). We must not misinterpret the significance of this fact: Cobban warns us against thinking that having Fould's support meant that Bonaparte was supported by the financiers and industrialists in general. He points out that these were predominantly Orleanist, and more firmly so than the politicians (Cobban 1965, Vol. 2, pp. 151–2). This accords with the apparently opposed fact that, as de Luna points out, the Party of Order originally favoured Cavaignac over Bonaparte, until it became clearer and clearer that only the latter could absorb and redirect the threat from the lower orders (see De Luna, pp. 370ff.).

Bonaparte at this stage was the suitor bearing a gift, rather than the bridegroom receiving his dowry. One important factor motivating the big bourgeoisie, which is central to Marx's explanations but which he does not emphasise, is the sheer terror provoked in their hearts by the June confrontation with the workers (whether or not they had provoked it themselves). They were not calm, calculating masters of the situation: they were trying to stem revolution in a country which only two generations before had conducted revolution by the guillotine. In the calm of hindsight we might judge that the revolutionary threat had been suppressed for many years to come, but this is not how things would have seemed at the time, particularly when the reds won 20 out of the 30 seats in the by-elections in March 1850 to fill the places of the deputies imprisoned for June 1849. Marx tells us that around this time Bonaparte seemed to be at the nadir of his popularity, and the bourgeoisie was in total political control (*EBLB*, p. 187). Only the fear aroused in them by the radicalisation of the lower classes, and the measures necessary to repress this, can explain how Order eventually abdicated in favour of the apparently 'innocuous man'.

The extent of radicalisation is hardly to be doubted. We have already seen why the workers would have little love for Order, except in that they defeated the victors of June 1848. The petty bourgeoisie would not see in the bankocracy even this derivate and circuitous virtue. As for the peasant, he found the new government at least as ready as its predecessors to tax him to pay for the state debt. 'When the French farmer talks of the devil, he pictures him in the guise of a tax collector' (*CSF*, p. 113).

Gradually we have seen peasants, petty bourgeois, the middle estates in general, siding with the proletariat, driven into open conflict with the official republic and treated by it as antagonists. *Resistance to bourgeois dictatorship, need for a change in society, retention of democratic institutions as a means to this end, regrouping around the proletariat as the decisive revolutionary force* – these are the common characteristics of the *so-called party of social democracy, the party of the red republic.* (*CSF*, p. 121; translation from *MEW* vii, p. 87 slightly amended)

This coalition was not unlike the 'red' party formed for the Legislative elections of 1849, except that it had rather more numerous and more radical peasants, and that for a change it was the petty-bourgeois democrats who were demoralised and the workers' representatives who took the lead. Marx saw that in the face of this threat from the workers, and also from 'its vassal, small property, [which] seeks its salvation in the camp of the propertyless' (*CSF*, p. 126), the bourgeoisie would be driven to abolish universal suffrage. He exulted over such a prospect, reckoning that this proposal would be just what was needed both to bond and to motivate the 'red' coalition: 'Universal suffrage is the banquet question of the new revolution', (*CSF*, p. 128) he declared, referring to the banquets which had been the original arena of the liberal bourgeoisie's political movement. But of course it was not to be so.

At this juncture the textual point about *CSF* which we have already noted becomes of theoretical significance. Chapters 1, 2 and 3 of *CSF* were written for the *Neue Rheinische Zeitung Revue* for, respectively, January, February and March 1850, and actually appeared in March and April of that year. Chapter 3, from which our last quotation above is taken, thus coincides with the famous 'March Address' to the Communist League, in which Marx and Engels envisage an imminent rising of the lower orders against the reaction in various European countries. This was one of Lenin's favourite Marxian texts, as it is one of the few instances where Marx seems to endorse simultaneously the 'writing-off' of the bourgeoisie as a revolutionary force, and conspiratorial organisation by those who do make the revolution (but see Evans, p. 30). In the course of the next six months, in any case, Marx was greatly to modify this position, and it cannot be taken as definitive on questions of political strategy (see Hunt, especially chapter 7, for an exhaustive discussion). The French elections of March 1850 must clearly have been as much a factor in his optimism, as was the 'calme majestueux' with which the petty-bourgeois parliamentarians greeted abolition in his disappointment. For the moment, we shall remain in the perspective of *CSF*, chapter 3, and note an interesting contrast between its periodisation and that of *EBLB* (see diagram, p. 101). *CSF* 3, as we saw, ends in March 1850, and its final sub-period is that of the 'dissolution of the constitutional republic'. Here the contrast emerges with *EBLB*, which speaks of June 1849–May 1850 as 'parliamentary dictatorship of Party of Order'. We might be tempted to see the last sub-period of *EBLB* – 'struggle of Party of Order against Bonaparte' – as a parallel to the last sub-section of *CSF* 3, 'dissolution of the republic', but we would be totally mistaken in this. The reason is that the 'dissolution' envisaged by *CSF* 3 is the overthrow of the whole bourgeois order by the rising of the lower classes envisaged in the 'March Address', *to which there is no parallel in EBLB*, written after it failed to materialise and Marx had ceased to expect it. Thus the periodisation in *CSF* 3 must not be taken as simply an incomplete version, completed by that of *EBLB*, at least on this vital point, since the later work deals with a quite different 'dissolution', namely that of the 'dictatorship' of the big bourgeoisie, and does not deal with a total social revolution of the kind envisaged in the middle of 1850.

We have noted earlier in this chapter (see p. 77 above) that what we know as 'chapter 4' of *CSF* is in fact two extracts from a review of general European economics and politics which was written in late 1850 for the May–October issue of the *NRZ-Revue*. The selection was made by Engels when he published it along with the first three chapters intentionally written as a unit, under the general title of *CSF*, in 1895. If we do not advert to this 'scissors-and-paste' provenance, we will make the mistake of seeing *CSF* as an integral work, and miss the fact that its final 'chapter' dates from well after Marx's disappointment and change of mind. This explains why chapter 4 has more in common with the perspectives of *EBLB* than has either with the first three chapters of *CSF*. There is however one difference which holds even between chapter 4 and *EBLB*. Whereas in chapter 4 Marx no longer predicts imminent catastrophe, he equally does not predict the coup which Bonaparte staged in December 1851, and which *EBLB* can deal with happily in retrospect. In both *CSF*, chapter 4, and an article for Ernest Jones's *Notes to the People* written about June 1851

Third period: Constitutional republic

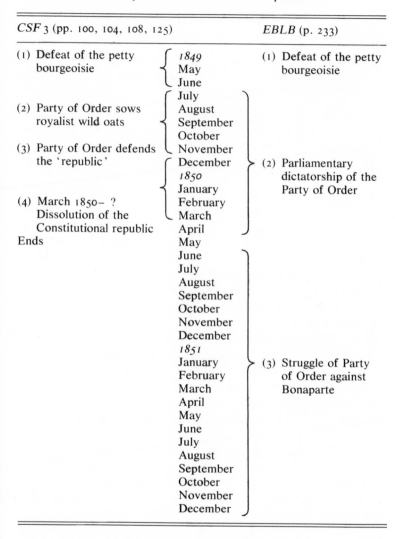

CSF 3 (pp. 100, 104, 108, 125)		EBLB (p. 233)
(1) Defeat of the petty bourgeoisie	*1849* May June	(1) Defeat of the petty bourgeoisie
(2) Party of Order sows royalist wild oats	July August September October November	
(3) Party of Order defends the 'republic'	December *1850* January February March April	(2) Parliamentary dictatorship of the Party of Order
(4) March 1850– ? Dissolution of the Constitutional republic Ends	May June July August September October November December *1851* January February March April May June July August September October November December	(3) Struggle of Party of Order against Bonaparte

(*CFR*), Marx predicts stalemate between Bonaparte and Order. Even if Order could agree on a single candidate for the scheduled presidential elections in May 1852, he says, he would be beaten by Bonaparte. But to tear up the constitution prescribing the elections would re-open all the old revolutionary questions. Nor can Bonaparte risk a *coup*, which would similarly raise the old questions, and moreover would encourage pretenders with better claims than his.

> The only possible solution for the bourgeoisie is the postponement of a solution. It can only save the constitutional republic by a violation of the constitution, by a prolongation of the powers of the President... Essentially, the old game cannot help but continue. In spite of the cries from the sticklers for principle in its various fractions the majority of Order will be forced to prolong the power of the President. Similarly, despite all temporary protestations, Bonaparte will be obliged to accept this extension of power simply as a delegation from the National Assembly (if only for lack of money). (*CSF*, pp. 139, 142)

He was, moreover, quite dismissive about Bonaparte in late 1850 (see *CSF*, pp. 139–41) in a manner quite different from his more judicious and balanced account of his personality '*après coup*' (see *EBLB*, p. 198). The article for Ernest Jones is important here, since it was most probably written about June 1851, that is a mere six months before the coup (see *MEW* VII, p. 623, note 327). It is difficult to maintain that some startlingly new factor, which Marx could not have foreseen, supervened between then and December 1851, so we must regard it as a 'black mark' that he did not give the *coup* a better chance as outcome of the stalemate (although he notes the pressures impelling Bonaparte to such a move; see p. 104 below). But if he did not foresee the cure, he certainly gave a convincing picture of the disease: the inability of the big bourgeoisie to rule in conditions of class conflict, without reliance on a strong executive authority which put themselves in danger.

The bourgeoisie's fear of openly ruling as a class explains their not being able to make use of the 'irretrievable' moment, after the March 1850 elections, when Bonaparte in panic offered even to let them name their own government. 'Instead of boldly taking possession of the power offered, it did not even force Bonaparte to reinstate the ministry dismissed on 1 November' (*EBLB*, p. 192). The reason for this, and for the long decline whose process we are studying, is that 'the French bourgeoisie was...compelled by its class position to liquidate the conditions of existence of all parliamentary power, including its own, and to make its opponent, the executive, irresistible' (*EBLB*, p. 186).

31 May 1850 to 2 December 1851. This is the final sub-period of *EBLB*, during which all the pressures which we have already seen in operation forced Order more and more to abdicate to the President. Marx further sub-divides this sub-period into four sections, but we need not concern ourselves with them, since they represent only successive stages in a continuous and cumulative decline: Order's loss, respectively, of control over the army, of its parliamentary majority and of the support of its own class, and finally the open breach with Bonaparte, leading to the *coup.*

The confrontation over the army was in large part caused by Bonaparte's attempts to bribe them with material rewards and promises of glory. When the Assembly attacked Bonaparte's Minister of War over imperialist demonstrations at army reviews, Bonaparte managed to make scapegoats of his subordinates without abandoning his projects. At the same time he made public declarations of his submissiveness to 'the People' – thus implicitly revoking the abolition of universal suffrage – and made it quietly but firmly clear that the President had sole control over the army. The Party of Order was seething with fury, but at the same time was terrified at conjuring up further political storms which it would be blamed for causing. Nor would it fight on issues where it could gain popular support, because 'a nation on the move was what it feared most of all' (*EBLB*, p. 204). Thus in January 1850 it had to accept the humbling and dismissal of Changarnier, the general who had defeated the petty bourgeoisie in June 1849 and whom Order saw as their only saviour. This Marx interprets as a public declaration that 'the bourgeoisie had lost its vocation to rule' (*EBLB*, p. 208). He depicts the Assembly as only now entering the war with Bonaparte, after it had yielded up or lost its army, public opinion, even (through abolition) its popular mandate; it had sunk to the status of 'an old French *parlement*, which had to leave action to the government and make do with growling' (*EBLB*, p. 209). When Bonaparte appointed a new ministry of his own personnel, opposed to the party of Order, the latter could not muster a majority of their own to condemn this: fear, compromise-mania, egoism, dependency on state positions, and speculation on future office were detaching individuals from the declining parliamentary bourgeois party (*EBLB*, p. 210). At the same time, and crucially, the non-parliamentary bourgeoisie, motivated by the discontent of the lower classes, were becoming more and more vociferous in their demands for tranquillity, strong government and administration. Marx vividly represents Bonaparte's growing contempt for parliamentary censure by describing the ministries of November 1849, January 1851 and April 1851 as, respectively, the un-parliamentary, extra-parliamentary and anti-parliamentary ministries (*EBLB*, p. 213).

Marx depicts Order's dilemma. They could not revise the con- stitution, thus avoiding the 1852 election, because the republicans had the quarter of votes needed for a veto; no revision at all, or a merely partial extension of his authority, would tempt Bonaparte to a *coup*. 'Total revision', that is, abolition of the republic, raised the question of whether the monarchy restored should be Legitimist or Orleanist: attempts to fuse the two houses at this time were actually counter-productive, increasing the fragmentation of the bourgeois forces. There was thus a situation of stalemate, where the bourgeoisie could not abolish the republic because the repub- licans had the crucial majority of votes, and, while the republic lasted, the 'contradiction' of Assembly and Presidency was in- soluble (see p. 121 above). At this point Order more or less gave up, adjourning from August to November 1851. During the ad- journment the majority of *départements* voted for revision of the constitution (that is, opted for Bonaparte against the party of Order) and the non-parliamentary bourgeoisie openly declared itself to be for Bonaparte, whom *The Economist* in an issue of the time dubbed the 'guardian of order' (see *EBLB*, pp. 221–2). In October, Bonaparte proposed the restoration of universal suff- rage. This was an ideal move for him, since he stood to gain either a nationwide constituency or a sharp decline in his opponents' already low popularity. In November the Assembly rejected the proposal. On 25 November the non-parliamentary bourgeoisie, at, appropriately enough, an industrial prize-giving, loudly applauded Bonaparte's speech regretting how political intrigue was frus- trating France's potential for growth and stability.

The stage was thus set for the *coup*, which took place on the night of 1 to 2 December, 1851. Nobody could pretend to be very surprised by this event, which 'cast its shadow forward well in advance of its occurrence' (*EBLB*, p. 228). Some strategic arrests were made, and some blood was spilt, but the takeover was relatively peaceful, especially as the masses were quite unprepared to fight once again for the bourgeoisie (*EBLB*, p. 235; see Cobban 1965, Vol. 2, p. 157). Bonaparte announced the danger from which he had just saved the republic, to which he declared loyalty. This convinced nobody, and the Empire, approved by 7,800,000 votes to 250,000 in November 1852, was proclaimed on 1 December of that year.

The role of artisan protest: Germany and France

We must briefly discuss what the large artisan movements in both Germany and France in 1848 mean for Marx's political theory. There is no problem for him in the mere fact that, at a time of bourgeois revolution, most workers should be artisan rather than proletarian; quite the reverse, in fact. This means that the numbers of German artisans do not falsify Marx's expectations, although we shall have to deal with the fact that in France the artisans survived well after *the* 'bourgeois revolution' in a way which Marx did not expect. Nor is it a problem for him that the artisans should be opposed to the bourgeoisie: destined to be proletarians, as on his theory they are, they cannot have much enthusiasm for capitalist industry. What is crucial for Marx is that 'workers' – whether artisan or proletarian – should support the bourgeoisie in the 'revolutionary' sense already mentioned (see p. 42 above). This is where his problems begin, at least in Germany.

In that country, factory workers played only a small and sub-ordinate role in the political movements of 1848 (see Noyes, e.g., p. 281). We have already noted that there were divisions within the artisan movement, but also that the overwhelming mass of artisans, from masters to journeymen, were opposed to the further extension of industry and economic freedom (see p. 52 above). They thus offered the bourgeoisie not 'revolutionary support' but 'reactionary opposition'. Hamerow criticizes Marx and his followers for their remoteness from this movement, saying that 'if socialism had been willing to exploit their grievances as liberalism had done, it too might have won a great victory on the barricades of a new insurrection' (p. 140). But this charge is difficult to sustain. Marx could hardly have mobilised the artisans *for* the bourgeois revolution, and if he had mobilised them *against* it few people to the left of G. K. Chesterton would seriously have maintained that the result was socialist. Marx may well have been naive in expecting 'revolutionary support' for the bourgeoisie from the artisans, but it is not clear what else *he* could have looked for from them. His problem was that they were quite disinclined to give it, a disinclination encouraged by the absence of an established republican tradition in politics and by the presence of other strong reactionary social groups.

France presents a quite different case: a bourgeois society undergoing a political transformation, but not '*the* bourgeois revolution'. It is possible of course to deny that the economy was 'bourgeois', at least in respect of the artisans, but there are arguments against. If we are simply to deny that the artisan sector was part of the bourgeois economy in 1848, we would probably also have to do so at least as late as 1866, when the same small scale of production still predominated (see Edwards, p. 6). Johnson reminds us that 'hand work is not necessarily non-capitalist work' (p. 89), and, in the case of the tailoring trade, details the way in which artisan activity was being increasingly penetrated, at the middle of the century, by commercial, that is bourgeois, pressures. Not only was bespoke tailoring being threatened by the growth of 'readymade' production ('*confection*'), but the bespoke tailoring which survived was being forced to concentrate, and was dominated by a new breed of 'merchant tailors' (see Johnson, pp. 88–96). Rather than simply excluding the artisan sector from the bourgeois economy, we should recognise the evolution towards the peculiarly French kind of small-scale capitalism, which was to endure for many decades to come.

Our main concern here is the artisans' response to this process. In the case of the tailors, there was in 1848 a common artisan oposition to the readymade producers, one of whose establishments was burnt to the ground in June (Johnson, p. 93). But there was a crucial divergence within that opposition: 'while still seeking the upper hand with their workers [the masters] proposed "corporate" measures of master–worker alliance. The workers for their part shifted their main antagonism to *confection* but never put their trust in the masters either. They went over, *en masse*, to the concepts of socialist worker association.' (Johnson, p. 102). Johnson concludes that the masters may perhaps be called 'reactionary', but that the other artisan tailors looked forwards to schemes of large-scale co-operation, rather than back to outmoded guild structures, for their salvation (p. 109). Tilly and Lees make a similar point for the movement in general: it wanted a new social order which would make an economic reality of republican principles (Tilly and Lees, p. 181). Bernard Moss generalises further, to deny that what took place in 1848 was either an 'elite' or an 'amorphous' movement, and to stress the presence in it of 'a socialist and class conscious Parisian proletariat' (Moss, p. 73). Moss has put his finger on a crucial fact about French artisan radicalism, but his *explanation* of it is less than convincing. He adduces the evidence of 'economic misery' amongst Parisian artisans under the July Monarchy, and tells us that they 'experienced industrialisation as a deterioration, as the process of proletarianisation *that tended to unite them with new elements of the working class*' (Moss, p. 78; emphasis added).

The problem is that there can be no straightforward inference from the fact that artisans are suffering impoverishment and proletarianisation to the conclusion that they are 'socialist' rather than 'reactionary'. If this were so, and especially since Moss adduces bourgeois opposition to them as evidence that the workers' demands were socialist, we would on both counts have to regard the German artisan movement as even more socialist than the French one, which is absurd. If French artisans did indeed adopt crucial perspectives of socialism, the explanation lies not in the fact of their proletarianisation, but more likely in *other* factors off-setting its negative effects. It lies partly in the fact that many of the artisan workshops, though affected by the new competition and other pressures, were able to achieve some *modus vivendi* within them, experiencing 'a broad exposure to capitalism without being decapitated by it' (Johnson, p. 107; see also Kuczynski, p. 197). Equally, of course, we must note the presence in France of a political tradition which could orient artisans, even the masters to a degree (see Johnson, p. 108), in a forward-looking direction, and the absence of a landed class with the reactionary tendencies of the Prussian Junkers. With such experience, in such a context, many of the French artisans were capable of seeking salvation in a vision which, even if frequently utopian, transcended rather than simply rejected capitalist industrialism.

None of this settles the question of the attitude of the factory proletariat, which is the crucial one in terms of Marx's long-term perspectives. As we shall see in chapter 7, Marx was often to be disappointed in his hopes that they would become increasingly radical as they became more numerous (see pp. 178–9 below). So much was this the case that one might almost conclude that political radicalism of the kind encountered in June 1848 pertains to a peculiar phase of artisan development, and was not to be expected amongst the proletarians of the more developed economies. We shall return to a discussion of Marx's theoretical perspectives on proletarian revolution in chapter 6 below.

Conclusion: the prospects for reaction

It is often said that 'the events of 1848' forced Marx to change his mind. This is true, but not precise enough (see Krieger, p. 384). While Germany falsified Marx's notion that the bourgeoisie would *acquire* political power, France falsifies his claim about how they would be able to *retain* it. Before the year of revolutions, Marx had told us that the English and French bourgeoisies had won their decisive political victories over the old order in, respectively, 1832 and 1830 (see *CM*, p. 88). As we have already noted in chapter 2, he sees the acquisition of political power not as the last word in the bourgeoisie's advancement, but as something which they use to achieve their maturity (see p. 00 above). It is here that things go wrong in France. Where the 'ideal' progression is for industry to come to dominate the economy, and the industrial bourgeoisie consequently to dominate the bourgeois polity, the actual development in France was retarded in these respects. When the internal conflict between the financial and the other fractions of the bourgeoisie broke out in 1847–8, the bourgeois republicans were not strong enough – for want perhaps of a strong industrial bourgeoisie behind them – to impose themselves as the natural leaders of their class. The problem was aggravated by the coincidence of this internal struggle with one between the bourgeoisie as a class and its enemies. These were peasants, petty bourgeoisie and (mainly artisan) workers. Unlike the case of Germany, they were almost entirely structural rather than transitional groups, so that the *coup d'etat* of 1851 reflects on the notion of bourgeois rule within bourgeois society rather than on the notion of the bourgeois acquisition of political power.

Marx's account seems at its weakest when dealing with the internal divisions of the bourgeoisie. On his theory the various bourgeois fractions should have had one great interest leading them to sink their royalist differences in a common front against the external class enemy. But in the first place, as we shall see, Marx does present the bourgeois fractions' differing royalist allegiances as, at the crucial point, instrumental, rather than based on blind loyalty (see pp. 117ff. below). In the second place, he tells us that the 'common front' was tried, and failed. That front was the republic, where each fraction abandoned its exclusive claim to rule on the condition that others did so too: 'they enforced that form of society in which particular claims of the various parties were held in check and neutralised – *the republic*' (*CSF*, p. 108). But the republic in 'democratic' form proved too dangerous because it empowered its own enemies, and the attempt to transform it into a direct weapon of class war destroyed it. It is interesting that this is the argument which Marx applies after a twenty-year lapse of time: 'If the Parliamentary Republic, as M. Thiers said, "divided them (the different fractions of the ruling class) least", it opened an abyss between that class and the whole body of society outside their spare ranks' (*CWF*, p. 71).

Marx emphasises that the continual recourse to presidential authority and the watering-down of legislative checks, were acts done by the bourgeoisie themselves; the abolition of universal suffrage in May 1850 was 'a necessity of the class struggle' (*EBLB*, p. 194). The non-political bourgeoisie grew increasingly impatient with its political representatives, and disowned the struggle 'to maintain its *public* interests, its own *class interests*, its *political power*' (p. 223) because this troubled business. The *coup* was a result of an option for authority, for the replacement of the political market by *fiat*. The Assembly 'subjected itself to the superior command of an alien will, to authority. The opposition between the executive and legislature expresses the opposition between a nation's heteronomy and its autonomy' (*EBLB*, p. 236). It will be clear then that the relevant overview is the 'structural contradiction' one: a pretentious state has here emerged from the way in which the bourgeoisie were forced to use already-acquired political power (see Price 1975, pp. 54–6). As Marx says, the bourgeoisie increasingly used 'the sabre and the musket...to judge and administer, to guard and to censor, to play the part of policeman and night-watchman'. He asks, as we have foreseen in chapter 1 (see pp. 22ff above):

Was it not inevitable that barracks and bivouac, sabre and musket, moustache and uniform, would finally hit on the idea of saving society once and for all by proclaiming the supremacy of their own regime and thus entirely freeing civil society from the trouble of ruling itself? (*EBLB*, p. 163)

This noble intention was no stranger to that of receiving a more adequate reward for services which the bourgeoisie were apt to use but to under-value; here was Bonaparte's opening for winning over the army. At the same time, 'his possession of executive power had caused a number of interests to group around him', and fuelled his ambition of forcing the bourgeoisie to 'a recognition of the *neutral pretender*' (*CSF*, p. 108; see also p. 139).

Marx devotes the last chapter of *EBLB* to discussing the French executive, with its 'immense bureaucratic and military organisation, an artificial and broadly based state machinery, and an army of half a million officials alongside the actual army, which numbers a further half million' (*EBLB*, p. 237; translation amended in light of *MEW* VIII, p. 196). He wants to explain how it came to its present position, where it 'surrounds the body of French society like a caul and stops up all its pores' (*ibid.*). Under the absolute monarchy, which arose from and accelerated the decline of feudalism, seignorial privileges became attributes of the state power, feudal dignitaries becoming state officials. Since the revolution of 1789 set itself to abolish the remnants of feudal restrictions, it promoted this tendency for the central power to grow, and 'Napoleon perfected this state machinery' (*ibid.*). The Restoration and July monarchies merely added to the size of the executive, without qualitative alteration. Finally, the recent parliamentary republic had to rely more and more on state power in 'its struggle against the revolution' (p. 238). The upshot of this history is that 'All political upheavals perfected this machinery instead of smashing it' (*ibid.*). Marx distinguishes two phases in this long process: under the absolute monarchy, the revolution and Napoleon the growth of the executive prepared the way for the rising bourgeoisie, whereas under the Restoration, the July Monarchy and the Second Republic 'it was the instrument of the ruling class, however much it strove for power in its own right' (*ibid.*). Only after 1851 does the third phase begin, in which 'the state seems to have attained a completely autonomous position'.

While allowing for the sense in which the state has become

autonomous of the bourgeoisie, Marx argues that it does not 'hover in mid-air'. He says that Bonaparte represents the peasants, the majority group in French society. These constitute a class, insofar as the millions of peasant proprietors live in identical smallholdings, thus having a distinct economic position, a distinct culture, distinct interests and an opposition to other classes. But they lack the dimension of unified class consciousness and action, insofar as all the identical smallholdings are related to one another only 'by the simple addition of isomorphous magnitudes, much as potatoes in a sack form a sack of potatoes' (p. 239). Thus although they have common interests, they do not communicate them, and rather than being in a position to articulate and impose their interest 'they must be represented. Their representative must appear simultaneously as their master', as a strong authority ruling not only them but also all their enemies. 'The political influence of the small peasant proprietors is therefore ultimately expressed in the executive subordinating society to itself' (*ibid.*).

Marx sees the coup of 1851 as the long-delayed realisation of the peasants' vote of December 1848, where they chose Bonaparte against the 'republic of the rich' which had increased rather than abolished their tax burden. To this extent, Bonaparte's appeal to the peasants as his central constituency is an appeal to the enemies of bourgeois society, and the strength of that appeal is a consequence of the development of the bourgeoisie. For, while Napoleon I consolidated the small-holdings which the bourgeois revolution won for the peasants, 'the interests of the peasants are no longer consonant with the interests of the bourgeoisie' (p. 242) who exploit them through the profit, interest and rent extracted from the peasant's pocket. If Bonaparte thinks that he can fulfil the peasants' dream of a return to the age of glory, 'his experiments will burst like soap bubbles at their first contact with the relations of production' (p. 241). Another idea associated with Napoleon I is that of strong government; but that government will now be parasitic on the peasants, who will soon abandon their '*idées Napoléoniennes*'. 'All the Napoleonic ideas are ideas of the underdeveloped smallholding in its heyday' (p. 244), and the smallholding cannot be protected against the ravages of the bourgeoisie.

It is an integral part of Bonaparte's appeal that his strong government will uphold the bourgeois order. But insofar as he accepts that bourgeois industry must develop and grow to dominate the social order, while at the same time repressing the political activity of the bourgeoisie, Bonaparte has put himself in an insoluble dilemma: 'by protecting the material power he recreates the political power. The cause must accordingly be kept alive, but the effect must be done away with wherever it appears' (p. 245). Not only does Bonaparte see it as part of his mission to protect the bourgeois economy: he also depends on it for the resources nourishing himself, his bureaucracy and his army. His programme then is one of materially encouraging while politically repressing the bourgeoisie, depending the while for political support on a peasantry whose interests are at loggerheads with his material encouragement of the bourgeoisie. 'Bonaparte would like to appear as the patriarchal benefactor of all classes. But he cannot give to one class without taking from another' (p. 247). Marx predicts that his regime will ultimately collapse under the tension of these contradictory commitments. We shall look at how he treats the regime, and how his predictions fare, in chapter 7 below.

5. Problems of political action

This chapter will examine some of the more fundamental assumptions of the theories which we have seen Marx evolving in the course of the last two chapters. It will deal with the fact that, after his highly optimistic expectations as to what political groups would want to do were disappointed, Marx was forced to elaborate a more complex approach to explaining and predicting political action than he had applied before 1848.

The first section will explain why the pre-1848 approach was at least apparently so mechanistic and naive. It will suggest that Marx was not in fact committed to a 'mechanistic' position before 1848, but that his naive expectations allowed him to ignore the complexities of human motivation. The second section will look at the vexed question of whether Marx holds, or needs to hold, that 'all motivation is economic'. It suggests that it is difficult to make such a claim both coherent and plausible, and that in any case there is good evidence that Marx did not hold it, but rather held that in situations of crisis people will defend their economic position at the expense, if necessary, of their loftier principles. The third section will look at the issue of 'necessity' in Marx's political explanations. It will argue that he normally allows that people have, or had, freedom to act in different ways, and attempts to reconcile this position with the claim that how they do act can be explained. While this may be a philosophically incoherent enterprise, it is one in which many others join Marx, and if he is wrong it is for general reasons rather than because of some peculiar claim of his own. While the philosophical issue will not be settled in a study of this nature, the investigation gives us a valuable insight into the complexities of Marx's post-1848 account of political action.

The impact of disappointment

We have already seen on a number of occasions that Marx in his pre-1848 writings discusses how the bourgeois revolution happened, and especially how it can be repeated. He quite often compares the bourgeois revolution to the future workers' one (see, e.g., *PP*, pp. 172–3). In the *Manifesto* he does so to the advantage of the latter. He tells us that the unity 'to attain which the burghers of the Middle Ages, with their miserable highways, required centuries, the modern proletarians, thanks to railways, achieve in a few years' (*CM*, p. 76). But in the course of 1848–51 he is driven to reconsider both terms of this comparison. By December 1848, as we saw, he is driven to declare bourgeois rule impossible for Germany (*R1848*, p. 212). In 1852 he draws a contrast between bourgeois revolutions which 'storm quickly from success to success', and the nineteenth-century proletarian revolutions which 'constantly engage in self-criticism, and repeated interruptions of their own course' (*EBLB*, p. 150). The bourgeois revolution becomes much harder to repeat, and its successor the proletarian one looks a much slower and harder affair than before 1848. We shall be concerned here with the revisions which these disapointments imposed on Marx.

We need not seek very far to find the reason why the pre-1848 theory is so naively optimistic. It lies in the fact that Marx, at least on the very eve of the year of revolutions, either failed to see or ignored the possibilities of tension between the bourgeoisie and their revolutionary allies. He was not always unaware of these possibilities (see pp. 60–1 above), but when he did perceive them he normally ignored or glossed over them, so as to stiffen the sinews of the bourgeoisie. This accounts for the apparently crudely mechanistic psychology of these writings. Taken in by the ease of conceptually reconstructing an already-completed historical process, he tended to overlook the pitfalls of implicitly assuming that the future reality would reproduce the idea of the past (see pp. 32 above and 205ff. below). It is understandable that in the interlude between reflection on past revolutions and participation in future ones Marx should have had over-tidy and over-optimistic ideas; the interest of our present discussion is in seeing his response to the untidy and depressing reality.

This argument revises the popular view that Marx 'really' held very rigid and mechanistic assumptions about human action and was only forced to modify them by the reality of events such as the revolutions of 1848. It is much nearer the truth to say that, because he believed (or chose to pretend) that the *choices* facing the parties would be clear and simple, he did not need to spell out any assumptions as to how choices are made. The pre-1848 writings envisage the bourgeoisie, and then the proletariat, as finding themselves in pretty much the same situation as a small child confronted by a large cake: we need little in the way of theory to predict and explain what will happen. But in 1848 the cake was replaced by a hot potato, and the world began to look much more complex. At this point the need for a more reflective account of action became apparent. As we indicated at the end of chapter 2, and saw in some detail in chapters 3 and 4, most of the groups involved were faced with difficult choices: the bourgeoisie, between dangerous allies and seductive foes; the petty bourgeoisie, between a precarious existence in the *status quo* and the dangers of revolution; and the workers, between 'their enemies [and] the enemies of their enemies' (*CM*, p. 75).

It might be argued that the works which we are considering do not merit, or should not be subjected to, too close a scrutiny. Thus Evans tells us that *CSF* and *EBLB* 'though often referred to as historical accounts, are in fact contemporary political polemics' (Evans, p. 51). But in the first place, if they *are* polemics, they attack nobody in particular, unlike for example *MCCM* and *Herr Vogt*. In the second place, they are written just after Marx has announced, in his Prospectus for the *NRZ-Revue*, that the period of apparent standstill following 1848 must be used

to get a clear understanding of the revolutionary period just lived through, of the character of the contending parties, of the social relationships which condition the being and the struggle of these parties. (*MEW* VII, p. 7)

CSF, indeed, occupies a large part of the *NRZ-Revue*, and is thus Marx's attempt to achieve just this clarification of the being ('*Dasein*') and struggle ('*Kampf*') of the various parties. Moreover, *EBLB* was written over a fairly long period of months after Bonaparte's coup; when republishing it in 1869 Marx made no apologies for it, while stating that it had clearly been written 'under the immediate pressure of events' (*SE*, p. 143). It is thus entirely fair to judge Marx's reactions to 1848 by what he says in these works, which does not of course mean that we regard the development of his theory as culminating in late 1852.

The *Neue Rheinische Zeitung* articles discussed in chapter 3 might be regarded as less suitable for scrutiny. But in dealing with them I was careful always to take out broad and recurrent lines of argument, rather than to seize on isolated sentences or outbursts. Moreover, and more significantly, we have to hand a work which does for Germany much of what *CSF* and *EBLB* do for France. That is, *Germany: Revolution and Counter-Revolution*, a series of articles written by Engels for the *New York Daily Tribune* in 1851–2. These were until recently believed to have been written by Marx, who in fact commissioned them from Engels on account of his own poor written English and preoccupation with economic studies (see Marx to Engels, *MEW* XXVII, pp. 296, 314). Eleanor Marx, who was clearly taken in by the pretended authorship when she published *RCR* in book form in 1896, tells us that her father had no opportunity of checking the proofs (*RCR*, p. ix). There is however no evidence of Marx's dissenting from Engels's analysis – which he most probably read when transmitting it to New York – and he was always happy for the series to be credited to his authorship. I shall thus treat *RCR* in this chapter as though it were a work of Marx's own hand. It is important to refer to it, since it is an indication whether Marx significantly altered his attitude to events in Germany in the more reflective period after 1849, by comparison with the *NRZ* articles written at the time of revolution.

It is suggested by what has already been said that what 1848 forces on Marx is much less a revision of his assumptions about 'how people face problems' (whatever that may mean) than of the kinds of problem which they will have to face. Both before and after 1848 the assumption is that people act in what Percy Cohen helpfully designates as an 'instrumental rationalist' manner (Cohen, P. S., pp. 79–81): in other words, Marx sees people as acting so as to achieve what they perceive as their interest, in the situation in question. For example, Marx explains the failure of both the party of Order and Bonaparte to bring matters to a head with an attempted *coup* in 1849 or 1850 by showing that neither side could be sure that it could achieve what it wanted, and thus neither had a good reason for taking the risks involved (see e.g. *CSF*, pp. 82–3). Equally, Marx explains the June insurrection of

1848 by saying that the Provisional Government's policy meant that 'the workers were left with no choice; they had either to starve or to strike out' (*CSF*, p. 58). It was not in every sense inevitable that the workers should have responded by striking out, but it is difficult to imagine what *reason* they could have for not trying resistance rather than starving. It is important to stress the 'instrumental rationalist' character of explanations like this, since some of them, especially where they explain 'do-or-die' decisions like that of the workers in June, might look assimilable to a much more mechanistic model of explanation, which correlates situations and actions without regard to any intervening perceptions or deliberation on the actor's part. That such a model does not handle Marx's range of explanations is clear from the number of times when Marx makes people's perceptions of a situation (often because of previous relevantly similar experiences, such as for example the previous treachery of a potential ally) central to how it comes out. The distinction in question between the two models comes down to that between what Fleischer calls 'the necessity of events' (which is all that the mechanistic model will countenance) and the 'necessity of action' which brings men to recognise that they must pursue certain ends and/or that if they wish certain ends they must adopt certain means (Fleischer, pp. 119–20). It is the latter necessity which Marx invokes in explaining human actions in crisis situations, as when he says that the workers had a compelling reason not to starve, and thus had a compelling reason to adopt the means of insurrection to achieve the end of not-starving.

The 'economic' motivation of action

In this section we shall deal with one of the most notorious problems about Marx's theory of action, that of whether he holds that all motivations either are 'materialistic' or 'economic', or else can be accounted for as merely 'manifestations' of 'real' motivations which themselves are economic. The best case to take is Marx's explanations of the allegiance of the landed bourgeoisie in France to the Legitimist cause, and that of the urban bourgeoisie to the Orleanists. He says that it was not so-called principles which divided the two houses, but rather 'their material conditions of existence, two distinct sorts of property; it was the old opposition between town and country, the old rivalry between capital and

landed property' (*EBLB*, p. 173). But immediately Marx answers
the anticipated objection: 'Who would deny that at the same time
old memories, personal enmities, fears and hopes, prejudices and
illusions, sympathies and antipathies, convictions, articles of faith
and principles bound them to one or to the other royal house?'
It is important to note that not all the factors adduced here are
said to be 'untrue' or 'mere appearances' – people really have
memories, antipathies, fears and so on, and really act on them.
Marx does not deny them, but rather maintains that certain points
of view arise in certain situations, and that forms of consciousness
thus correspond to class situations:

A whole superstructure of different and specifically formed feelings,
illusions, modes of thought and views of life arises on the basis of the
different forms of property, of the social conditions of existence. The
whole class creates and forms these out of its material foundations and
the corresponding social relations.

This 'superstructure' of consciousness is then the class's way of
living its particular situation, and, rather than being an automatic
product of the social relationships or material foundations, is
created and *formed* by the class. But at this point Marx seems to
come down very clearly on the 'all motivation is really economic'
side:

The single individual, who derives these feelings, etc. through tradition
and upbringing, may well imagine that they form the real determinants
and the starting-point of his activity. The Orleanist and Legitimist fractions each tried to make out to their opponents and to themselves that
they were divided by their adherence to the two royal houses; facts later
proved that it was rather the division between their interests which
forbade the unification of the royal houses. A distinction is made in
private life between what a man thinks and says of himself and what he
really is and does. In historical struggles one must make a still sharper
distinction between the phrases and fantasies of the parties and their real
organisation and real interests, between their conception of themselves
and what they really are. (p. 174)

The first sentence of this passage certainly suggests that Marx
believes that we can and should always read individuals' stated
motivations as a code for an underlying, 'really decisive' economic interest which they are unaware of or do not acknowledge.
I am however not inclined to accept this conclusion. In the first
place, there are indications elsewhere in Marx's writings that he
did not consistently write off 'non-economic' motivations in such

a way. In the most theoretical series of articles written for the *NRZ*, Marx gives the familiar picture of the bourgeois mode of production developing to the point where it must be backed up by political dominance or be frustrated. He adds, however, that the bourgeoisie 'was also ambitious enough to wish to conquer a political position commensurate with its social position, once it had deprived the bureaucracy of the monopoly of so-called culture' (*R1848*, p. 189). On many other occasions in the *NRZ* writings he states that the resistance of army, crown and bureaucracy to the bourgeois challenge is motivated by the desire to retain political power and social position; he makes no serious attempt to translate these motivations directly into 'manifestations' of ulterior, 'really economic' ones.

In the second place, some of Marx's most crucial arguments in this area can be made intelligible only by *rejecting* the 'all motivation is economic' thesis. To return to our main case, that of the Orleanists and Legitimists, let us consider how Marx spells out his argument that, when they claimed dynastic loyalties, this 'had no other meaning than that each of the *two great interests* into which the bourgeoisie is divided – landed property and capital – was endeavouring to restore its own supremacy and the subordination of the other interests' (*EBLB*, p. 174). He proceeds to illustrate his point by saying that while the Tories in England thought they were enthusiasts for crown, church and constitution, 'the day of danger wrung from them the confession that they were only enthusiastic about *ground rent*' (*ibid.*). This argument crucially depends on a shift from non-economic to economic interests, or at least on a shift in priority between them. If all motivations are economic, Marx is here talking nonsense. If we attempted to rescue the thesis by saying that maybe not all prima facie motivations are economic but they are however manifestations of uniformly economic *second-order* motivations, we still cannot account for the crucial shift. We would have to be able to show why some second-order economic motivations manifest themselves in *prima facie* non-economic ones, and some not, and in explaining the shift between them we would be in danger of an infinite regress of 'orders' of motivation. Neither in its '*prima facie*' nor in its 'second-order' version can the thesis that all motivation is economic make sense of the shift which Marx here makes central to his explanation.

This analysis suggests an interpretation which more successfully covers all the assertions which Marx wants to make. The main point is that although people's ideas about themselves and the world arise within a particular class-situation, they are most of the time unaware of this fact, and tend to believe that their ideas have a trans-class, trans-historical validity.

The occupation assumes an independent existence owing to division of labour – everyone believes his craft to be the true one. The very nature of their craft causes them to succumb the more easily to illusions regarding the connection between their craft and reality...The Judge, for example, applies the code, he therefore regards legislation as the real, active driving force. (Addenda to *GI* in *GI*, pp. 671–2)

The crucial point here is that what people are said to overlook, or be deluded about, is the *connection* ('*Zusammenhang*' *MEW* III, p. 539) *between* their particular craft and social reality. This illusion can develop to such a point in the case for example of specialised ideologues and their class that there arises 'a certain opposition and hostility between the two parts' (*GI*, p. 62). While Marx somewhat optimistically asserts that in the case where this cleavage endangers the class it 'automatically comes to nothing' (*ibid*.), the central point at the moment is the fact that it arises in the first place: that, in other words, people can fail to see the connection between their ideas and their social position. If we now return to the passage in *EBLB* which we are analysing, we find that Marx does not flatly assert that the distinction between a class's illusions and its real position can always be clearly grasped: he says that this distinction emerges '*in historical struggles*' (*EBLB*, p. 174; my emphasis). The whole point of a significant historical struggle for Marx is that it arises when the position of a particular dominant class, with its ideas and political forms resting on its characteristic social relations, is being threatened by society's development beyond that class's conditions of life. It is just such a 'day of danger' (*ibid*.) that will concentrate a class's mind, and make it realise how dependent on a particular economic position are ideas, powers and privileges which it had previously thought to be self-subsistent. It is because of these arguments that I interpret Marx's 'economically-based theory of politics' as assuming (a) that people act on motivations which can be related to the economic situation in which they arose and (b) that in political crises classes will realise the dependence of their way of life on their economic position, and will act to preserve or further that position.

Free action and necessity

Having characterised Marx's approach to action as an instrumental rationalist one, and argued that the factors which he sees as motivating people are not necessarily or always economic ones, we must next discuss the sense in which he sees his approach as yielding determinate explanations. Dismissing explanations of the coup in 1851 which appealed to Bonaparte's peculiar cunning or the Assembly's being taken by surprise, Marx insisted that 'if it succeeded, it was as a necessary and inevitable result of the previous development' (*EBLB*, p. 229). The question arises whether Marx sees the outcome of the political events of 1848–51 as fatalistically predetermined and, if not, what is the sense in which he sees it as 'necessary and inevitable'. A similar question, of course, arises about Germany's reaction.

In the first place we must take account of the fact that Marx frequently uses language which sorts ill with a fatalistic perpective. On many occasions during the German events he argues, as we have seen, that things might go one way or another depending on the choice, determination and courage of the different parties involved. Not only does he say many such things, which imply that people *could* act in a variety of possible ways: he also frequently tells people that they *should* act in one way rather than another. Thus he exhorts the Frankfurt Assembly to take a firm stand against the King's reactionary intrigues (*R1848*, p. 182), and the people are told that it is up to them to apply 'at the right moment and fearlessly' (*NRZ*, p. 175) the lessons of the previous months, if they wish to achieve their ends. But, of course, the fact that someone uses exhortatory language before the event does not establish that he is not a fatalist. Given the psychic leap-frogging of one's own shadow involved in treating one's decisions as subject to fatalistic causation (see Berlin), it is possible for the exhorter to regard his own exhortations as causally-produced moves which themselves are part of the causal antecedents of the eventual outcome. He might also, of course, explain his exhortations as absurd but irrepressible, rather like the impulse to scream warnings at the celluloid image of a film-actor although we know quite well that the film is literally cut and dried well before we see it. We need more evidence of non-fatalism than *ex ante* exhortations.

Such evidence is available in Marx's case. He very frequently, after the event, states or implies that people *could have*, sometimes also *should have*, done otherwise than they did; there is evidence that he is not more fatalistic after than before the event. Despite previous errors and setbacks, we are told,

the present situation in Germany offered the Assembly the opportunity of overcoming its unfortunate material position. It needed only to oppose the reactionary encroachments of the antiquated German governments in a dictatorial fashion, and it would have conquered a position in the public esteem impregnable to bayonets and rifle-butts. (*R1848*, p. 121)

It might be argued that this passage, written in June 1848, is still in the midst of events, even if after the precise events which it deals with, and is thus a roundabout case of 'fatalistic exhortation'. But, given that we may accept *RCR* as evidence of Marx's as well as Engels's views, and that it was written well after the events with which it deals, we may be more confident as to Marx's non-fatalism. We find exactly the same point being made: if the Assembly had had the least bit of energy

It would, above all, have secured for itself an organised and armed force in the country sufficient to put down any opposition on the parts of the Governments. And all this was easy, very easy, at that early period of the Revolution. (*RCR*, p. 40)

When the Reich Constitution Campaign of 1849 gave the Assembly an undeserved 'second chance', resolute action 'might have opened chances both for the insurrection and for the National Assembly' (*RCR*, p. 98). The Berlin Assembly 'ought to have had the ministers arrested' (*R1848*, p. 179); in France, the Party of Order

instead of letting itself be intimidated by the executive's perspective of new disorders...should have allowed the class struggle some latitude, so as to keep the executive dependent on itself. (*EBLB*, p. 212)

Reflecting on the reaction's successes in late 1848, Engels tells us that whether the cause of democracy was already lost, or whether a vigorous resistance might have won over some of the army and driven on to success 'is a question which may never be solved. But in revolution as in war...it is of the highest necessity to stake everything on the decisive moment, whatever the odds may be'

(*RCR*, pp. 71–2). Here we ought to comment on the strange fact that one of the two men associated with an allegedly mechanistic economic determinism spent much of his life studying military strategy, and with a far from purely historical approach. It is also of interest, incidentally, that Marx himself, in relation to a quite important moment in the French events, points to a phenomenon often adduced as falsifying his alleged theory of action:

A revolt in Paris would have permitted [the Government] to proclaim a state of siege in Paris...The Government set to work. At the beginning of February 1850, provocation of the people by chopping down the liberty trees. In vain...Finally, the prophecy of a revolution on 24 February was also in vain. The result of the government's prophecy was that the people ignored 24 February. (*CSF*, pp. 123–4)

Marx's account of political action, then, is an instrumental rationalist one, which makes economic motivation crucial but neither universal nor 'essential', and which allows, both before and after the event, that people really make choices and decisions which might have gone other ways. None of this denies that he is a determinist, given that determinism is the thesis that there are no inexplicable events. Nor do I deny that being a determinist who wants to speak of some kind of freedom of action probably lands Marx in philosophical difficulties. But these difficulties have apparently not yet been solved by the philosophers (see e.g., various essays in Honderich, ed. 1973). It seems unlikely that they will be solved by a study of Marx's account of action in its own right, since Marx rarely if ever attended to these difficulties at a philosophical level. The best we can do is to allow him to pursue the *prima facie* sensible project of explaining people's actions on the twin assumptions that we cannot either before or after the event rule out their having done otherwise, and that nevertheless the precise way they did act is not to be regarded as a mere 'visitation' barring the door to further inquiry. If this is an inherently absurd project, it is so for philosophical reasons which indict most of the rest of us along with Marx, and which therefore say nothing of particular interest about Marx's particular account of the matter. We shall learn more from watching him try to carry it out than from translating his explanations into the conceptual vocabulary proper to the question whether it should be attempted at all.

The kinds of *explananda* confronting Marx all relate to the failure of the various French and German parties to act in a way which would have realised the hopes and prophecies of the *Communist Manifesto*, as summarised in chapter 2 above. If Marx sees people as acting to achieve their interest as perceived in the situation, how does he explain their not acting in line with his predictions? He rarely if ever invokes simple mistakes, where people for example might afterwards say 'I now realise that I didn't want to be hit on the head after all' or 'I now realise that it was silly to expect him to give me his gun and surrender.' But he does invoke two kinds of 'failure of perception' which we shall mention now and return to at a later point. The first is what I call 'not-yet-seeing', as where the Austrian bourgeoisie in 1848 simply did not believe the stories from France about opposition between the interests of workers and bourgeois, because the possibility of such conflict, although real, had not yet actualised itself in their own experience (see *RCR*, pp. 30–1). The second is self-deception as to the nature of the situation, as where the French Assembly allowed Bonaparte's ministers to tell it lies about the real nature of the Rome expedition, 'not daring to know what the constituted republic had to do' (*CSF*, p. 87). For the moment, I wish to concentrate on the core of Marx's explanations of people's not acting as they 'ought' to have; these two 'failures of perception' will be integrated into the account.

The chief way in which Marx explains political actions in the 1848–51 period is along the line that, while people act to achieve their perceived interest in the situation

(a) the situation can be complex and the interest of a group difficult to interpret:

When interests so varied, so conflicting, so strangely crossing each other, are brought into violent collision... what else is to be expected but that the contest will dissolve itself into a mass of unconnected struggles in which an enormous quantity of blood, energy and capital is spent, but which for all that remains without any decisive results? (*RCR*, p. 8)

and

(b) people may in fact have not one clear, but two competing interests in the situation. Marx for example rejects the claim that in consolidating rather than prosecuting the revolution the liberal German bourgeoisie was betraying its principles (*R1848*, pp. 189–90); it was rather pursuing its economic interest by trying to quieten the political storms. As it was thrust on it that this course would undermine its *political* interest in control of government, the bourgeoisie indulged in self-deception so as to ignore this danger, precisely because the material interest in property outweighed a political interest which could be safeguarded only with the help of the propertyless. A similar option was forced on the French bourgeoisie in even starker terms:

the bourgeoisie confesses that its own interest requires its deliverance from the peril of its own self-government;. . . that its political power must be broken in order to preserve its social power intact. . . and that in order to save its purse the crown must be struck off its head. (*EBLB*, p. 190)

(c) There is the additional complication that (a) can interact with (b): the more distinct parties there are, trying to discern their one interest, or to choose between their competing interests, the more difficult are both the discernment and the choice for each party. (This much is implied in our quotation from *RCR* under (a) above.)

Out of these three related facets of the situation, Marx tends to concentrate on (b). In other words, rather than seeing people as simply bewildered by the situation, he sees them as being pretty well aware of the tension between their interest in protecting their initial or acquired position and the dangers of further political activity. This latter danger is in most cases that of giving increased political freedoms and powers to groups with interests inimical to those of the group in question.

Marx variously categorises what we might call the 'neglected interest', the one on which people fail to act. Sometimes he suggests that it is a 'general interest' of a number of classes or fractions of classes, which a group fails to act on because of being too 'caught up in its own immediate, narrowest interest' (*R1848*, p. 209), or it is an altruistic interest, which is not served because of a group's 'lamentable, cowardly, narrow-minded egoism' (*ibid.*). But this way of categorising the neglected interest cannot be seriously maintained, at least by such a consistent debunker of ideological enthusiasms as Marx. It is of interest in this regard that as early as his *Rheinische Zeitung* articles of 1842 Marx had noted the absence of such inter-class enthusiasm in Germany; he bewailed the selfishness of the various Estates, saying that 'the Rhinelander ought to have been victorious over the estate, the human being ought to have been victorious over the forest owner'

(*RZ*, October–November 1842, in *MECW* I, p. 262). In 1844, as we have seen, he concludes that 'all classes lack that breadth of spirit which identifies itself, if only for a moment, with the spirit of the people' (*CCHPRI*, p. 254), adding that Germany is pervaded by a 'modest egoism', and the middle class represents only the narrow and limited mediocrity of all the other classes (p. 255). But our discussion of the writings on 1848–51 makes it quite clear that, whatever regrets he might have had in the early 1840s about the disappearance of general enthusiasm, Marx the debunker can hardly shed many tears over its grave. Insofar as groups are not-yet-aware of their particular interests, an enthusiasm might persist for the time necessary to achieve revolution; but there could be no question either of condoning, or of thinking remotely conceivable, the *reconstruction* of an enthusiasm already dead or still-born. Marx brings us little closer to a solution in the eloquent pages contrasting the narrow-minded Prussian bourgeoisie with the English bourgeoisie of the 1640s and the French one of 1789, whose revolutions 'expressed the needs of the whole world, as it existed then' (*R1848*, p. 193). This lamentation is but a redescription of the problem. The problem is that the social situation made impossible in Germany in 1848 what had been possible in previous eras in England and France; the cure cannot be to try to make people unlearn what they now know, but rather must be to find how to make a revolution without illusions.

When Marx analyses, rather than just bemoans, the absence of enthusiasm, he presents a group's option as being between their present, social particular interest and their future, political particular interest (as we saw in the case of the French bourgeoisie on p. 125 above). We are now concerned with what Marx sees as determining that option. Georges Lefebvre says of the revolutionaries of 1789 that: 'Other men with the same reasons to fight have resigned themselves. Revolutionary action takes place in the realm of the spirit' (Lefebvre, p. 179). This, to my mind, typifies the kind of explanation which Marx will do his very best to avoid having to give. Rather than simply setting up a situation, and then leaving the parties' 'courage' or 'determination' or so forth to decide its outcome, Marx seems to want to deal with 'courage' etc. in a much more *material* way, as kinds of behaviour occurring in kinds of situations. We are told that the German bourgeoisie was 'inclined from the outset to treachery against the people and compromise with the crowned representative of the old society, because it itself already belonged to the old society' (*R1848*, p. 194). After the failure of the revolution, Marx prophesies that

the treacherous role that the German liberal bourgeoisie played against the people in 1848 will be assumed in the coming revolution by the democratic petty bourgeoisie, which now occupies the same position in the opposition as the liberal bourgeoisie did before 1848. (*March Address* in *R1848*, p. 321)

When explaining the failure of the Quaestor's Bill, by which the Assembly tried to re-assert control over the army shortly before Bonaparte's coup, Marx says that the deciding factor was the petty bourgeoisie's opting against the bill. He says that the petty-bourgeoisie *Montagne* was like Buridan's ass, except that it was caught between showers of blows, one from Changarnier, the other from Bonaparte. He adds: 'One must admit that the circumstances were not conducive to heroism' (*EBLB*, p. 230). This sentence sums up Marx's approach to this point, which is to try always to pin down more exactly the circumstances making for 'courage', 'treachery' and so on, rather than to see the circumstances as merely creating the space within which these attributes will play out their drama.

It might be argued that the many occasions on which Marx talks of the courage of the parties as deciding things, accord to courage a much more autonomous status than I have allowed. He says for example, on the eve of a crucial struggle in Prussia, that:

Which of the two sides gains the victory will depend on the attitude of the people, and in particular on the attitude of the democratic party. The democrats must choose... The intention is there, certainly, but what is needed is the courage to act. (*R1848*, pp. 159–60)

Towards the end of the same article he says that 'He who is most courageous and consistent will gain the victory' (p. 163). But whatever our final judgement about Marx's account of action, these statements are not conclusive evidence. That is not because they are exhortatory, but rather because the assertion that courage will be the determining factor in no way rules out the belief that the courage itself is fatalistically pre-determined; it is rather like a physicist who says 'whichever magnet is stronger will attract the particle'. I do not believe that Marx assimilates people's attitudes to the attractive power of magnets, but the role which he *attributes to* those attitudes will not settle the question.

Having made all these negative points about the autonomy of peoples' attitudes, we must attend to two pieces of counter-evidence. The first is, that Marx does seem to allow of situations in which, even after we have set up the socio-political situation, the interference of factors which are random from the socio-political point of view may distort the outcome away from what we would have predicted. Such a case could perhaps be constructed out of the following explanation which Marx offers for the proletariat's relative passivity in June 1849 in France.

To begin the insurrection at this moment against the will of the Montagne would have meant for the proletariat – decimated, moreover, by cholera and driven out of Paris in considerable numbers by unemployment – a useless repetition of the June days of 1848, without the situation which had forced that desperate struggle. The proletarian delegates did the only rational thing. (*CSF*, p. 97)

In an article written on 21 June 1849, right after the events, Marx had given the workers' memories of Ledru-Rollin's ambiguity, and 'finally the cholera' (*MEW* VI, p. 528) as explanations. It seems virtually impossible to build medical factors such as cholera into a socio-political theory, which latter must therefore accept that all its predictions will have to cover such factors by a '*ceteris paribus*' clause. By extending this point one could, I believe, lead Marx to accept that in principle one could have delineated a socio-political situation in which the behaviour of the groups turned out less 'determined' or 'courageous' than expected, for non-socio-political reasons such as the cowardice of a particular leader at a certain point, or even an outbreak of debilitating illness. I believe that he would, if forced, allow of this, but point out that it related to factors lying, by definition, outside the pale of the social and political scientist.

There is one further, and that an important, sense in which 'courage' might be said to be autonomous of 'the situation'. We have hitherto assumed that the 'courage-input' of a group is a parameter of the explanation, and have ignored the question of its value. We must now address that question. Courage may be divided into two sorts. Each of them is relevant to the fact that, in the political situations which interest us here, groups are offered a choice. One option is to remain in (and if necessary defend) their present position. The other is to press forward politically, to achieve a different position. In the relevant situations, the second option carries a loading of pain and/or risk. A group can exhibit more or less *pain-bearing courage* – the readiness to accept assured discomfort in attaining an assured goal – and more or less *risk-bearing courage* – the readiness to pay costs (in terms of effort, pain-bearing and so on) for a goal which is not assured. In situations where the goal is not assured (or not thought to be assured) pain-bearing courage of course still applies, since we must assess what pain the group would bear in relation to various probabilities of gaining the goal. The extent to which a group has either or both of these types of courage will determine its assessments of its best interest in a situation. A case in point is Engels's explanation of the petty bourgeoisie's political activity, which suggests that we can explain the extent (or rather absence) of their political courage in terms of the character of their social experience *before the political crisis arose*:

The *mesquin* character of its commercial transactions and its credit operations is eminently apt to stamp its character with a want of energy and enterprise; it is then, to be expected that similar qualities will mark its political career... [it showed] in politics the same short-sighted, pusillanimous, wavering spirit, which is characteristic of its commercial operations. (*RCR*, pp. 93, 101)

Whilst Marx's and Engels's peculiar scorn for the petty bourgeoisie might have been somewhat exaggerated in the direct aftermath of 1848, the general kind of correlation suggested here is of great interest.

A further question arises, as to the sense in which Marx allows that a political situation might have one of a number of outcomes. We have already seen enough instances of his saying 'things will go one way, or another', especially in the *NRZ* writings, and need not repeat them. The point of interest to us here is that it is fairly clear that Marx allows of things conceivably going in various ways after as well as before the event. In his speech for the defence when he and others were on trial in February 1849 – well after the events of Autumn 1848 – Marx said that the Berlin Assembly might have answered the counter-revolution's moves by adopting a passive stance or by following 'the revolutionary course – which it did not adopt, as the gentlemen did not want to risk their necks' (*R1848*, p. 263). Engels's remarks about what the Frankfurt Assembly might have done at the early stages, which we have already discussed, adopt a similar approach, where we explain

why people went one way rather than another, but not fatalistically. This 'one way or the other' argument might, however, be
either strong or weak. The weak version would allow that, even
to define an event as such and such, we must refer to other kinds
of events which it is not, and would make the 'either–or' an empty
tautology. I believe that Marx's version is a stronger one, which
allows of the real possibility that things might have gone otherwise, and explains why they did not.

We thus return to our earlier question, about the sense in which
Marx sees events like the coup of 1851 as 'necessary and
inevitable' results of previous events. In the first place, it is
important to note that in the passage in question he is concerned
to rule out explanations which appeal to mere accident, or oversight, and to draw attention to how the events of 1848 created a
situation to which the coup was the most likely answer. In the
second place, it is possible now to give the process underlying the
'growing inevitability' which we have observed in chapters 3 and
4. Inevitability increases because of the kind of decision and
option which people make in the kind of situation in which they
find themselves. It is thus an inevitability created and nurtured
by people's own rational (but perhaps imperfectly rational) reactions to their position: the Berlin Assembly found itself unable to
assert its will in the hour of danger 'precisely because it failed
to have a will and to assert it at the proper time' (*R1848*, p. 257).
Lastly, as we have seen in our discussion of France, the
inevitability in question is not an absolutely remorseless and
unilinear process. When the Constituent Assembly opposed
Bonaparte's encroachments in early 1849, it became a focus
for renewed revolutionary hopes: 'the crystallisations of the
revolutionary movement became fluid again' (*SE*, p. 80, amended
in light of *MEW* VII, p. 51). The March 1850 elections raised the
possibility of a proletarian–petty-bourgeois–peasant rising. These
possibilities came to nothing, but only, in Marx's eyes, because
of the non-revolutionary course favoured by certain groups. It was
no more completely excluded here than at any other point in his
account that, with some different conditions, they might have seen
things differently and so acted differently. The 'inevitability' which
Marx invokes is not an overarching iron necessity; but it does
demand that we show how groups might have acted in a significantly different way, given the precise situation.

We may conclude this long section on political action by comparing the botched revolutions studied in chapters 3 and 4 with the paradigmatic French Revolution studied in chapter 2. In Marx's eyes, the bourgeoisie of 1789 had been able to press forward to the point where their interests, at the time, were fulfilled; this did not happen in 1848, in either Germany or France. This should not lead us to think that, on Marx's model, the successful 1789 bourgeoisie did not face problems of individual and group recalcitrance. Individual bourgeois might well have become cowardly or self-seeking at crucial times; the point is that the bourgeoisie as a whole were able either to suppress or to survive the threat. Nor did non-bourgeois groups always pursue goals which coincided with the precise goals of the bourgeoisie, as we have seen in chapter 2. In an article of December 1848 Marx makes the point that even when the workers, and other non-bourgeois urban groups, stood out for their own interests, as in 1793 and 1794, 'they were in fact fighting for the implementation of the interests of the bourgeoisie' (*R1848*, p. 192). The fact that even other groups pursuing other ends furthered the bourgeoisie's rise, induced in the latter the kind of unreflective confidence which Marx sees as essential in the successful revolution:

As soon as it has risen up, a class in which the revolutionary interests of society are concentrated finds the substance and material of its revolutionary activity in its own immediate situation: enemies to be struck down; measures to be taken, dictated by the needs of its struggle – the consequences of its own actions drive it on. It does not conduct theoretical investigations into its task. (*CSF*, p. 45)

The successful bourgeoisie did not operate in every sense without illusions: Marx tells us that the English sought in the Bible, and the French in ancient Rome, the images needed to raise them to the 'heroism, self-sacrifice, terror, civil war and battles' (*EBLB*, p. 148) involved in setting up bourgeois rule. The point about these images, however, is that they were the theatrical devices whereby a confident revolutionary class raised itself to the pitch of enthusiasm needed for courageous action; they involved no distortion of their class-situation, no depiction of retreat as 'consolidation', or of consolidation as 'progress'. This heroic illusion is, of course, closely bound up with the 'enthusiasm' which obtained between the various groups in the sucessful revolution.

As always, the question is whether such a sense of unity can occur in the post-French Revolution world.

As regards the modern bourgeoisies, Marx clearly rules out their creating such an enthusiasm. The Viennese movement stayed enthusiatic for a while precisely because the Austrian bourgeoisie was not aware of the tensions which progress would open up between it and its allies; progress beyond the barricades of March quickly dispelled this innocence. Even this initial illusion was denied to the French republican bourgeoisie, which won government power through repression of the people: 'The fruit fell into its lap from the tree of knowledge, not from the tree of life' (*EBLB*, p. 158). In some places, such as Vienna, social development was not matched by the bourgeoisie's political awareness; in some others, political awareness of discordant interests was more developed than the concrete conditions of the groups; but in all, by 1848, the combination of a more developed objective antagonism between the bourgeoisie and the people, and a heightened subjective awareness of such antagonism, made a repeat of the 1789 enthusiasm unlikely.

Will the proletarian revolution be without illusions? One thing which we come to realise in reading Marx's politics is that, on his theory, the proletariat in a mature capitalist economy is the only class which can gaze on its own interest, and pursue it, without hesitation or flinching. This does not rule out that the proletariat should employ 'theatrical' images, designed to raise and sustain its enthusiasm and courage; but it 'can only create its poetry from the future, not from the past' (*EBLB*, p. 149). Insofar as, during the period 1848–51, Marx sees the alternative to bourgeois revolution not as a pure proletarian revolution but as a rising of the proletariat, petty bourgeoisie and peasants, he does not seem to think that all the members of this alliance will share the same conviction, courage and fixity of view:

The *general* pretext dulls the perceptions of the half-revolutionary classes; it enables them to deceive themselves as to the *specific character* of the coming revolution, as to the consequences of its own deeds. Every revolution needs a banquet question (*CSF*, p. 128)

But this brings us onto later questions of strategy, which will be touched on in chapter 6.

A crucial document: Engels on the Prussian military question

Having examined the many complexities with which Marx
grappled in the area of political action in the direct aftermath of
1848, we must finally ask whether these remain characteristic of
his later approach. The brief answer is that they do. There exists a
document which admirably and concisely demonstrates this. As
in the case of *RCR*, this also is written by Engels: a brochure
entitled *The Prussian Military Question and the German Workers'
Party* (*PMQ*). It was written in 1865, in the midst of the 'constitutional conflict' between the German progressive bourgeoisie
and Bismarck. The main points of that conflict will be given in
chapter 7 below (see pp. 193ff.). Here we are less interested in
the historical details than in the significance of Engels' interpretation for our topic of political action. There is even less doubt
that the work represents *Marx's* views than there is in the case
of *RCR* (see p. 116 above). Rubel and Manale tell us that 'Marx
had originally encouraged Engels to undertake [it]' (p. 206). In a
letter to Engels of 11 February 1865 Marx, after suggesting two
alterations which do not affect our argument (and which Engels
in any case made), said that 'as a whole the thing is very good'
(*MESC*, p. 153). The pamphlet, after discussing the details of the
proposed army reorganisation (see p. 193 below), deals first with
the position of the bourgeoisie and then with that of the workers'
party. Each discussion is significant for our topic.

Engels begins his section on the bourgeoisie by summarising
their 'sell-out' of the 1848 revolution. In so doing he tends to
over-state both the extent to which the bourgeoisie in March 1848
was 'master of the situation' (pp. 121–2) and the reasons which
should have prompted them not to abandon the revolution (p. 123);
he also conveniently speaks of 'the workers' party' without
referring to the artisans. But what is of importance here is that
Engels goes on to depict the period of reaction which, he says,
was the 'inevitable consequence' of their pusillanimity (p. 122).
When there was a brief interlude, on the accession of Prince
William as Regent (see p. 192 below) the bourgeoisie was fooled
into thinking that it was again in control. It completely forgot that
'it had itself reinstated all the forces hostile to it, which, having
gathered their strength, now controlled the real power in the state
just as they had before 1848' (*ibid.*). Having given this sober

picture of the bourgeoisie's situation, Engels goes on to ask what
was the best attitude for them to adopt 'from a purely bourgeois
standpoint' and in all the circumstances (p. 124). It is very important to grasp the conditions which Engels puts on his answer,
since otherwise it will smack of the most cynical *Realpolitik*. He
says that the bourgeois opposition, rather than staying aloof and
trying to win concessions which their former cowardice had long
rendered impossible, should have 'been on its guard against taking
up, right from the start, a position opposed to the reorganisation...it should have made use of this reorganisation and the
money to be voted for it in order to purchase from the "New Era"
as many equivalent concessions as possible and to convert the nine
or ten million thalers of new taxation into as much political power
for itself as possible' (p. 125). All of this is premissed on the
judgement that it is in fact impossible to prevent the reorganisation
from being made (p. 124): the government has been allowed to
become too contemptuous of the opposition. Given that fact, if
it is a fact, Engels is saying that the bourgeoisie should have used
their constitutional right of consent to the plan as a means to
introduce *some* beneficial elements into it, such as universal
conscription and an increased bourgeois role in the officer corps.

Here we clearly have the same kind of retrospective judgements
as to what people could or should have done as we encountered
just after 1848. On the other side of the coin, we have the same
correlation of the political group's courage with its previous
experience and its situation. This emerges when Engels argues
that, things having been let go so far, the bourgeoisie now ought
to persist in its oppositional attitude, and fight the question as a
constitutional one. 'But anyone who expects such powers of en-
durance does not know our bourgeoisie' he tells us. 'In political
matters the courage of the bourgeoisie is always in direct proportion to its importance in society. In Germany the social power
of the bourgeoisie is far less than in England or even France; it
has neither allied itself with the old aristocracy, as in England,
nor has it destroyed the aristocracy with the help of the peasants
and the workers, as in France' (p. 132). Given the narrowness of
its sphere of social activity 'it is no wonder that its whole mentality
is equally petty! Where is it to find the courage to fight an issue
out to the bitter end?' (*ibid.*). Here we see, incidentally, the
consequences of the Prussian bourgeoisie's failure to win political

supremacy: while it does not literally 'perish' (see p. 58 above), the lack of political power reacts back on its social advancement, in a way which we shall consider in chapter 7 below.

The final section of *PMQ*, concerning the workers' party, is worth mentioning here, since it signals a crucial move in Marx's and Engels' thinking in the decades after 1848. This might be described as their 'loss of faith in the bourgeoisie'. It is often noted as paradoxical that Marx's description of the rise of the bourgeoisie in the *Manifesto* is one of their greatest eulogies; it is less often noted that it embodied absurdly high estimates of the *political* capacity of that class. The German and French happenings which we have analysed led Marx to regard the continental bourgeoisies as having in various ways failed in their 'historical vocation': the Germans could not create, and the French could not handle, bourgeois hegemony. But then, as we shall see in Chapter 7, the English bourgeoisie also failed to live up to his heroically unflagging optimism about their readiness to sweep aside both Whig and Tory and establish a purely bourgeois regime. Not, of course, that Marx ever had an *allegiance* to the bourgeoisie as such: he always analysed their actions from the point of view of their contribution to the workers' revolution. But in the earlier part of his career he was normally confident that the bourgeoisie could be relied upon to pursue their own clear interest, which would involve the creation of a political democracy which the workers could then use to overthrow them. It would be a mistake to say that he even then saw the bourgeoisie as in total untroubled control of their world: even the *Holy Family* of 1844 presents them as victims of the cunning of reason whereby they produce their own gravediggers; but he did not expect them to flinch because he did not expect them to see this outcome of their actions. As time went on however, the dominant imagery of his thinking ceases to be that of the torch being passed from a fairly competent bourgeoisie to a totally competent proletariat, and is rather that of the proletariat alone making sense of a world which even its 'creators', the bourgeoisie, can neither comprehend nor master.

Engels' discussion in *PMQ* clearly reflects this development. One might almost believe that he wrote its third section with the *Manifesto* in front of him, for all of its phrases recur here. There is however a crucial difference, in that here we read of what *ought to have* happened, not what will assuredly happen. Engels at one point attributes what has not yet happened to the fact that Germany's industrial revolution 'is still taking place' (p. 134). But this is a disingenuous plea, since as we saw in earlier chapters the bourgeois conquest of political power should *precede* the real efflorescence of industry. In any case, Engels for the most part recognises the peculiar set-backs in Germany, when for example he speaks of the structural petty bourgeoisie's 'mission. . .to spur the bourgeoisie on in its struggle with the remnants of the old society and, in particular, against its own weaknesses and cowardice' (p. 135). This brings Engels to a discussion of the temptations held out to the workers by the reactionary party in this struggle. He points out, as did Marx in both the *Manifesto* and the *NRZ* writings, in the first place that such an alliance is unrealistic for the workers, involving an attempt to undo industrial development, and secondly that the government is in no way well-disposed to the workers: '[it] will never summon up all its strength and seize power from the bourgeoisie merely to hand over this power to the proletariat!' (p. 140). As both of them did before 1848, Engels now repeats the Marxian position that the workers must not for a moment join any reactionary crusade against the bourgeoisie, who 'cannot gain political supremacy and express this in the form of a constitution and laws without, at the same time, arming the proletariat. . .It is in the interests of the workers, therefore, to support the bourgeoisie in its struggle against all reactionary elements, *on condition that it remain true to itself*' (p. 144). The final clause, which Engels underlines here, is the nub: the workers will have to *force* the bourgeoisie to carry out the bourgeois mission of the *Communist Manifesto*! Should the bourgeoisie betray 'its own class interests and the principles arising from these interests' (*ibid*), the workers still must maintain their pressure on them, rather than simply abdicate from the struggle for free association, universal suffrage and the other 'bourgeois' freedoms. In this section Engels also deals briefly with Bonapartism, which he characterises in much the same way as we did in the conclusion of chapter 4, as a kind of reaction arising within bourgeois society after the bourgeois conquest of political power. He warns the workers that it would be 'the height of folly to expect any more for the workers from a government which merely exists to hold in check their struggle against the bourgeoisie' (pp. 139–40).

His overall position is summed up in a letter to Marx in the following year:

It is becoming more and more clear to me that the bourgeoisie has not the stuff in it to rule directly itself, and that therefore unless there is an oligarchy, as here in England, capable of taking over, for good pay, the management of state and society in the interests of the bourgeoisie, a Bonapartist semi-dictatorship is the normal form. (13 April 1866; *MESC*, p. 166)

Conclusion

This chapter has charted the presuppositions of Marx's analysis of the revolutionary fiascos of 1848 in Europe. It has thus had to do largely with the revisions forced on him in his highly optimistic assumptions as to how and why the different parties outlined in the *Manifesto* would act. In the course of studying this question, we saw that Marx's position on political action is not a 'mechanistic' one; he does not maintain that all motivations are economic, and allows of a real sense in which people have freedom of action and things can thus turn out in really different ways. This does not prevent him from trying to explain how they do act, and relating their 'courage' or lack thereof to their social history and immediate situation. Finally, we looked at a writing of Engels which, as well as showing that this kind of approach to political action endures through Marx's career (for Marx read and approved the manuscript), presents the crucial movement from faith in the bourgeoisie as revolutionary class to faith in the proletariat as the only group capable of that role. In the following chapter we shall see how Marx grounds this commitment to revolutionary proletarian action in his mature economic theory.

6. Politics in the mature economic theory

In this chapter, we see Marx grappling with a reality different in kind from the problems which he faced in the period preceding, and directly following, the failure of 1848. That reality is the longevity of the bourgeois form of society, especially in England. All the pre-1848 writings, even those on economics, envisage the speedy and inevitable breakdown of the capitalist mode of production and, thus, of the bourgeois social formation. Only during the 1850s and 1860s, in his prolonged studies on economics which produced the *Grundrisse* (1857–8), *A Contribution to the Critique of Political Economy* (1859), *Theories of Surplus Value* (1861–3) and *Capital* (1863 onwards), did he probe the depths, ramifications, strengths and inner weaknesses of the capitalist organism. These studies showed him that capitalism lived by crises, and even drew new strength from what, in 1847 and 1848, he had thought were its death throes. But his analysis of this cyclical process of [crisis → new upsurge → new crisis] at the same time showed how each new beginning was made at a higher level of development, concentration and (albeit perverted) socialisation of the forces of production. He claimed to have evolved an account of how capitalist production relations would render themselves superfluous, or rather actually antagonistic, to the further development of wealth.

We must not however overstate the 'catastrophism' of the pre-1850s attitude to politics. Given that that attitude was not yet underpinned by a deep study of the economic structure of capitalism, and that Marx was over-optimistic about capitalist breakdown, his approach was still realistic, even 'gradualist' in the eyes of some. Even before 1848 he had broken with Weitling who would not accept that bourgeois rule must precede communist revolution in Germany (see McLellan 1973, pp. 155–7). Marx did not require conversion, after 1848, to the idea of a politics grounded in economic analysis. He did need to grasp that the economic analysis, and consequently the politics, must be much more complex than he had imagined. The kind of economic analysis suggested by the 'Hungry Forties', when bourgeois society seemed to be digging its own grave by pauperising the masses, was understandably simplistic. It led to a concentration on the moment of insurrectionary politics, premised on the certainty that the economy would obligingly explode at the required time. This understandable, but mistaken, inference from the experience of early capitalist crisis does not, however, place Marx in the Jacobin tradition. I have already argued in Chapter 1 (see pp. 10–11 above) that Marx regarded the Jacobin project as tragically impossible, because it was an attempt to make bourgeois society live up to its earliest and most generous ideological proclamations. He did not have to drop Jacobin, Blanquist or other insurrectionary assumptions after the failure of 1848. He had to assimilate the insight that the ripening of conditions on which his politics was always characteristically premised was both further away, and more dependent on the political intervention of the working class, than the *Communist Manifesto* had declared it to be.

Exploitation and ideology

There is a passage in Volume III of *Theories of Surplus Value* which has the merit of bringing together, in summary form, the main lines of Marx's treatment of capitalism. It treats the topic in three phases. The first is the 'historical genesis of capital, the *historical* process of separation which transforms the conditions of labour into capital and labour into wage-labour. This provides the basis for capitalist production' (*TSV* III, p. 315). There then proceeds accumulation of capital on this basis, which 'reproduces the separation and the independent existence of material wealth as against labour on an ever increasing scale' (*ibid*). But this very expansion of capitalist wealth leads to concentration, the replacement of many small by a few large capitals. 'It is in this extreme form of the contradiction and conflict that production – even though in alienated form – is transformed into social production.' (*ibid*.) The capitalists become structurally superfluous, but none the less overbearing, and their extraction of wealth changes from being in some sense payment for services rendered to being 'mere outdated and inappropriate privileges' (*ibid*.). This is, in broad outline, the story which Marx tells in the mature social theory: in an emergent, disordered totality in the *Grundrisse* and more systematically in *Capital*. Capitalism is born out of fraud and violence, and when it has 'done its job' it eventually succumbs to the proletariat, but not without political reaction which must be overcome politically. Between these two extremes, capitalism is a functioning, ongoing system reproducing itself by its own action.

We shall be concerned with all three of these phases of capitalism. But we start with the second, with capitalism as an established system. Some of the reasons for adopting this approach may be summed up in Marx's dictum that 'analysis is the necessary prerequisite of genetical presentation, and of the understanding of the real formative process in its different phases' (*TSV* III, p. 500; for further discussion, see pp. 205ff below.) This approach is broadly adopted by Marx himself. In Volume I of *Capital* we are given the essential characteristics of capitalist production as a going concern; only at the end of the volume does Marx go into the 'so-called original accumulation' from which the system emerged. Volume II goes in detail into the regular functioning, the reproduction, of capital, given the existence of many capitals and different kinds of production. In Volume III, alongside an account of the concrete day-to-day reality of capitalist economy and society, we have an account of the essential contradictions of this mode of production, and the way in which it makes itself superfluous. My presentation in this chapter will follow the sequence: *functioning* system, *genesis* of system, *breakdown* of system.

As early as the *EPM*, Marx was in a position to dispute the rosy picture of capitalist society put forward by its apologists. Not only this, but he could do so in terms of the assumptions of classical bourgeois political economy itself, showing the contradictions between that science's premiss of labour as the source of value and the actual position of the labourer which it accepted. But with the conceptual apparatus available to him (and to the rest of political economy) at the time, he could do no more than act as the heretic within an established paradigm, pointing to the uncomfortable facts brushed under the carpet by others. It was however Marx himself who supplied the conceptual novelty which solved the problem. Classical political economy had correctly postulated that between capitalist and worker there took place an exchange of equivalents. It had however wrongly claimed that the equivalents involved were 'wages' and 'labour'. So long as these were indeed the equivalents exchanged, there was no conceptual space for the claim that the worker was defrauded: however badly he did, he got no less than he gave. Marx's insight was, while keeping the conceptual framework of exchange, to point out that the exchange involving the worker had to take place prior to the beginning of production, to allow the worker to get at the conditions of production (machinery and materials) which he did not own or control. But if he had to make an exchange *before* the production period in order to produce at all, he was in fact exchanging with the capitalist not his labour (which was not yet performed, let alone 'objectified' in a product), but merely his capacity to create products, his labour-*power*. In the classical model, whose assumptions as we have seen Marx is adopting, commodities exchange for the equivalent of the amount of labour socially necessary to produce (or re-produce) them. If the worker owned his conditions of labour, he could exchange his *products* for the socially necessary labour embodied in them, including the full equivalent of his own added, living labour. But as he does not own the conditions of labour, he must exchange his labour-*power* for wages. But the value of labour-power, as that of any other commodity, is what it would cost to produce, or re-produce, the labourer capable of working. This is the amount necessary for physical subsistence, plus an added 'moral' element which differs in different societies. This amount has no intrinsic connection whatever with the amount of labour which the worker will do after striking the bargain with the capitalist. If he embodies in his products less labour than was embodied in the wages (or more strictly, wage goods) which he is paid, then he has gained. If the wage goods represent x hours of socially necessary labour, and the labourer does x hours work for the capitalist, he is, by sheer *coincidence*, getting a straight equivalent for the labour done. But anything done over the x hours gives to the capitalist products which he is able to sell on the market at their value (i.e. the hours of socially necessary labour done by the labourer) without having paid any counter-value to the labourer for the hours of living labour which these products embody. The value realised in the sale of this surplus-product is *surplus-value*; it is created by the worker, who however does not receive for it any counter-value or equivalent in wages. In reality, the worker in capitalist society will almost never get away with working less than, or just as much as, the labour-time (i.e. value) represented by his wages. He is not in a position to dictate what shall be regarded as the normal working-day, and labour is productive enough to produce its own living requirements in less than even a humane and bearable working-period. The capitalist, however deficient his grasp of classical political economy, can recognise this gain, and is defined by his pursuit of it:

The expansion of value...becomes his subjective aim, and it is only insofar as the appropriation of more and more wealth in the abstract becomes the sole motive of his operations, that he functions as a capitalist, that is, as capital personified and endowed with consciousness and a will. (*Capital* I, p. 130)

As the capitalist's initial stock of capital is replaced, it comes about that even the conditions of labour by which it is enslaved are produced by labour itself. Marx expressly brings out the parallel between this subjection of labour to its own alienated creation, and the notion of religious alienation: 'As, in religion, man is governed by the products of his own brain, so in capitalistic production he is governed by the products of his own hand' (*Capital* I, pp. 634–5). I have used the phrase 'it comes about' rather than the phrase 'it emerges', since the point which Marx has here proposed is far from evident to anyone but the scientist equipped with the theory of surplus-value. In *Capital* III especially Marx goes at great length into the enormously complex host of surface phenomena which intervene between this essential, depth process of capitalist production and the apparent, day-to-day, surface process of life in capitalist society. The upshot is that it appears that capital is the dynamic, active factor, 'giving employment' to labour, and endowing the labourer with productive powers which are its own creation. Thus: 'this social form of the labour-process presents itself, as a method employed by capital for the more profitable exploitation of labour, by increasing that labour's productiveness' (*Capital* I, p. 326). In this chapter we are concerned with the relation between this depth process and the exchange between wage-worker and capitalist.

In coming to this topic, we must note an important development in Marx's total conception of society and polity, between the 1840s and the *Grundrisse*. In an earlier study of Marx's Paris writings, I noted that the model of state and civil society employed up to and including the *Contribution to a Critique of Hegel's 'Philosophy of Right': Introduction* of 1844 gives way, in and after the Paris Manuscripts, to a model of capitalists and proletarians in civil society. I said that this model 'takes over from the first' (Maguire 1972, p. 66). The reality, when we switch our canvas to the whole of Marx's development, is more complicated. Where the 1844 writings on politics use the two-level model of state and civil society, the mature social theory uses a three-level one. This is best presented in the '1859 Preface'. In that Preface Marx tells us that men necessarily enter into relations of production which can be explained as being 'appropriate to a given stage in the development of their material forces of production' (*CCPE*, p. 20). These relations, explicable in terms of the needs of the forces of production, constitute 'the economic structure of society, the real foundation, on which arises a legal and political superstructure' (*ibid*). What was 'civil society' in the Paris writings – and Marx expressly uses the term again here – is reconceptualised as the 'economic structure', since civil society's 'anatomy . . . has to be sought in political economy'. Although Marx's categories in this passage are not defined with complete clarity, a central vision emerges: first, the process of production in which the forces of production act; second, the relations into which men have entered in the course of developing production, the totality of which are the 'economic structure' when viewed from the point of view of production, and 'civil society' when viewed as day-to-day life in the bourgeois social formation; third, the public institutions of state and law. The really important point is that the essence of Marx's mature politics, insofar as it contains new developments beyond what we have already observed and analysed, concerns the middle of these three terms, rather than the formal structures of law and the state. Where the earlier picture located exploitation in the social, and ideology in the political order, we now have as it were a 'double dose' of ideology. The ideology is centrally produced by the relations holding within civil society, and is thus not a direct product of the state sphere. But this does not mean that the state's functions *vis-à-vis* the working class may be written down from two (ideological and repressive) to one, that is, simple repression. In the first place, the ideological representations of civil society have to be codified and hallowed in legislation if they are to hold in cases of dispute without direct coercion. In the second place, the 'civil ideology' of the market still needs the backing of the 'political ideology' which represents each citizen as equally sharing in political power and decisions, and therefore as equally having 'contracted' into the present form of society. The centre of gravity may have been displaced from official politics to civil society in Marx's mature model, but it still requires the context and support of political ideology. While a lot of conceptual precision would be required to clear up all the details of the transition, the central point is clear. In evolving his mature theory, Marx has come to see that the central, though not the only, questions for politics are about the kinds and degrees of power conferred by the production relations constitutive of bourgeois society.

Before discussing how the surface process of market-exchange camouflages the depth-process of exploitation, we must note Marx's repeated insistence that the conjunction of these two processes is anything but accidental. In the argument of the *Grundrisse*, Marx promises, 'it will ultimately be shown that private property in the product of one's own labour is identical with the separation of labour and property, so that labour will create alien property and property will command alien labour' (*G*, 238). There are several stages in the argument by which Marx does in fact establish this conclusion. One is the general argument that exchange, as distinct from production for use-value in direct consumption, either remains unimportant in a community, or dissolves the mode of production and releases elements making for the capitalist mode of production (although Marx does admit that this is a complex question, admitting of a variety of answers, largely dependent on the nature of the prevailing mode of production; (see e.g. *Capital* III, pp. 327 and 583 and *G*, pp. 256–7)). But the precise argument which interests us here is that the very conditions which define the labourer as exchanging his labour-power as a commodity presuppose that he does not own or control the conditions of production. If he did, he would have no reason to work for wages rather than exchange the finished product, i.e. the whole of his materialised labour, for a full equivalent. The capitalist encounters a labourer who is 'free in the double sense, that as a free man he can dispose of his labour-power as his own commodity, and that on the other hand he has no other commodity for sale, is short of everything necessary for the realisation of his labour-power' (*Capital* 1, p. 147; see also *RIPP*, pp. 949–54, 1019–24 and 1062–64).

Marx tells us at a number of points that, because of the conditions under which it takes place (he is 'compelled to sell it voluntarily' (p. 761) and the nature of the object involved ('it gives its possessor. . .the power to appropriate alien labour *without exchange, without equivalent*' (*G*, 551), it becomes systematically misleading to call the worker–capitalist transaction an 'exchange' at all (see *RIPP*, pp. 1014–15). But by this he does not mean that the conceptual vocabulary of exchange, value, equivalent and so on does not apply to the surface appearance of the transaction: 'when it is regarded in isolation from capital, as it appears on the surface, as an independent system, then it is a mere *illusion*, but a *necessary illusion*' (*G*, 509). This can best be understood if we make a distinction between *illusion* as a systematically misleading aspect of surface reality, and *hallucination* as a seeming reality which does not exist at all (see p. 82 above). It is the former notion which Marx quite clearly applies to the wage-contract. It is real, and is real as described under the rubrics of exchange; but that reality and its description in fact systematically camouflage the other, deeper aspects of the matter, which bring us into a world far beyond exchange of equivalents. Marx sees the dependence of the labourer in the apparently free exchange not as static, but as deepening over time. By the very fact of working under alienated conditions the worker becomes a less rounded person, with only a single, narrow partial skill: 'by nature unfitted to make anything independently, the manufacturing labourer develops productive activity as a mere appendage of the capitalist's workshop' (*Capital* 1, p. 355). Marx summarises this whole development in a striking passage:

by a peculiar logic, the right of property undergoes a dialectical inversion . . .The exchange of equivalents. . .has become turned round in such a way that the exchange by one side is now only illusory. . .The complete separation between property, and, even more so, wealth, and labour, now appears as a consequence of the law which began with their identity. (*G*, 458)

This must be a reply, either explicit or by unconscious recollection, to Hegel's equally triumphant but optimistic conclusion about the same kind of society:

by a dialectical advance, subjective self-seeking turns into. . .the result that each man in earning, producing, and enjoying on his own account is *eo ipso* producing and earning for the enjoyment of everyone else. (*Philosophy of Right*, pp. 129–30, Par. 199)

We come now to what is, in a sense, the central problem of Marx's mature politics: how capitalism, founded as it is on exploitation, nevertheless survives, and moreover does so not through the imposition of martial law but with at least the passive consent of the workers. In the *Communist Manifesto*, Marx questioned how this could happen in practice: 'It is unfit to rule because it is incompetent to ensure an existence to its slave within his slavery' (*CM*, p. 79). In the first place, capitalism proved not incompetent in this respect, as Marx himself came to realise; he in fact switched the emphasis of his claims from absolute to relative impoverishment, as we shall discuss later in this chapter. But in the second place, we need to appeal to some further factor, for even relative impoverishment (the growth of social inequality, albeit on a rising base-line) if observed in the raw should, at least on Marx's theory, be enough to provoke vast disenchantment if not direct action. In short, we have to advert to the *ideological* hold of capitalism.

Marx believes that an ideology is a set of ideas which naturally, intelligibly, evolves from a set of established social relationships. It is not the case that the agents in capitalist production simply *imagine*, or that one set of agents (the capitalists) somehow *persuade* the others (workers) that things are so-and-so; the agents believe that they are so-and-so because that is the reality of their day-to-day experience. For example, the misguided notion that every part of a capital yields a uniform profit, 'expresses a practical fact' (*Capital* III, p. 167), namely that the calculation of surplus value in relation to the *whole* capital, constant *plus* variable,[1] although it obscures the origin of surplus value in living labour, is how profit appears on the surface of the capitalist circulation process. In general, although it is a 'merely *historical* necessity', the situation in which labour finds itself, a situation of dependence on its own alienated powers, 'is a *real* [phenomenon], not a merely *supposed one* existing merely in the imagination of the workers and the capitalists' (*G*, p. 831).

The reconciliation of irrational forms in which certain economic relations appear and assert themselves in practice does not concern the active

[1]　Constant capital is laid out on machines and materials, variable capital on wages.

agents of these relations in their everyday life. And since they are accustomed to move about in such relations, they find nothing strange therein. A complete contradiction offers not the least mystery to them. They feel as much at home as a fish in water among manifestations which are separated from their internal connections and absurd when isolated by themselves. (*Capital* III, p. 760).

And here it becomes crucial that, as Marx frequently asserts, capitalism is not simply a system of material reproduction, but one which reproduces its own presuppositions by its circular process. By acting in the role of worker and capitalist, worker and capitalist return constantly in those roles at the start of new circuits:

the capitalist mode of production, like any other, does not merely constantly reproduce the material product, but also the social and economic relations, the characteristic economic forms of its creation. Its result, therefore, appears just as constantly presupposed by it, as its presuppositions appear as its results. (*Capital* III, pp. 849–50)

But in the functioning capitalist system, then, we must conceive also of the agents' own image of their world as a moment in this reproduction; the agents of capitalist production can be like 'fish in water' precisely because recurrent, everyday experience does not clash with the ideology: capitalists really do 'give employment' to workers who have no work, and – because of the establishment of an average rate of profit (see *Capital* III, chapters 9 and 10) – bigger capitals do make bigger profits, regardless of how much surplus-value they directly exploit.

The mystification inherent in the *capital-relation* emerges at this point. The value-sustaining power of labour appears as the self-supporting power of capital; the value-creating power of labour as the self-valorizing power of capital and, in general, in accordance with its concept, *living* labour appears to be put to work by *objectified* labour. (*RIPP*, pp. 1020–1)

Primitive accumulation: capitalism and force

Before tracing the growth of the power by which the workers transform capitalist society, we must advert to the power by which the bourgeoisie set it up in the first place. Marx tends to distinguish two kinds of power. One, which he calls *Macht*, and which we shall continue to render as 'power', normally stands for what an agent is able to achieve *within* a structure of roles, relations and expectations. The other is *Gewalt*, which we shall render as 'force'; it covers situations in which agents are trying to establish, defend or change the relations and expectations in question. Marx does not clearly define 'power' and 'force' as I have done here, nor does he observe a strict rule as to usage;[1] but the conceptual isolation of 'force/*Gewalt*' as proper to creating/defending/destroying relationships is faithful to his theory. After giving the first broad account of how capitalism functions, Marx turns, towards the end of *Capital* I, to the nature of its historical emergence. He argues that

In the tender annals of Political Economy, the idyllic reigns from time immemorial. Right and 'labour' were from all time the sole means of enrichment, the present year of course always excepted. As a matter of fact, the methods of primitive accumulation are anything but idyllic. (*Capital* I, p. 737)

In most of the passages where he discusses this historical, forceful phase of capitalism, Marx refers to E. G. Wakefield's *A View of the Art of Colonization*, published in 1849. This book, Marx tells us, represents a bourgeois writer's realisation in the case of England's colonies of the brutal facts which are both historically and ideologically submerged as regards her own past. Wakefield discovers that the mere importation of the means of production into a colony does not permit their owner to function as a capitalist, so long as he does not create 'the wage-worker, the other man who is compelled to sell himself of his own free-will' (*Capital* I, p. 791). In the *Grundrisse* Marx gloats over 'an utterly delightful cry of outrage on the part of the West-Indian plantation owner', who complains in *The Times* 'how the *Quashees* (the free blacks of Jamaica) content themselves with producing only what is strictly necessary for their own consumption' (*G*, p. 325). Wakefield's book describes how it is necessary to use force in order to separate these independent producers from their property in the means of production, so that they can then produce only on condition of creating surplus value for the capitalist. But Marx argues that, in the centuries during which English capitalist production was establishing itself, similar forceful means were used to 'transform the propertyless into *workers* at conditions advantageous for capital... (Very bloody means of coercion of

---

[1] For 'Macht' see *MEW* IV, pp. 476–7, *MEW* VI, p. 414 and *MEW* XXV, pp. 629, 765. For 'Gewalt' and cognates, see *MEW* IV, p. 473, *MEW* XXIII, p. 249, *CWF*, p. 75 and *EN*, pp. 315–16.

this sort employed under Henry VIII *et al*.)' (*G*, p. 736; see also p. 769 and *GI*, p. 72).

Marx explicitly draws a distinction, in discussing the agricultural revolution in England, between its 'purely economic causes' and the 'forcible means employed' (*Capital* I, p. 746). This calls to mind the oft-quoted assertion, elsewhere in the same long discussion of the genesis of capitalism, that 'Force is the midwife of every old society pregnant with a new one. It is an economic power' (p. 776). But the passage, when quoted out of its theoretical context, is misleading, The second sentence, especially, is no more than an aphorism, as is suggested by the fact that the German reads that 'die Gewalt' is 'eine ökonomische Potenz' (*MEW* XXIII, p. 779). Here 'force' is subsumed under a wide category of 'power' or 'potency', one which Marx does not normally employ in this context. The point of the aphorism is clear enough: that force contributes, is indeed essential, to economic transformation. But the distinction between force and economic relations (as it were, economic power) is not abandoned. This becomes clear from what is perhaps the nearest attempt to an explicit theorisation which Marx gives us:

The dull compulsion [*der stumme Zwang*] of economic relations completes the subjection of the labourer to the capitalist. Direct force, outside economic conditions [*Außerökonomische, unmittelbare Gewalt*] is of course still used, but only exceptionally. In the ordinary run of things, the labourer can be left to the 'natural laws of production', i.e., to his dependence on capital, a dependence springing from, and guaranteed in perpetuity by, the conditions of production themselves. It is otherwise during the historic genesis of capitalist production. (*Capital* I, p. 761; *MEW* XXIII, p. 765)

This historical genesis is completed when the worker is separated from his conditions of production, and has at least sullenly acquiesced in this fact, to the extent of no longer requiring forcible subjection. He becomes a captivated '*Träger*' (bearer) of the role of wage-worker:

The direct producer is driven rather by force of circumstances than by direct coercion, through legal enactment rather than the whip, to perform it on his own responsibility. (*Capital* III, p. 775).

The labour movement

The economy politicised

Marx does not hold that the workers are irretrievably locked within this ideology, however. While he does not provide an explicit account of the process from ideology to revolution, defining each stage clearly, he does envisage a sequence of attitudes which the worker can have to his role in the wage-relationship. I shall briefly reconstruct this sequence of attitudes here, and we shall see how Marx believes that the objective development of capitalism will create at least the necessary conditions for their emergence in a later section. We might call the first attitude the 'captive one'. Marx at one point tells us that even the best of the classical economists remain more or less 'in the grip' (*Capital* III, p. 809) ['*befangen*' (*MEW* XXV, p. 838)] of capitalist illusions; it is all the more natural that the actual agents of the process – workers and capitalists – should be similarly imprisoned. 'The advance of capitalist production develops a working-class, which by education, tradition, habit, looks upon the conditions of that mode of production as self-evident laws of nature' (*Capital* I, p. 761).

If the 'captive' worker sees everything about his position as 'natural' (which does not rule out his grousing *against nature*), the worker in the second attitude accepts the wage-relationship, but takes a combative approach to his fate within it. He is aware that, within certain extremes, the level of wages 'is only settled by the continuous struggle between capital and labour' (*WPP*, p. 223). Realising that the outcome will depend on the 'respective powers of the combatants' (*ibid.*), the workers organise themselves into trades unions to bargain, and if necessary strike, for better pay or fewer hours of work. Marx very frequently uses military metaphors for industrial struggles, and relates the attitude which we are here depicting to 'a guerilla war against the effects of the existing system' (p. 226).

If the 'guerilla' attitude reacts to the effects of the system by waging a power struggle, there is a further attitude which, while still accepting the basic relationship, goes one step further and tries to use established political structures to set general limits to the power of the individual capitalists. Pursuing the military analogy, Marx tells us that the limitation of the working day in

England (which we shall examine in more detail below) was 'the product of a protracted civil war, more or less dissembled, between the capitalist class and the working class' (*Capital* 1, p. 285). As early as 1847 Marx had made a similar point about the evolution of the unions:

In this struggle – a veritable civil war – all the elements necessary for a coming battle unite and develop. Once it has reached this point, association takes on a political character. (*PP*, p. 173)

This gives us an insight into the meaning of 'politics', on Marx's account: the drive of the ruling class is to 'depoliticise' as much as possible, so long as the workers are acquiescent; the tendency of militant workers is to politicise what the bourgeoisie would have us accept as natural. There is thus no ultimate institutional definition of politics. A 'sphere' of society becomes part of politics when the workers cease to regard it as a given and begin to analyze and challenge its conditions of existence. To move from individual isolation to combination is a step in this direction, and the step to public organisation on a national scale is a qualitatively further one.

The fourth and final attitude implicit in Marx's account is the one which he himself purveys: the revolutionary one. Here the whole capitalist structure is challenged by a working class imbued with the analysis which we are discussing in this chapter, and working along the strategic lines which we shall see in our last sub-section below.

The 'Civil war' phase: factory legislation in England

It will emerge from the previous section that Marx's theory does not draw as rigid a distinction between law and force as might be inferred from some of his general statements about the secondary status of law (see, e.g., *GI*, pp. 252, 382–3, 671). When English landowners and manufacturers forced vagabonds to become workers, they used the compulsion of state legislation to do so. The kinship of such 'bloody legislation' (*Capital* 1, p. 758) to the force which it barely disguises is well conveyed in the observation of Townsend that 'legal constraint to labour is attended with too much trouble, violence, and noise, creates illwill etc.' (quoted *G*, p. 845), while the silent pressure of hunger is far more efficient. It will emerge in this section, equally, that legislation can represent a victory for labour in the class struggle, and is then also far from a mere reflection of the *status quo ante*. I do not believe that these points conflict with Marx's general observations on the status of law. His central point still stands, that modes of production, and thus social formations, are not changed merely by writing new laws; if the endogenous development of the conditions of production, or the balance of forces in the class struggle, do not accommodate or support the legislation, it is a literal dead letter. In Marx's system, the shift from structure to politics is a far more important shift than the more conventional distinction between 'law' and 'force'. We are here concerned with the first stage in this shift from structure to politics.

As we have seen, the capitalist is motivated to make more and more profit. His two chief considerations will be the level of wages, setting his labour costs, and the length of the working day, limiting his surplus value (leaving aside questions of the *intensity of labour* for the moment). It would be interesting, in the light of contemporary politics, to hear how Marx would restate his claim that ' so long as wages are still regulated by statute, it cannot yet be said either that capital has subsumed production under itself as capital, or that wage labour has attained the mode of labour adequate to it' (*G*, p. 736). Be that as it may, we shall postpone our discussion of wage-levels until the end of the section, since as Marx points out it was the length of the working-day which was the object of general political conflict and legislation in the capitalism of his day.

Given that the capitalist wants more and more profit, where will he stop using his power to exact a longer and longer working day in return for the conditions of labour? Marx says that, of itself, the capitalist class will never call a halt to this prolongation; even when concessions have been extracted from the class in the 1860s legislation, he notes 'the hesitation, the repugnance, and the bad faith with which it lent itself to the task of carrying these measures into practice' (*Capital* 1, p. 501). Marx tells us that the prolongation of the working-day reached its peak in a frenzied orgy which destroyed 'all bounds of morals and nature, age and sex, day and night' in the last third of the eighteenth century (p. 264). 'In its blind unrestrainable passion, its were-wolf hunger for surplus-labour, capital oversteps not only the moral, but even the merely physical maximum bounds of the working-day' (p. 250). This reference to the conception of a 'moral' limit to the exploitation of labour raises a theoretical problem. At a number of points, Marx appears to be arguing that the capitalists themselves either have a change of heart, or else are made ashamed of themselves. 'Malthus, by no means a man whom you would suspect of a maudlin sentimentalism, declared in a pamphlet, published about 1845, that if this sort of thing was to go on the nation would be attacked at its very source' (*WPP*, p. 219). Marx tells us that the report of a commission on mining in 1840 'made revelations so terrible, so shocking, and creating such a scandal all over Europe, that to salve its conscience Parliament passed the Mining Act of 1842' (*Capital* I, p. 501). But we must carefully analyse these arguments.

In the first place, we should not overlook the divisions within the bourgeoisie, the potential opposition to the interest of industrial capital which has been noted already in chapter 2 (p. 30 above). This is relevant to the protest of Malthus, who 'defends the interests of the industrial bourgeoisie only insofar as they are identical with the interests of landed property, of the aristocracy' (*TSV* II, p. 115). On the question of Repeal of the Corn Laws, Marx points out, 'the majority of the monied interest and some even of the commercial interest (Liverpool for instance) were to be found amongst the *allies* of the landed interest against the manufacturing interest' (*ibid.*, p. 123). Thus Parliament's actions are by no means always calculated expressions of the industrial bourgeosie's best interests; Marx elsewhere quotes Palmerston's triumphalist declaration that 'The House of Commons is a house of landed proprietors' (quoted *Capital* III, p. 611). This explains the otherwise puzzling argument that the destructive effects of machinery on the alleged free wage contract 'afforded the English Parliament an excuse, founded on juridical principles, for the interference of the state with factories' (*Capital* I, p. 394). But of course I have so far omitted the fundamental factor which gives this inner 'class-struggle' within the bourgeoisie its context; that is, the class-struggle with the working class.

As soon as the working class, stunned at first by the noise and turmoil of the new system of production, recovered, in some measure, its senses, its resistance began, and first in the native land of machinism, in England. (*Capital*, I, p. 264).

While Marx's theory does not invoke the shame, or moral conversion, of the capitalists as a class, it does not seem to rule out the salutary effect of moral, or perhaps ideological, *discomfiture*. When the bourgeoisie finds itself confronted with a potentially radical or revolutionary working-class, it is willy-nilly in the arena of politics, of publicity, of *spelling out* its actions and their justification. I do not mean that the bourgeoisie would be seriously worried at discrepancies in its account of the world, and motivated thereby to bring practice into line with principle. What matters is that a successful spelling-out, or half-ideology, half-spelling-out, is the alternative to *forceful confrontation*; sometimes even a reform of practice is preferable to that!

The various forces involved led to the Factory Act of 1844. The working-class were organised and threatening, under the banner of Chartism. The conflict of land and industry over the Corn Laws was coming to a head, and the landed interest was using the sins of industrial capital to discredit the latter's demands for Repeal.

However much the individual manufacturer might give the rein to his old lust for gain, the spokesmen and political leaders of the manufacturing class ordered a change of front and of speech towards the workpeople. They had entered upon the contest for the repeal of the Corn Laws, and needed the workers to help them to victory. (*Capital* I, p. 267)

Once the Repeal had been won in 1846, and the working class had suffered the twin blows of the collapse of Chartism in 1848 and the simultaneous collapse of the French proletariat and the German revolution, the manufacturers changed their tune. They openly flouted even the letter of the Act, sitting in judgement on their own cases as magistrates. But when, in 1850, the Court of Exchequer handed down a decision giving the apparently decisive legal victory to the manufacturers, there 'followed at once a revulsion' (*Capital* I, p. 278). Even the Factory Inspectors in their official reports warned the government of the dangerous degree of resentment, and the likelihood of active opposition. The result was a compromise, the Factory Act of 1850, which was completed by an Act of 1853 covering loopholes.

It will be easily understood that after the factory magnates had resigned themselves and become reconciled to the inevitable, the power of resistance of capital gradually weakened, whilst at the same time the power of attack of the working class grew with the number of its allies in the classes of society not immediately interested in the question. (p. 282)

Thus Marx concludes that the factory acts were a 'meagre concession wrung from capital' (p. 494), that they would not have come about without the resistance and threatened use of force by the working class, and that even then the capitalists tried to evade in practice what they had had to concede publicly in principle. In this class struggle, the internal oppositions of the bourgeoisie were crucial, as shown by the lack of reform in mining:

an industry distinguished from others by the exceptional characteristic that the interests of landlord and capitalist there join hands. The antagonism of these two interests had been favourable to factory legislation, while on the other hand the absence of that antagonism is sufficient to explain the delays and chicanery of the legislation on mines. (p. 501)

Without inferring a cut-and-dried law from a single passage, we may suggest that the basic factor in the whole process is the organised opposition of the working class, its conduct of 'a protracted civil war, more or less dissembled, between the capitalist class and the working class' (p. 285). But for this organised opposition to be successful short of violent confrontation, the internal divisions of the bourgeoisie were a further necessary condition. They were favourable to ('hatte...begünstigt' [*MEW* XXIII, p. 519]) factory legislation, and their absence sufficed to explain ('reicht hin...zu erklären' [*ibid.*]) its non-emergence, delayed emergence or emasculation.

Wages are settled between the employer and those seeking employment. The former's strength is that he owns the conditions needed for the latter to work at all; their countervailing power is the strike, the refusal to put those conditions into action. As we have seen, Marx is happy enough to call this business an 'exchange', although he emphasises that its outcome is the resultant of two hostile forces, rather than the harmonic encounter of 'demand' and 'supply' envisaged by the classical economists. In this respect, his mature account is faithful to the dramatic opening sentence of the 1844 *EPM*: '*Wages* are determined by the fierce struggle between capitalist and worker' (*EPM*, p. 282). As his work, both theoretical and practical, in the International showed, Marx did not regard the strength of the worker as a simple given quantity: to the extent that trades unions grew and ramified, the capitalist was less able to set off one group of workers against another. But before and during the period of the International Marx encountered opponents who, while anti-capitalists of one kind or another, accepted the classical political economy's assertion that there was a *natural* level to which wages tended to return if they deviated from it. In 1847 Marx criticised Proudhon's assertion that any rise in wages would, by raising costs, bring about an equal rise in prices with chaotic consequences nullifying the initial gain. One might suspect that, even if he had had at this time little or no theoretical justification for his position, Marx would have found it impossible to condone the quietism flowing from Proudhon's claim. But as a matter of fact he did propose a theoretical argument, and one which strikingly anticipates the developed theory of surplus-value. He poured scorn on Proudhon's notion of an equal and general rise in prices, arguing that it was a question of the proportion of costs represented by wages in different lines of production. Those employing relatively less labour (here we have implicitly the category of variable capital) will have less added cost, and therefore higher profits than before, and *vice versa*. Marx went on to note that competition will tend to wipe out the excess of profits in the first case. I do not propose to dwell on the picture presented in this discussion, because it is clear that Marx has not arrived at anything like the subtlety of his post-1850 view of the matter. What is interesting is his grasp, even at this stage, that

the rise and fall of profits and wages expresses merely the proportion in which capitalists and workers share in the products of a day's work, without influencing in most instances the price of the product. (*PP*, p. 167)

Here is Marx's earliest explicit grasp of the distinction which we employed earlier in this chapter, between the sphere in which the capitalist sells the product on the market for the value embodied in it (or necessary for its reproduction, if these two differ) and the entirely separate sphere in which the capitalist and the worker settle how much of that value will go to each of them. This distinction, and the distinction of constant and variable capital, have both been developed into the theory of surplus-value by the time of Marx's debate against Weston in the International Workingmen's Association in 1865, which was published posthumously as *Wages, Price and Profit*. By this stage (especially in *TSV*, various sections) Marx has clarified his rejection of any notion of profits as an amount added to the costs of production by the capitalist. He goes into a fairly complex analysis, although one presented in pedagogically admirable terms, of the effects of wage rises in sectors with different ratios of wages (variable capital) to other costs (constant capital). We need not here go into all the points of the argument (which are summarised, along with a general survey of Marx's thought on wages, in chapter 9 of Mandel 1971). What matters is that Marx concludes that trades-union activity to raise wages is both possible and necessary. It is possible in the sense that actual rises of wages can be brought about, without the chaotic consequences envisaged by Proudhon and Weston. (Marx is, however, pessimistic as to the possibility of large, widespread, permanent wage rises, as we shall note in the next section.) But such activity is also necessary, as follows from the reiteration of the earlier point from the *EPM*, that wages are in any case set by *struggle*. In *WPP* Marx argues that 99 out of 100 disputes are cases of labour's *reacting* against an attempted advance by capital:

[should the working class] renounce their resistance against the encroachments of capital, and abandon their attempts at making the best of the occasional chances for their temporary improvement? If they did, they would be degraded to one level mass of broken wretches past salvation. (*WPP*, p. 225).

Thus we may briefly sum up Marx's position on this question (some further features of which will appear in the next section). It is not true, he claims, that wage rises automatically cause price rises and market effects which reduce wages to their former levels. This means that trades union activity is worthwhile, and can bring about at least sustained wage rises. But in any case trades unions are necessary in order to prevent the capitalists from further depressing wages or raising hours. And in *WPP* Marx adds a dimension which was present also in *PP*: even apart from their strictly economic role, the unions are a necessary school for the development of class-consciousness and more directly political forms of organisation and activity: 'By cowardly giving way in their everyday conflict with capital, they would certainly disqualify themselves for the initiating of any larger movement.' (*WPP*, p. 225; see *PP*, pp. 172–5).

The proletarian revolution

In this section we shall discuss the relevance of Marx's mature economic theory to specifically revolutionary working-class action, the 'large movement' of building communist society. Its first sub-section will examine some specific details of how the economic theory grounds Marx's approach to revolution, and the second will look briefly at some of the strategic implications.

The grounds of revolution

As we have already noted, Marx's early approach was based on the firm expectation that the lot of the worker would become dramatically worse. The recovery of capitalism which Marx had to study in the 1850s and 1860s forced him to accept that this was not necessarily so. It seems to me however, that there is a danger of exaggerating the extent to which Marx's early claims about the wage-relation are exhausted by the claim about pauperisation. There is, for example, a passage in the *EPM* where he claims that, even if the worker becomes better off, this is at the cost of 'overwork and early death, reduction to a machine, enslavement to capital which piles up in threatening opposition to him, fresh competition, and starvation or beggary for a section of the workers' (*EPM*, pp. 285–6). This argument is very important. While it does not disprove Mandel's judgement that up to the *Manifesto* Marx and Engels 'remain wedded' to pauperisation (Mandel 1971, p. 143), it shows that even at this stage, had they been shown a case of steadily rising wages, they would still have had plenty to say about what was wrong with capitalism from the worker's point of view. That matters quite a lot, since it corrects any impression that, being forced to give way on the question of absolute wage-levels, Marx then truculently looked about him for other sticks with which to belabour the bourgeoisie.

Undoubtedly, of course, there was development on this front, and perhaps the chief point is the switch of emphasis from absolute to relative poverty. Marx spells out this point in the 1860s: 'The position of the classes to one another depends more on relative wages than on the absolute amount of wages' (*TSV* II, p. 419; see also *TSV* III, pp. 33–4). Sometimes the worker can get a rise in living standards, allowing him to participate in 'the higher, even cultural satisfactions, the agitation for his own interests, newspaper subscriptions, attending lectures, educating his children, developing his taste, etc.' (*G*, p. 287; see also p. 438). But the crisis phase of the industrial cycle hits even 'the best-paid, the aristocracy [*ihre Aristokratie*] of the working-class' (*Capital* I, p. 685, from *MEW* XXIII, p. 697). In *Wage-labour and Capital*, delivered in 1847 and published in 1849, Marx had already used the famous comparison of a cottage and a palace to illustrate the point about *relative* wages, and asked whether the working-class should be content with forging the 'golden chains by which the bourgeoisie drags it in its train' (*WLC*, p. 87). The *Grundrisse* continues this trend towards concern with the *nature* of the wage-relation, whatever the size of the wage. The worker, we are told, 'necessarily impoverishes himself...because the creative power of his labour establishes itself as the power of capital, as an *alien power* confronting him' (*G*, p. 307). Moreover, every worker is *essentially* a pauper, suspended over the pit of unemployment, even if he successfully renews that suspension every day of his working-life (see *G*, p. 604).

We are less concerned with the validity of these claims – lying as they do in the area of Marxian economics – than with their *nature*. What is relevant about them is that they form part of a general development in Marx's thinking, away from the vision of a single total collapse of capitalism and towards an exploration of its internal tensions and contradictions. Within this perspective, Marx can allow of wage rises, but point to the standing conditions of insecurity under which they are achieved, and the periodic crises and consequent wage cuts in which that insecurity manifests itself. This leads us to the topic of his theory of crisis and breakdown.

Here again we are concerned with the nature rather than the validity of Marx's claims. He elaborates an extremely complex picture, but one in which there is one absolutely central tension. This is between the pursuit of profit, which is the capitalist's motive, and the gratuitous development of wealth. At first these coincide, so that a single process of development falls under both descriptions; but gradually the first becomes a fetter on the second.

The means – unconditional development of the productive forces of society – comes continually into conflict with the limited purpose, the self-expansion of the existing capital. The capitalist mode of production is, for this reason, a historical means of developing the material forces of production and creating an appropriate world-market, and is, at the same time, a continual conflict between this its historical task and its own corresponding relations of social production. (*Capital* III, p. 245)

At this juncture, a short textual point is in order. Since the appearance of English selections in 1971 and a complete English edition in 1973, much has been made of the light thrown on Marx's mature theory by the *Grundrisse*, his notebooks of 1857–8. It is difficult to suppress the suspicion that much of the excitement – amounting almost to a 'fetishism of the *Grundrisse*' – is the product of an insufficient reading of what has been available for years in *Capital*. Much of the interest of the earlier work, indeed, is to see Marx painstakingly working away at problems which he had largely solved, and could formulate more clearly, in the later one (for example, many of the calculations about production- and circulation-time in *Capital* II). A good case in point is the chapter in *Capital* III entitled 'Exposition of the Internal Contradictions of the Law' (*Capital* III, Chapter 15). Here, in the space of twenty-odd pages, Marx sums up a number of passages in the *Grundrisse*, all of which deal with the tension between profit and production. In both discussions, Marx lays great emphasis on the tensions resulting from capitalism's attempts to *use* as much labour as possible, and *pay* as little of it as possible. After giving an account of the various secondary tensions to which capitalism gives rise, Marx later concludes that nevertheless 'the ultimate reason for all real crises always remains the poverty and restricted consumption of the masses as opposed to the drive of capitalist production to develop the productive forces as though only the absolute consuming power of society constituted their limit' (*Capital* III, pp. 472–3). The important thing about all these arguments, from our point of view, is that they lay emphasis not on an overnight collapse of capitalism, but on its growing unmanageability, on the way in which successive crises give it advice 'to be gone and to give room to a higher stage of social production' (*G*, p. 750).

But there remains one other problem in this area: that of the *necessity* of revolution. Having argued that Marx allows for a fairly complex development of capitalism, and not for an overnight collapse, we face the problem of the sense in which its downfall is nevertheless 'inevitable', as he was fond of claiming.

This is one member of a family of problems, another one of which has been raised recently by Professor Charles Taylor. He claims that there is in general in Marx's theory a gulf between 'revolution' and 'science'. He says that Marx fails to reconcile his insistence on the need for revolution with his scientific account of 'how men are caught up in structures and a dynamic which they neither understand nor control' (Taylor, C., p. 553). If men are so caught up in alienated structures, how can they ever achieve the prior liberation necessary for revolution? We may take Taylor's problem first. The answer to it is that it overestimates the extent to which Marx regards capitalism as being a total, coherent, self-maintaining system. Our discussion of the role of ideology is relevant here. We might say that, in Marx's eyes, capitalism is coherent, but crucially on two levels rather than one. It is coherent, that is intelligible, to the scientist, in an *explanatory* manner: he can explain its depth process, and explain the surface process as an appearance of it. To the people living in it, it is also coherent but only in an *experiential* way, as a lived ideology whose systematically misleading expectations are justified because their conditions are recurrently reproduced by the depth process which they distort. This is quite unlike the situation which he envisages for communism, where the mystical veil will be stripped from society because material production 'is treated as production by freely associated men, and is consciously regulated by them in accordance with a settled plan' (*Capital* 1, p. 51). The whole point of Marx's theory of crisis is to show that capitalist roles are such that people cannot forever rest happy in the ideology attaching to them, because *the roles themselves undermine the ideology*. As a matter of fact, capitalism works itself into crises which jerk people out of their complacency, because – or so Marx claims – the ideology becomes incapable of stretching to cover, for example, mass unemployment, suppression of strikes and such realities. If this were not so, then Taylor would be right, and Marx would have fallen into the trap of giving so coherent an account of how capitalism works that its downfall is inconceivable.

But of course we have got Marx off one charge here only by raising another: his alleged naivety in believing that the working class *would* be jerked out of complacency by capitalist developments. Fully to answer this question would involve a study of industrial relations over the last century or so, and that is well outside our scope. But we may shed light on Marx's thinking, and return to the problems of the 'necessity' of revolution, by specifying exactly what problem this point raises for him. It is all too easy to forget why and for whom Marx wrote *Capital*. While making a contribution to economic science, he did so in the interest of the group whose cause he believed that the contribution justified: the workers. This is why, in the 'Preface to the French Edition', he applauded the idea of publishing it in serial form, whereby it would be 'more accessible to the working class, a consideration which to me outweighs everything else' (*Capital*, Volume I (Harmondsworth 1976), p. 104). A lot of the 'inevitabilism' of Marx's economic writings becomes both more understandable and more acceptable if we read it as prefaced by the assumption 'given that there is an organised working class seeing its interest and pursuing it'. In other words, you do not begin a handbook on golf by a long attack on the counter-attractions of tennis: you are entitled to assume that people, committed to your goal, are interested in how to achieve it. In the same way, Marx was writing a study the truth of some of whose assertions depended on the complicity of the reader: it is a handbook for a (presumably) revolutionary working class. In this sense, we may say that objectively Marx's science shows – if correct – no more than that crisis is inevitable in the capitalist system. But crisis is no more than the moment for revolution, and is not synonymous therewith. There are of course occasions when Marx is simply unrealistic, and there is no point in denying that. But much more sense can be made of his theories if we understand for whom, and on what assumptions, they were presented. This does not mean that Marx's assumption turned out to be justified. The theory of working-class organisation was to prove to be as much more complicated than he supposed, in the century after his death, as did the theory of 'bourgeois organisation' in his own lifetime. My clarifications here are intended not to acquit Marx of all charges of naivety, but rather to show where precisely the charges should lie: not in his supposed extreme 'inevitabilism', but in his optimism that the working class would in fact become revolutionary.

Implications for strategy

Marx's positions in the many and complex strategic debates in which he was engaged, especially during the period of the International, are being treated to an exhaustive study by Professor Hunt (see Hunt, Vol. 1 [1974] and Vol. 2 [forthcoming]). They are concerned with theory of a different kind from what we have encountered so far, in that they are 'action-guiding' rather than explanatory. They do not lie outside the scope of our inquiry for that reason, however, since to divorce 'practical' and 'explanatory' theory would be a disservice to Marx's notion of *praxis*. A satisfactory discussion of them – over and above Professor Hunt's meticulous compilation, and comparison with some post-Marxian positions – would require a study of revolutionary theory since Marx, since he was not to participate in the envisaged proletarian revolution during his lifetime. The present section is intended to bring out some of the main points of Marx's strategic position, as they relate to the theoretical grounding which we have so far studied in this chapter. I shall present the discussion by relating Marx's own thinking to a number of different strategic tendencies which he opposed.

(1) *Economic abstentionism.* We have already referred to Marx's debate with Weston (see pp. 156–57 above). Weston's attitude typifies a whole approach which declares the economy, for one reason or another, 'out of bounds' to human interference. We have already seen that Marx argues that such interference is not only possible, but crucially necessary if wages are to be protected or raised. What interests us here is the political significance of Marx's insistence on the role of the unions. He tells us that 'if we do not find concealed in society as it is the material conditions of production and the corresponding relations of exchange pre-requisite for a classless society, then all attempts to explode it would be quixotic' (*G*, p. 159). In other words, no political change can 'bite' if it does not achieve a redefinition of the roles and relations constituting capitalist society. But this can be guaranteed only by an organisation of the workers as such, the occupants, as it were, of the roles and relations. To concede the 'economic abstentionists'' point would be to vitiate Marx's approach to politics at its very root.

(2) *Political abstentionism.* In 1873, after the effective dissolution of the International, Marx wrote an article for an Italian journal, on the subject of 'Political Indifferentism'. It starts with a long satire on his opponents, whom he represents as laying down that:

> The working class must not constitute itself a political party; it must not, under any pretext, engage in political action, for to combat the State is to recognise the State: and this is contrary to eternal principles. Workers must not go on strike; for to struggle to increase one's wages or to prevent their decrease is like recognising *Wages*: and this is contrary to the eternal principle of the emancipation of the working class! (*PI*, p. 20)

What Marx here satirises is what we might call the 'ultra' variety of abstentionism: a claim to be so revolutionary that any truck with bourgeois society is unacceptable. It is very probable that many of those who held this view did so for the less noble but quite understandable reason that political activity of a working-class kind, in nineteenth-century Europe, was at times an extremely dangerous business (see Lichtheim 1975, pp. 68–9). An 'ultra-revolutionary' attitude to politics and economics could save both skin and conscience from dangerous involvement. A related position is that of strictly *political* abstentionism, which perhaps is quite militant in the economic sphere but rules out all political confrontation as involving a compromising assumption of bourgeois political forms. It is essential to complement Marx's rejection of economic abstentionism by stressing that he would have no time for a *merely economic* militancy: action at the strictly economic level is necessary but far from sufficient. Even on purely economic grounds it would be self-defeating, for when economic gains become serious 'the lords of land and the lords of capital will always use their political privileges for the defence and perpetuation of their economical monopolies' (*IA*, p. 80). In other words, as soon as the workers' gains begin to call in question the power built into the existing economic relationships, the bourgeoisie will resort to *force* to restore it (see pp. 147ff. above). If the workers cannot match that force in political terms, they will be defeated even in the economic sphere.

(3) *Anarchism.* The most spectacular confrontation within the International was that between Marx and Michael Bakunin, the

Russian anarchist. Not only ideas, but two forceful personalities were involved. Nationalism also played a part in this dispute between a russophobe German and a germanophobe Russian. Both men, and the adherents of both men, stooped to intrigue, although Marx seems to have done so less consistently than Bakunin. In this brief account, I shall abstract two of the chief theoretical issues concerned, and make no attempt to give the historical and personal details. The first strand in the anarchist critique of Marx's position was the opposition to participation, not so much in politics as such, but in *bourgeois* politics. To that argument, Marx made the answer which we have looked at under political abstentionism in general, although he had also to meet the specific charge of 'bourgeoisification'; it will be easier to look at his position on the latter issue under our fifth and final heading. Here I shall concentrate on the more important issue raised by the anarchists, that of 'authoritarianism'. Bakunin charged that the Marxian ideas on how to organise the revolution were authoritarian, and thus stifled the mass spontaneity essential to a real defeat of political authority. He alleged that this, if it did not destroy all chance of revolution, would mean that there would evolve a new state structure which would oppress the workers every bit as much as does the bourgeois one. We may usefully distinguish his opposition to authority in the making and to authority in the aftermath of the revolution, although as we shall see he claims that the one follows from the other.

As regards Marx's own practice as a revolutionary, it was much less authoritarian than Bakunin and his followers claim (as Hunt has exhaustively documented [see Hunt, chapter 8]). It is significant that Marx's famous letter to Freiligrath, disowning any notion of 'the party' in any but the broadest sense, was written in 1860, long before the Bakuninist charges had been directed against him; it can therefore be taken as a genuine disclaimer, and not just a polemical self-defence (see Hunt, p. 283). It is also interesting that, in writing about the Spanish revolution in 1854, Marx comments that because of the localised nature of the many revolutionary movements 'a wholesome anarchy prevails' in the provinces. 'This anarchical state of the provinces' he adds, 'is of great advantage to the cause of the revolution, as it prevents its being confiscated at the capital' (*NYDT*, 1 September 1854, in *RS*, p. 119). In the following article he contrasts the Spanish situation with French centralisation, and says that it means that capitulation at the centre cannot successfully sell out the movement 'so long as that state of "anarchy" survives there without which no revolution can succeed' (*NYDT*, 4 September 1854, in *RS*, p. 122). We are of course not entitled to erect a whole theoretical point on these indications. They are however interesting suggestions as to the positive reaction of Marx to the element of 'revolutionary anarchism' before the Bakuninist attack rendered the word anathema. This is not to say that Marx even in 1854 regarded total anarchism as a possible way of achieving a successful revolution. Spain indeed is a good example of the point which he would put to Bakunin: whatever one's attitude to authority after the revolution, it is pointless to render the revolution itself impotent by not preparing it to match the organised onslaught which its enemies will not hesitate to launch (see e.g., *ASI*, p. 407). Bakunin himself talks of the need to 'seize' and 'smash' the state (Bakunin, pp. 283–5). It is difficult to imagine how this can be achieved by unorganised spontaneity, still less how the almost inevitable reaction can be crushed without at least the massive *threat* of organised force.

Where Bakunin makes his most telling points is on the issue of whether the 'revolutionary workers' state' will be, as Marx maintains, a purely transitional and self-destructive one. There can be little doubt that Marx was as sincerely an opponent of the state as was Bakunin. He differed from him in believing that the task of defending the revolution against counter-revolution would necessitate a transitional workers' state, and it is difficult not to side with him on that issue. Bakunin however argues with force that this state will in the process become a power *over* the workers, and will simply refuse to step down when the time comes. Marx has in general the merit of trying to theorise, that is to make explicit and defend, his point of view, while Bakunin writes in a brilliant and erratic manner, almost of all of his 'theoretical content' being borrowings from Marx's historical materialism. But Marx's theory is less than overwhelming in its pronouncement that 'once the aim of the proletarian movement, i.e. abolition of classes, is attained, the power of the state, which serves to keep the great majority of producers in bondage to a very small exploiter minority, disappears, and the functions of government become simple administrative functions' (*ASI*, p. 407). The defect in Bakunin is that he does not match Marx by trying to give us a theory of the *conditions* under which the state acquires power over men, and how those conditions can be abolished. This incidentally leaves it theoretically possible that an authoritarian state could emerge at any moment even after *his* spontaneous mass revolution. Given this weakness, we must conclude that while he pierces the Marxian optimism with some most disquieting *aperçus* as to post-revolutionary authority, he himself gives no clear argument as to how to dispense with it, and in any case gives us little reason to believe that his kind of a revolution could succeed in the first place (for further discussion of the abolition of the state, see pp. 229ff. below).

(4) *Reactionary socialism.* We shall later examine in some detail the political failure of the German bourgoisie in the 1850s and 1860s (see pp. 190–96 below). The emergence of Bismarck, achieving the 'bourgeois' aims through an authoritarian state, posed a very great temptation to the German workers: that of allying themselves with the state against the bourgeoisie, in return for social welfare and other such concessions. Marx had encountered the proposal for such an alliance even before the 1848 revolution, when Hermann Wagener launched a well-founded attack on the liberals' hypocrisy, and argued that only the monarchy had the interest of the people at heart. Marx excoriated the whole project, along lines which we have already referred to (*KRB*, pp. 191–203; see also *GI*, p. 629 and p. 61 above). This was his chief bone of contention with Lassalle who, before his death in 1864, had held secret talks with Bismarck along such lines (see Mann, pp. 167–8). When the more 'Marxist' wing of the German workers joined with the Lassalleans in 1875, Marx wrote scathing comments on the resultant programme. He attacked its wilful misinterpretation of the *Manifesto* as declaring everyone non-proletarian to be part of a 'single reactionary mass', whereas it had said that the proletariat alone was a consistently revolutionary class (see *CM*, p. 77 and *CGP*, pp. 348–9). The misinterpretation allowed the Lassalleans to write off the bourgeoisie as themselves simply 'reactionary' and thus with a good conscience to compromise with a state which denied the bourgeois political freedoms. Throughout his career Marx held to the line which we have already encountered, that whatever opposition to the bourgeoisie a socialist may have, he

had nothing to gain from joining the reaction in repressing bourgeois political development.

(5) *Reformist socialism*. It is curious that only four years after taking the authors of the Gotha Programme to task for being duped by anti-bourgeois reaction, Marx was criticising them for their subservience to the bourgeoisie, in his *Circular Letter* with Engels. In fact there is a clear answer to the puzzle: in the first instance, Marx was attacking the German party's lack of revolutionary opposition to the state, and in the second, their lack of revolutionary opposition to the bourgeoisie. Both faults, he believed, stemmed from the same root failure to establish the working class as an independent force capable of taking power from both bourgeois class and reactionary state. We need not document the instances of pusillanimity which Marx and Engels attack in this circular; what is of interest is the way in which it illustrates their general attitudes on a number of crucial questions. All of them are relevant to the danger so eloquently pointed out by Bakunin in *Etatisme et Anarchie* (*Statism and Anarchy*), that the working class would become incorporated by the forces which it was supposed to overthrow.

The general point of their criticism is that the Social Democrats are so afraid of appearing 'unrespectable' in the eyes of the bourgeoisie that they forget that they are meant not to attract but to defeat that class. Marx and Engels ask whether the party is infected by 'the parliamentary disease, and does it really believe that with the popular vote the Holy Ghost is poured out over the elect...?' (*Circular*, p. 366). We have seen in earlier chapters how he had to revise his notion that the 'normal' bourgeois form would be a representative state with universal suffrage, because of the danger which the lower orders posed to the bourgeoisie. But no sooner had he made this revision than he was faced with reactionary regimes which could quite safely use universal suffrage as an embellishment of their rule, and he therefore had to revise his estimate of its inherent revolutionary potential. Later on he was to declare that 'England was the only country where the working class was sufficiently developed and organised to turn universal suffrage to its proper account' (Report of Speech of 16 September 1871, in *FI*, p. 271).

The mention of England raises the related question of revolutionary violence. We have already seen that, in his economic and social theory, Marx holds the economic power of the ruling class to be backed by *force* which, although in abeyance during times of peace, is an ever-present recourse for them. In an interview given in 1871, Marx is reported as saying that the way to political power lay open to the working class in England, and: 'Insurrection would be madness where peaceful agitation would more swiftly and surely do the work' (' *World* Interview', p. 395). In a speech in Amsterdam the next year he added the United States and possibly Holland to the list (*SHC*, p. 324). But he was quick to counter the optimism of his ' *World*' interviewer about England:

The English middle class has always shown itself willing to accept the verdict of the majority so long as it enjoyed the monopoly of the voting power. But mark me, as soon as it finds itself outvoted on what it considers vital questions we shall see here a new slave-owners' war. (*WI*, p. 400)

Marx also criticises the German party for arguing from a tactical necessity of the moment to a general strategic principle as though:

if 500,000–600,000 Social-Democratic voters, one tenth to one eighth of the whole electorate, dispersed, furthermore, far and wide across the whole country, are sensible enough not to run their heads against a wall and to attempt a 'bloody revolution'. one against ten, this proves that they forever exclude the possibility of making use of a tremendous external event, of a sudden revolutionary upsurge which might result from it, indeed of a *victory* gained by the people in a conflict arising from it! (*Circular*, p. 370)

We might say then that Marx's criterion for a properly revolutionary movement (and this is his answer to Bakunin's charge of bourgeoisification) is, not that it should *make a point* of using violence, but that it should constitute the kind of independent threat to both bourgeoisie and state that *raises the question* of violent confrontation. If such a confrontation is *ruled out* of its thinking, a movement could not be revolutionary on Marx's terms. It seems to me that Engels speaks for Marx also when he says that a revolution will be an 'authoritarian' affair *vis-à-vis* the ruling class, imposing its will by means of 'rifles, bayonets and cannon', and that it will have to defend itself afterwards 'by means of the terror which its arms inspire in the reactionaries' (*OA*, p. 103). It is possible that this fear could mean that the arms need not be used in the first place, but impossible that one could win without at least having them available. Given the kind of mass organisation which he envisages for it, Marx can be sanguine that 'it is possible that the struggle between the workers and the capitalists will be less terrible and bloody than was once the struggle between the feudal lords and the capitalists in England and France. Let us hope so' (*RPL*, p. 204). Our scope does not include the subsequent history of German Social Democracy, but we may close this brief review of Marx's position by saying that that movement was constantly tempted to forget the stringent conditions under which alone he would concede that when the workers win victories through the bourgeois state structure they 'do not fortify governmental power...[but] transform that power, now used against them, into their own agency' (*IDGC*, p. 89).

Conclusion

In this chapter we have looked at the role of politics in the economic theory which Marx elaborated in the decades after 1848. We have seen how Marx's earlier distinction of state and civil society is amplified by an account of the depth-process of production, below the 'appearances' of market equality in civil society. Although capitalism was born in force, its structures of power are maintained without force, because of the grip of bourgeois ideology. It is the task of the labour movement to organise so as to contest those structures at increasingly deeper levels. There follows a discussion of the relationship between the bourgeois social structure and the revolutionary movement. Although Marx sees capitalist crisis as inevitable, he does not conclude that the revolution also is inevitable: it requires the activity of a conscious revolutionary movement. This 'repoliticisation' of society will inevitably raise the question of force; the last section gives an outline of the positions taken by Marx on this and related questions of revolutionary strategy.

7. The later political writings

In this chapter I want to look at how Marx's theory of politics fared in the same period as that covered in the previous chapter: the decades of relative political stability which followed the revolutionary storm. There is a danger in the kind of approach which I want to adopt, that the chapter might try to become a 'potted history' of the period, which would be absurd. What I have tried to do is to get a broad idea of the events which confronted Marx, so that we can understand how he tried to make sense of them, and what impact they had on the basic theory. In terms of Marx's biography, the years after 1850 divide into three periods: 1850–64, the 'retreat into the study' and the journalism; 1864–72, the International, and 1872–83, the last years, in which he was less politically active, but took a new interest in ethnography, as we shall see in the next chapter. In terms of sources for what I want to do, there is a significant break in the early 1860s, when Marx virtually gave up his journalism. I have however carried my fairly detailed examination beyond that date, up to about 1870, for reasons both historical and biographical. 1870 marks a turning-point for both France, whose Empire went down to military defeat, and Germany, whose Empire was born of victory, in that year. Shortly before, the 1867 Reform Act had signalled the ability of the British political system to adapt to new circumstances in a way quite contrary to Marx's expectations. In the three countries which mainly interested Marx, then, there is a break about this point. The period 1870–2 was a break for Marx too: 'The revolution had come and the International proved powerless[...] Marx could not face the prospect of a long period of painfully slow development as he had faced it in the thirties' (Collins and Abramsky, pp. 297–8). His powers of intellectual creation were failing too (see *ibid.*, and McLellan 1973, p. 422). I have not ignored events happening, or works written, after 1870, as will emerge. I have however concentrated on the decades 1850–70, as they represent also the high-point of Marx's theoretical, journalistic and political involvement.

A statement of the theory

Despite all the scorn which has been poured on it – the present study included – the unfortunate *Communist Manifesto* is always a good point to start a discussion of Marx's theories. This is true even for the treatment of politics after the setbacks of the revolutionary years. The reason is that in the *Manifesto* there emerges a correlation which in one way or another dominates Marx's thinking: the correlation between capitalist industry and bourgeois politics. Before looking at how his theory fared in the later period, it is useful to examine this correlation more closely.

Marx believed that the countries which he was dealing with – Britain, France and Germany – would all be forced to industrialise. The two latter would be so forced because of the need to compete with Britain, and Britain, having started the process, would suffer if she did not keep the lead in it. This would entail a growing social importance for the bourgeoisie, especially the industrial bourgeoisie. Marx believed that the bourgeoisie would become the politically ruling class as a result. If we take this claim at its face value, it fares disastrously in the period which we are examining, as will emerge. The French bourgeoisie lived under the Empire for two decades, replacing it by a republic only when it was externally defeated. If the British bourgeoisie became dominant in British politics, this was well into the 1870s, and not as Marx expected as a consequence of the 1832 Reform Act. The only argument about the German bourgeoisie is whether they achieved power in 1918 or in 1945. More sense can be made of Marx's claim, and a more useful inquiry can be made on the basis of it, if we divide it into two parts. The first will be about political *personnel*, and will posit that as the bourgeoisie becomes socially dominant it will want to take control of politics for itself. The second will predict that, whatever its personnel, the political system will have to serve the needs of the bourgeoisie, because of the demands of social development; this is a claim about the *function* of the state. This subdivision of Marx's claim has its dangers, as will emerge in our last section, but if properly used it can be most fruitful. We now turn to a brief consideration of the development of Britain, France and Germany in the 1850s and 1860s, and of Marx's response; after this we shall consider some theoretical implications.

Britain

There is little doubt that Britain fulfilled the first of Marx's claims: industry boomed from 1850 to 1873, with a short break in 1866–7 (see Kindleberger, pp. 10–12). But at the end of this period we still find politics dominated by Whig and Tory rather than by the new parties of land, money and labour which Marx expected (see *NYDT* 1 August 1854, in *AOB*, pp. 218–20). We shall look at the situation around 1850, at Marx's predictions and their failure, and at the reasons for his disappointment.

Britain in mid-century

One factor explaining the survival of so many 'feudal' and aristocratic styles in British politics was noted by Marx himself in his review of Guizot's book on the English Revolution in 1850. Marx speaks of

> the permanent alliance between the bourgeoisie and the greater part of the big landlords, an alliance which essentially differentiates the English Revolution from the French – the revolution that abolished big land-ownership by parcellation. Unlike the French feudal landowners of 1789, this class of big landed proprietors, which had allied itself with the bourgeoisie and which, incidentally, had arisen already under Henry VIII, was not antagonistic to but rather in complete accord with the conditions of life of the bourgeoisie. In actual fact their landed estates were not feudal but bourgeois property. On the one hand, the landed proprietors placed at the disposal of the industrial bourgeoisie the people necessary to operate its manufactories and, on the other, were in a position to develop agriculture in accordance with the state of industry and trade. Hence their common interests with the bourgeoisie; hence their alliance with it. (*RG*, in *AOB*, pp. 93–4).

In the sixteenth century, during and perhaps because of the Henrician Reformation and suppression of the monasteries, 'men began to treat land more and more as something that could be bought and sold, used and abused, in a word like modern capitalist private property' (Moore, p. 8). While there is continuing controversy over the class nature of the next century's revolution (see Evans, p. 140, for sources), by the end of the seventeenth century a crucial blow had been struck against the monarchy. 'The key to the English situation is that commercial life in both town and countryside during the sixteenth and seventeenth centuries grew up mainly though not entirely in opposition to the crown' (Moore, p. 7). When the development of industry got going in the eighteenth century, it had to fight neither wing of the Crown/ Junker alliance which, as we have seen, defeated the rising Prussian bourgeoisie in 1848. The landowners did not fear bourgeois society as such (whatever their later conflict with manufacturers) and, if they had, there was no absolute monarchy with which to league against it.

This development raises the question of whom Marx includes in 'the English bourgeoisie'. Sometimes he tends to stress the common economic position of 'capitalists – both landlords and moneylords' (*NYDT* 22 March 1853, in *AOB*, p. 164; see *IA*, p. 80 and *CWF*, p. 76). Then, 'the Tories, in the end, are bourgeois as much as the remainder', distinguished only by their *kind* of bourgeois property (*NYDT* 1 August 1852, in *AOB*, p. 114). But at other times, when a deep opposition between the two becomes important to his argument, he tends to distinguish between 'the bourgeoisie' and 'the aristocracy' (see *NOZ* 6 March 1855, in *AOB*, p. 222). If we keep this ambivalence in mind, Marx's arguments are not vitiated by it. It is important to stress how in Britain the landowners shared certain fundamentally bourgeois characteristics – as much economic as 'cultural' ones – with the urban bourgeoisie, and equally to note that within the bourgeoisie so widely defined there is still a deep cleavage between the interests of landed and other sectors. We may also note that where Marx talks of the 'middle class' in these writings he refers either to the non-landed bourgeoisie or, more specifically, to the manufacturing bourgeoisie.

We may set the scene finally by looking briefly at the two major issues of the preceding decades. The Reform Act of 1832 added another 217,000 to the 435,000 voters of England and Wales. Webb tells us that its provisions and results were 'too complicated' to allow of a simple summary (p. 196); the representation of land was little if at all damaged, while its influence increased (see Woodward, pp. 85, 87).

Nevertheless, it did recognise the right of the new bourgeoisie of manufacturing England to participate in a political structure previously dominated by land. While Woodward describes the controversy over the 1846 repeal of the Corn Laws as 'curiously out of proportion to the results obtained by repeal' (p. 119), it would be hard to exaggerate the measure's *political* importance. It was a successful attempt by the manufacturing bourgeoisie, backed by popular agitation, to subordinate the landed interest to the demand for cheaper food. While on both these major issues the landed interest had to be placated, by the middle of the century Britain had a political system whose landed elite had so far adapted remarkably to an age which they would never have chosen, and this explains their continued domination of politics. We may now look briefly at Marx's expectations for the future, which fall under three broad scenarios which are to an extent chronologically successive, although not completely so.

Marx's Three Scenarios

(A) *Tory reaction.* In an important article early in our period, Marx characterises the two main parties. Although the two come from the same social group – large landed property – they are different in the constituencies which they represent. While the Tories continue to represent the landed interest, the Whigs accept the need to trade concessions to the new bourgeoisie for continued political position. On these terms, the Whigs will help the middle class to gain 'all those concessions, which in the course of social and political development have shown themselves to have become *unavoidable* and *undelayable*' (*NYDT* 21 August 1852, in *AOB*, p. 112). Marx's analysis here is strongly supported by Lord John Russell's stated reasons for accepting Repeal (see Woodward, p. 116). Marx's expectation is that, as industry comes to engulf the economy, the Tories will try to stem the tide; they will try

to maintain a political power, the social foundation of which has ceased to exist. And how can this be attained? By nothing short of a *Counter-revolution*, that is to say, by a reaction of State against Society. They strive to retain forcibly institutions and a political power which were condemned from the very moment at which the rural population found itself outnumbered three times by the population of the towns. (*AOB*, pp. 110–11).

This reaction would confront the middle class, banded under the Free Traders, 'the official representatives of modern English society' (*NYDT* 25 August 1852, in *AOB*, p. 116), who would

reject royalty, Lords and standing army as '*faux frais* of production' (p. 117). Not only did the middle class not do that, but,
if they had, the Tories would have needed considerable prodding
to emulate the Junkers with whom Marx is clearly comparing
them. Some years later, he more cautiously qualifies the comparison by adding that 'broad lines of distinction must be drawn
between the English squire and the North German Junker' (*NOZ*
18 May 1855, in *SE*, p. 286). Many important concessions had been
made to free trade even in the *original* Corn Laws earlier in the
century (see Webb, p. 185), and Peel's budgetary policy of the
1840s meant that the prevailing climate was free-trade, so that
the landowners could not throw the charge of hypocrisy at the
manufacturers (see Woodward, p. 113). Above all, agriculture was
not seriously affected by Repeal, remaining prosperous until the
impact of US corn over twenty years later (see Woodward, p. 119).
One significant fact is that the Tories continued, with few
exceptions, to confine their resistance to legislation to the Commons, rather than to retreat to the Lords and provoke a constitutional conflict between Commons on one hand, and Lords and
Crown on the other (see Webb, p. 211).

(B) *Fall of the oligarchy*. The reference to the '*faux frais* of
production' sets the keynote of the second scenario. Whereas in
the first scenario the 'amphibious' Whigs (*AOB*, p. 111) would be
crushed in the struggle between Tories and middle class, in the
second one they share with the Tories in the general irrelevance
of the 'oligarchy' which they jointly compose. This oligarchy is
the 'governing caste' ('*regierende Kaste*') which the 'ruling class'
('*herrschende Klasse*'), that is the new bourgeoisie, have so far
tolerated (*SE*, p. 279, from *MEW* xi, p. 44; see also *MEW* xi,
p. 201). Marx depicts the confusion of the oligarchy, which will
be 'driven from one coalition to the next until it has given
conclusive proof that it is no longer destined to govern' (*ibid*.).
He believes that their downfall is sealed by the debacle of the
Crimean War, where the pointless luxury of aristocratic government was revealed as a positive liability. His account of the
political crisis is accurate. What happened the ordinary soldier
may have been no worse than in the wars of past times, but now
the telegraph meant that public opinion itself went to the front line,
and the revelations of *The Times* about the army's misfortunes

were shattering (see Webb, p. 304 and Woodward, pp. 254–5). Marx is equally accurate about the profound fragmentation of the party-system, where once-great parties now seemed to exist 'only in the form of coteries', unable either to coalesce or to distinguish themselves from one another (see *NOZ* 8 February 1855, in *SE*, p. 280). This confusion (see Woodward, pp. 154–5) can be understood as the result of the traumatic decisions of the past decades, symbolised in the 'Peelites' seeking a new conservatism for whose reforms even the Whigs were unprepared. Webb points out that the effects of the Reform Act produced a hiatus between the old smooth corruption and the future tight party discipline (p. 192). But Marx's second scenario equally proved false. There was no major change in political personnel until about 1875, that is, well after the *second* Reform Act (see Webb, p. 209). The undoubted incompetence revealed in the Crimea was the glaring exception to what was otherwise a period of considerable administrative improvement, and towards the end of the war some response even to the Crimea tragedy was possible. Perhaps most significant was the fact that economic prosperity was not endangered (see Kindleberger, p. 10), so that the middle class had less reason than Marx thought for seeking new representatives.

(C) *A Palmerstonian dictatorship*. If the oligarchy endured, so did the instability. The prolonged impossibility of forming a strong government prompted Marx, when Palmerston dissolved parliament and went to the country, to point to 'the similarity of the appeal made to France by Bonaparte in 1851 and the appeal to the United Kingdom made by Palmerston in 1857' (*NYDT* 6 April 1857, in *AOB*, p. 268). In both cases there was a single man putting *himself* forward over the heads of a refractory and privileged parliament; Sidney Herbert said at the time that however one might dislike him, Palmerston was 'the only public man in England who has a name' (Quoted in Woodward, p. 161). But the parallel is absurd on almost every other count. Whatever ambitions we attribute to Palmerston (ignoring for the moment the fact that he had risen *through* the parliamentary tradition), the context was just wrong. In France, parliament had proved dangerous to the bourgeoisie because it articulated their enemies' demands: not so in England. France had universal sufrage which enfranchised a large peasantry who hated above all *les riches*: not so in England. However popular he might be with some, the only successful usurper of parliament in English history was a distant figure: quite the opposite with Bonaparte's 'cult of the Uncle'. But beyond all these differences, there is a central feature which Marx gets wrong in the first and third of his scenarios, and is a vital explanation of their failure. When Marx speaks of the Tories' leading 'a reaction of the State against Society' one is inclined to ask 'what State?'. There had been the beginnings of a bureaucracy under Henry VII (see Bindoff, p. 56), but the growth of administration did not outstrip that of parliamentarism. The Crimea indeed showed the results of a fiscal orthodoxy which had starved the armed forces, and it was not only the Manchester radicals who regarded a large standing army as 'un-English'. This means that there simply were not the state forces there for either the Tories or Palmerston to use against civil society, had they wanted to in the first place (see Nairn, p. 7).

The Course of British Development. Throughout this period, Marx continued to proclaim his faith in a resurgence of the working class. In 1850 he had concluded that 'a new revolution is only possible as a result of a new crisis; but it will come, just as surely as the crisis itself' (*CSF*, p. 131). Although he had a profound grasp of the tensions and contradictions of capitalism, as we noted in the previous chapter, he spent a lot of time in his journalism proclaiming an 'approaching economic crisis' which almost always eluded him. The predicted crisis did appear in 1857, and again in the mid-1860s, but neither outbreak heralded the revolution or anything much like it. In the early 1850s, he set great store by the revival of Chartism, which he thought would be the new revolutionary workers' party, under his friend Ernest Jones. Only gradually was it borne in on him that Chartism was 'the end of an old world, not the beginning of a new' (Webb, p. 248). Marx believed in the importance of the British working class to any serious revolution in the capitalist world, and always insisted, as in his letter to Kugelmann of 23 February 1865, that his efforts were best placed in England (see *MESC*, p. 160). But in another letter which made the same point, Marx also had to admit the English workers' lack of 'the sense of generalisation and revolutionary passion' (Letter of General Council, January 1870, in *FI*, p. 116). The International failed even to win the affiliation of the crucial unions in the new expanding sectors. Not only were wages high, but the very factors which made them 'the most organised in the world' also made them 'comparatively unresponsive to the appeal of the International' (Collins and Abramsky, p. 89). As early as 1852 Marx had himself noted that the English workers were not 'a very malleable material for political agitation', and put this down to 'the political flaccidity and indifference consequent upon a period of material prosperity' (*NYDT* 2 November and 25 November 1852, in *AOB*, pp. 134 and 141 respectively).

Nor did the manufacturing middle class live up to Marx's hopes either. What we have just seen about the workers weakens Marx's explanation of this middle-class quietism in terms of that class's 'instinctive perception' of the fact that, after their struggle with the aristocracy, a struggle with the workers would ensue (*NYDT* 1 August 1854, in *AOB*, p. 219). In fact, the same thing explains the quietism of both classes: as Nairn puts it, 'the exhausted quiescence of the class struggle coincided with the maximum florescence of British society in the world outside' (p. 5). Marx himself indeed noted the 'fanaticism with which the *middle class* has thrown itself into the mighty process of industrial production', which explained how, while the Tories plotted their reaction, 'the Bourgeoisie...has no time to agitate, to revolt, not even to put up a proper show of indignation' (*NYDT* 2 November 1852, in *AOB*, pp. 134, 137).

If the middle classes did not become politically radical, this is largely because they did not need to, as the oligarchy saw the wisdom of adaptation. These are indeed the two sides of a single coin, which was forged before the Industrial Revolution got under way. 'It was possible because the economic position of the governing classes eroded slowly and in a way that allowed them to shift from one economic base to another with only a minimum of difficulty' (Moore, p. 39). If the oligarchy had dug in their heels, we may presume that the middle class would have become politically more radical. In the absence of reactionary artisans and a large-scale peasantry, they would probably have come much nearer than did the German bourgeoisie to Marx's ideal of the successful revolutionary class (see pp. 44ff. above). Prosperity and the adaptability of the oligarchy rendered this picture merely hypothetical, however. On the question of working-class radicalism, we must grant Marx the point that, even if the English workers were not revolutionary, the middle-class had before them the example of 1830 and 1848 on the Continent, and also the English agrarian unrest and Chartism of the thirties and forties. While the 'rising enemy' was rising both less quickly and less menacingly than Marx envisaged, it is likely that the quietism of the middle class had in it something of that preference for compromise with the 'vanishing opponent' (*AOB*, p. 118) which Marx alleges.

Out of this complex of forces emerged the Reform Act of 1867. In the years preceding the measure, it was by no means clear that the workers would acquiesce in too gradual an enlargement of the established polity. They felt a resentment at the smallness of their gains from the 1832 Reform Act (see Webb, pp. 236–7), and there was a resurgence of labour organisation after about 1860. The middle-class Reform Union was paralleled by a working-class-dominated Reform League which demanded universal manhood suffrage. This agitation coincided with an economic crisis: 'As in the thirties, economic distress and unemployment fed the fires of reform' (Webb, p. 324). The workers were by no means revolutionary, but there were enough signs of trouble for some politicians to sense that a wider version of the 1832 Reform was needed, this time accommodating workers' suffrage. Paradoxically, Disraeli introduced in 1867 a measure far more radical than the Bill which had unseated the Whigs. We might put this down to some extent to the flamboyance of his own personality, although it is significant that ever since Repeal Disraeli had worked to adapt conservatism to the modern world; moreover, Gladstone manoeuvred him into a position where he had either to advance, or to withdraw most of his proposals (see Woodward, p. 180). That he did advance was a triumph of the strategy of creative adaptation to the new circumstances which as we have seen Marx himself emphasised in his earliest writings on England, and which ironically undermined Marx's own expectations for the future. On one point Marx was acute: that it was usually under the Tories rather than under the Whigs that serious reforms would be made, since only when the Whigs were thrown out did the question of reform develop into a crisis of the regime (see *NOZ* 18 May 1855, in *SE*, p. 285).

Finally, we may consider why Marx got things so wrong about British political development. Fernbach traces the errors to his application to England of a political model worked out on the basis of continental experience...Marx had already had to recognise, with respect to Germany, that the general schema of the Manifesto could be distorted by relative backwardness, he did not yet understand that it could be equally distorted, in a different direction, by England's relative precocity. (Fernbach, Introduction to *SE*, p. 22)

Nairn, on whose analysis Fernbach bases his argument, tells us that Marx's interest lay in the economic rationality of England, to the exclusion of the 'conservative sheath' surrounding it, and that this was 'understandable in an intelligence which sought above all for laws of revolutionary motion' (p. 7n). It is explicable, but hardly justifiable in an intelligence professing to rise above all kinds of illusion and to grasp the movement of reality. What we see in Marx's analysis of Britain is a lingering attachment to the idealised picture of the *Manifesto*, a determination that if its components have fallen out in the continental revolutions they will surely stick together in Britain. What he did was not precisely to misread political data, but rather to misread their significance because of a belief that their *socio-economic context* was similar to the continental one. Some of his prognostications overlooked the absence of certain social groups such as reactionary artisans and peasants, and others overlooked the broad common interest between land and capital which he himself had perceived. Moreover, he underestimated the ability of mid-Victorian capitalism to 'ensure an existence to its slave within his slavery', and even to forge him some gilded chains in the process.

France

The period of the Second Empire was one of great economic growth in France: the national wealth probably doubled, savings increased greatly, and larger-scale enterprises increased. Although commentators differ as to detail, there is a consensus that the period was one of significant progress (see Kindleberger, pp. 5–7, Palmade, p. 172, Cobban 1965, Vol. 2, p. 165, and Edwards, pp. 3–6). The crucial development was the emergence of industry as such to a leading position, as reflected in the status of industrialists, who 'assumed a social importance and a place of merit as supreme representatives of the capitalist world. Previously, the bankers had been the only ones to aspire to such heights'

(Palmade, p. 152). We shall look first at the function which the regime fulfilled in relation to this expansion, and then at its political nature, with special reference to its controlling personnel.

The economic function of the Second Empire

The sheer diversity of personalities and aims involved in 'Bonapartism' is best conveyed by Bonaparte's cheerful remark that the Empress was Legitimist, his cousin was a republican, Morny was an Orleanist, he himself was a socialist, and Persigny, the only Bonapartist as such, was mad (see Zeldin, p. 46). We have already seen that Bonaparte took power under various conflicting pretexts (see pp. 108ff. above). In the following sub-section we shall see how it proved impossible for him to retain power by simple repression, by an alliance with workers and peasants, or by playing off each class against the others. For the moment, we shall accept that he thus could not keep the desired distance from the bourgeoisie, and see the consequences of this in his economic policy.

Bonaparte tried to make *virtù* out of this necessity: if the bourgeoisie could not be led where Bonaparte wanted, they must be *led* where they wanted to go anyway. He had a quite genuine ambition to be the initiator and patron of a new harmony and prosperity. This ambition was shared and encouraged by a number of Saint-Simonians who gathered around him (see Cobban 1965 Vol. 2, pp. 164–5), but there was also a more mundane rationale to it. If the Empire did not succeed in being – or appearing – indispensable to prosperity, then the bourgeoisie might start muttering about '*faux frais de production*' and try to take power for themselves. We shall take three chief features of Bonaparte's economic policy, and see to what extent he can be seen as the *initiator*, and to what extent the mere *servant*, of economic developments.

The first of these is the financial policy typified by the *Crédit Mobilier*, founded by Bonaparte's protégés, the Péreire brothers (see Palmade, pp. 130–1). It was conceived by them during an early confrontation with those established bankers and businessmen who were uneasy at the government's desire to let the economic boom continue unabated. It would free the government from the control of the *Bourse*, by drawing vast sums from the unused small savings of ordinary people. These it would invest in a wide range of industries, on the pattern of what we would call a 'unit trust', and it would be able to offset losses in any one branch against huge profits elsewhere. Marx ridicules the 'inverted pyramids of credit' which will be the monument of Bonaparte's reign (*NOZ* 8 October 1855, in *MEW* XI, p. 559), and gives a detailed account of the weakness of the scheme. It is bound to run into liquidity crises, as it belies its name by *immobilising* funds; it needs to maintain a dangerously vast disproportion between its assets and its commitments; its profits have to be 'exceptional' in *every* year (see *NYDT* 11 July 1856, in *MEW* XII, p. 33; *NYDT* 26 September 1857, in *MEW* XII, p. 290 and *NYDT* 30 May 1857 in *MEW* XII, p. 203). His comments tend to underestimate the significance of Bonaparte's credit policy (see Rubel, p. 63). Palmade tells us that the change of regime in 1851 was one of the rare occasions when 'a major political turning-point and a change of economic structure coincided' (p. 116), and there is evidence that the former contributed to the latter. We have noted on a number of occasions the conservatism, financial and otherwise, of the French economy. In the early years of the regime there was a change, in that finance started to become available to industrial development, and there is little doubt that the regime helped in this change. Marx does grant Bonaparte the achievement of having extended the scale of credit, while denying that he invented the principle behind it (see *NYDT* 11 July 1856, in *MEW* XII, pp. 33–4), but that is as far as he will go. He is not prepared to recognise the novelty of this kind of government policy, which we can recognise as precursor of many of the contrivances of the 'mixed economy'. But reference to modern state policy is sobering as regards the *effectiveness* of such contrivances, and here Marx has a good theoretical backing to his attitude. His comments in the journalism are extended in the long opening section of the *Grundrisse*, written during the economic crisis of 1857–8 (see *G*, pp. 116–74). There he expounds his argument that credit can run the economy smoothly only if we remove all the presuppositions which make the economy a capitalist one in the first place: it cannot control the crises inherent in such a contradictory system of production.

The Péreires met their severest difficulties during the crises of 1857 and 1866, and fell after the second; Marx is justified as to the inability of such an enterprise to insulate itself from depressions. The manner of their fall shows quite clearly the limits to the economic initiative of the regime; they were defeated by a group of bankers led by Rothschild, who prevailed on the Emperor to disown them in 1867 (see Palmade, pp. 143–9). It would be quite wrong to see this as a victory for unregenerate July–Monarchy financial conservatives. Palmade makes the point that we should not concentrate on the *Crédit Mobilier* to the extent of missing the fact that the *established* banks radically changed policy in the 1850s, and themselves began to lend to industry: 'They refused neither the tainted associations nor the seductions of share capital ' (p. 127). It is crucial that the Rothschilds were supported in defeating the Péreires by many leading *industrial* capitalists, including the archetypical Second-Empire industrialist, Eugène Schneider. The credit institutions of the Second Empire were a vital spur to the development of industry, but when they threatened to subordinate industry and ' sound finance ' to credit mania, influential bourgeois figures succeeded in undermining the Emperor's support for them. While Marx is ungenerous as to the originality of these ventures, his theoretical and journalistic scepticism is justified.

The second major feature of the regime's economic policy is the Free Trade Treaty signed with Britain in 1860. We have already noted the strong protectionism of the French economy (see p. 78 above). This leads Kindleberger to say that the treaty was imposed by Bonaparte and the economist Chevalier 'against the will of the *corps législatif*' (Kindleberger, p. 201). Cobban also says that the *corps*, 'weak as it was, would not abandon protective duties quietly', and speaks of the 'panic and fury' with which industrialists reacted (Cobban 1965, Vol. 2, p. 178). But Palmade, while noting the extent to which Bonaparte was encouraged into the measure by bureaucrats and Saint-Simonians, also points out that 'a section of the economic elite believed that France could compete with the most advanced economic power of the time' (p. 172). He lists merchants, shippers, bourgeoisie of the ports, producers of wine, cotton, silk and luxuries as supporters (p. 173). Thus it would appear that the treaty was not something which Bonaparte imposed on the *whole* bourgeoisie – there were significant sectors who wanted it – but there is no doubt that the regime took the initiative in this case.

Finally, we must note the disappointment of Bonaparte's

dreams of a really powerful state, commanding its own resources, actively restructuring both economy and society (see Palmade, p. 226). Cobban, after discussing the public works which were developed in the 1850s, warns us not to overestimate the share of the state in financing them (Cobban 1965 Vol. 2, p. 166), and Kindleberger tells us that 'governmental spending was limited during the Second Empire' (p. 186). Whatever initiative he took on policy, Bonaparte could directly execute very little of it, and this holds equally for his ambitious social welfare plans: particularly after the proceeds of the confiscation of Orleanist estates had been spent, Bonaparte was desperately in need of revenue, and his difficulty in raising it explains the 1860 liberalisation which we shall discuss in the next sub-section. He had to turn to the *corps législatif*, whose 'highly conservative majority . . . had little taste for the Emperor's reforms' (Boon, pp. 68–9); Edwards notes how his project of controlling rents 'was rejected as a fallacious socialist experiment' (p. 8).

We may thus conclude that Bonaparte had some initial success, but did not get very far, in his ambition of *directing* economic affairs. His credit projects coincided with a need of the economy, and contributed to its development; when they seriously endangered bourgeois security, the bourgeoisie brought him to heel. He did exercise an initiative on free trade, but at least a section of the bourgeoisie also supported it, as is shown by its survival during the first ten years of the Third Republic (see Woodward, p. 172n). Most crucially, the state never succeeded in getting a large part of the economy into its own hands, or in commanding a large sum of resources whose disposal it could decide. This is to a great extent due to Bonaparte's inability to operate a political strategy offsetting his dependence on the bourgeoisie, which we shall examine in the next sub-section.

The 'Bourgeois Empire': political strategy and personnel

As we have seen already, Marx stresses the fact that Bonaparte came to power with several declared aims, which were difficult to reconcile (see pp. 108ff. above, and *NYDT* 24 June 1856, in *MEW* XII, p. 26). He promised to save the different classes from one another, *and* to fulfil their several interests; he also promised a new order, which would rise above the squabbling of politics. There is a range of different strategies which he could have employed to fulfil some of these aims and yet retain his independence: he tried each of them to some extent, and each of them failed. At several points we shall see that the failure to achieve independence in economic policy entailed a failure to do so in political strategy, and vice versa.

One strategy was that of diverting people from their original concerns, by getting them to conceive of themselves under a new image. Although Bonaparte tried to achieve this, it was impossibly difficult, as his regime had been borne in and of a period of sharp social conflict, and people did not sink their differences just because they had allowed him to take power. Zeldin notes that the endorsement of the regime in the plebiscite of 1852 was much firmer than the support given to Bonapartist candidates in the election of that year (see Zeldin, p. 41), and Edwards notes a similar electoral schizophrenia between the plebiscite of 1870 and the election of 1869 (see Edwards, p. 35). At its beginning and its end, people supported the Empire as the alternative to chaos, but did not develop a 'loyalty' to it as such. Bonaparte's failure to achieve direction of the economy meant that he could not evoke a new 'corporate consciousness' by such means; the other method was success in foreign policy. In the Crimean War, as well as courting the Catholic vote by opposing Russia's protectorate of the Holy Places, Bonaparte was trying to achieve such a success (see Rubel, pp. 32–3). But the fall of Sebastopol was the sole and long-delayed relief in an undistinguished campaign, and by 1856 Marx noted that for the first time the French people seemed to have become indifferent to '*la gloire*' (see *NYDT* 25 February 1856, in *MEW* xi, p. 593). When Bonaparte attacked Austria allegedly in the name of Italian independence, Marx gave a convincing list of the factors making him less than resolute in the campaign, including the protests of 'high finance, industry, and trade' (Marx to Lassalle, 4 February 1859, in *MESC*, p. 108). Bonaparte did indeed call a halt with the Peace of Villafranca long before achieving his stated aim of freeing Italy. After this, as Cobban puts it, 'the French nation had fought in ten years two more wars than it wanted' (Cobban 1965 Vol. 2, p. 179), and the debacle of intervention in Mexico in the 1860s brought no fresh success (see *ibid.*, pp. 182–4).

If that strategy would not work, there was the closely related one of posing as 'patriarch' of the society by fulfilling *everybody's* interests. Marx accurately enough jibes that this was impossible, since it meant that he had to be the plunderer of each class if he were to be the patriarch of all, and would have to steal France in order then to buy her! (*NYDT* 24 June 1856, in *MEW* XII, p. 26). We have already seen how the bourgeoisie vetoed Bonaparte's plans for large social-welfare expenditure on the workers. Marx points out that as roughly two-thirds of France were peasants, Bonaparte's ambition of giving them cheap credit would mean an enormous tax burden on the remaining one-third (*NYDT* 7 February 1860, in *MEW* XV, p. 5). Marx seems to be wrong when on a number of occasions he insists that agriculture was doing badly under the Second Empire (see *ibid.*, p. 6, and *NYDT* 22 November 1856, in *MEW* XII, p. 77). It appears that agriculture as a sector of the economy shared in the economic prosperity of the period (see Kindleberger, pp. 212 ff., and Walter, p. 418). Marx however is justified in insisting that the lot of the mass of poor peasants did not improve; Walter tells us that 'the rich peasants became richer, the poor peasants poorer' (*ibid.*). Moreover, he is right in his claim that Bonaparte could not raise the funds to do much to help alleviate this misery. As Marx had correctly predicted, he did not succeed in becoming the 'patriarchal benefactor of all classes' (*EBLB*, p. 247; see p. 112 above).

Another strategy, if he could not satisfy all classes, was to *repress* all classes. There was repression at the inception of the Empire, the victims of which were mainly workers and peasants rather than bourgeois. When discontent mounted during the crisis of 1857–8, and after Orsini's assassination attempt, Bonaparte introduced an increased military note into his strategy by dividing France into five regions, each with a military commander, and by replacing a number of civilian prefects by military ones. Marx dubs this the 'rule of the Praetorians', and says that it signifies that Bonaparte will henceforth depend not on the French people but on his 600,000 bayonets. He goes so far as to say that whereas all previous regimes ruled through the army, this move represents the army coming to rule in its own right: a reaction of state against society (*NYDT* 12 March 1858, in *MEW* XII, pp. 399–400). This is in fact an exaggerated argument, in view of the fact that Bonaparte was well aware of the limits on his ability to flout the wishes of his subjects; Marx indeed makes just that point himself (*NYDT* 13 February 1859, in *MEW* XIII, p. 174). Having entered

that *caveat*, Marx is justified in saying that the posture of opposition to all classes is an element of Bonaparte's 'system' (*MEW*
XII, p. 402). It did not serve however as the basis of his rule.

Bonaparte was reduced to a strategy less ambitious than the
preceding ones, of tacitly allying himself to one class while in one
way or another keeping his distance from it. The peasants were
not a promising candidate for this role of 'most favoured class',
since any serious redistribution of income in their direction would
provoke the united opposition of workers and bourgeoisie. As the
working class began to recover some of its energies in the 1860s,
Bonaparte was tempted to try to channel their opposition to the
bourgeoisie into such a strategy, even financing the French labour
delegation to England which was, ironically, one of the initiators
of the International (see McLellan 1973, p. 361). Most of the
workers had an implacable opposition to anything tainted by
association with the Emperor, and Bonaparte had as we have seen
insufficient funds to try to bribe them: 'It is fair to conclude that
Napoleon III's attempts to reconcile the working class ended in
complete failure' (Boon, p. 76). A third bout of repression began
in the later 1860s, directed specifically against the working class.
This fitted in with the fact that it was with the bourgeoisie that
Bonaparte had to try to operate his 'most favoured class' strategy.
We have already noted the pressures operating in this direction
in the area of economic and welfare policy. Bonaparte tried to use
the bourgeoisie's fear of the workers to offset his dependence on
them, but the bourgeoisie were regaining confidence in their own
ability to run things (see Rubel, pp. 64–5). The economic crisis
of 1857–8 was traumatic for the regime, and after it 'the co-
operation of the legislature became more than ever necessary'
(Zeldin, p. 103).

In return for this co-operation Bonaparte had to make some
concessions, and in 1860 he promised a greater role for the
deputies in discussing legislation. Marx dismissed this as a mere
pretence, saying that any real constitutional control of finance
would destroy the Empire (see *Die Presse*, 19 November 1861, in
MEW XV, p. 379). Certainly it was not a major step, but it is
indicative of Bonaparte's growing dependence on the bourgeoisie.
A major factor in this dependence was his failure to evolve a
political party, or a group of politically dominant personnel, of
his own. He had to disown such 'Bonapartist party' as there even

was in 1852, and attempt a reverse takeover by picking influential non-Bonapartists and running them as 'Official Candidates' with full government backing. In the assembly which resulted he could count only one third as real followers, the rest, apart from the few opposition members, being 'very independent allies' (Zeldin, p. 33). Significantly, the characteristic of representatives under the Empire was the 'relatively large number of them engaged in trade, industry and commerce' (Zeldin, p. 56): Bonaparte had to give an increasing voice to these people. Their rise was symbolised in the fact that Eugène Schneider, the 'iron king', became President of the *corps législatif*. Bonaparte never succeeded in forging his own body of political personnel, and at successive elections his fortunes worsened. Zeldin quite correctly stresses that even the 1852 election was no sham, as with abstentions the government won only 53% of the total electorate (see Zeldin, pp. 39–45). 1857 was no better, and this time the opposition was republican rather than Legitimist, a disturbing sign (p. 66). The 1863 elections were a massive numerical 'win' for the government, but the opposition vote doubled, and the republicans won 8 out of the 9 Paris seats (p. 116). Again the government 'won' handsomely in 1869, but with an internally decomposing vote and against increased opposition (pp. 140–2). There were even 30 'red' republicans, who broke with those inclined to co-operate with the government. Bonaparte had little choice but to opt for a 'liberal empire' under Emile Ollivier as virtual Prime Minister in 1869. The complexities of a government with dual responsibility – to the Emperor and to the legislature – had not been ironed out when Bismarck rendered them irrelevant. Whether the bourgeoisie could have made a reality of the 'liberal empire', turning Bonaparte into a presidential figurehead, or even could have replaced the regime by a republic on their own initiative, is difficult to tell, since it was military defeat which destroyed the Empire. But Marx is quite justified in his picture of Bonaparte's dire straits even before war began (see Marx to Engels, 10 and 18 May 1870, in *MEW* XXXII, pp. 504–5 and 516; see also Rubel, chapters 9 and 12). In those straits he was increasingly compelled to make real political concessions to the bourgeoisie.

Germany

A chief problem of the 1850s and 1860s was to give a meaning to the word 'Germany', which the revolution had failed to do. The period abounds in divisions and conflicts, only some of which Marx had the time or energy to chart in his journalism. Here I shall focus largely on the development of Prussia, since it was her development which was to prove decisive for the new Germany, and to stamp it with its peculiar character. As with Britain and France, there is little doubt that Marx's claim about industrial growth was fulfilled in Germany in this period (see Schweinitz, p. 166, Mann, p. 199 and Hamerow, p. 122). He is justified when, at the end of the 1850s, he reflects that the decade has brought unparallelled economic growth, and decidedly transformed Germany from an agricultural into an industrial country (*NYDT* 10 June 1859, in *MEW* XIII, p. 354). This meant a decline in the proportion of peasants and artisans (see Holborn, p. 122 and Hamerow, pp. 227, 241–3). While the wave of emigration to the US showed the limits of industry's absorptive capacity, it also increased the relative importance of industry in the remaining population.

As regards the political consequences of this development, the results in Prussia are superficially like those in Britain: no radical change in political personnel, but successful adaptation to new functions. But, as well as the socio-economic context, even the political process is different, since there was an attempt at an anti-industrial reaction, and adaptation followed only on its failure. We shall look briefly at Marx's reactions to the three phases of Prussian history in our period.

(A) *1850–8: Manteuffel and Reaction*

As we have seen in chapter 3, the year of revolutions made Frederick William IV aware as never before of the threat which the new society posed to him; he turned to non-bourgeois groups to support his regime. It is probable that the Junkers became more influential than they had been before 1848, but it is difficult to measure their power against that of the bureaucracy. Marx at one point suggests that the two are equal (*NYDT* 27 October 1858, in *MEW* XII, p. 606), and at another that the landowners' power is greater (*NYDT* 5 May 1856, in *MEW* XI, p. 638). More generally however, he stresses that the regime is dominated by the bureaucracy (see *MEW* XII, pp. 616, 619 and 685). This is in line with Mann's emphasis on the narrow, regional outlook of the Junkers (p. 128), as with that of Holborn, who concludes that 'Prussia did not lose her character as a bureaucratic absolute state' (p. 108).

With regard to the defeated bourgeoisie, the regime was confidently repressive. Allowing the liberals the show of a say in the lower house, it transformed the upper house into a *Herrenhaus* or House of Lords. The regime's policy was to thwart the development of industry and economic freedom. With government backing, 4,000 guilds were either restored or created anew in Prussia alone (see Hamerow, p. 229). One area, however, where neither government nor Junkers tried to turn the tide was agriculture: the reaction itself concluded the destruction of manorialism. This was not unwise, since the development of latifundia went ahead in the East, and in the West the commutation to money burdens made the peasant as dependent as before, often more so. Marx accurately notes that the peasants' disappointment with emancipation rendered impossible a repeat of their brief alliance with the liberals (*NYDT* 5 May 1856, in *MEW* XI, p. 640). It would be a mistake, as Holborn warns us, to write off this reaction as an 'unpleasant but brief interlude' between revolution and unification (p. 114; see also Hamerow, pp. 213–14). But by the late 1850s, two facts emerged: one, that industrial progress could not in fact be halted by the guild restoration, and two, that more rather than less of it was needed anyway to fulfil Prussia's ambitions as a state. Any success which Prussia had had in foreign policy in the 1850s – in the thwarting and downgrading of Austria – had rested on her economic influence over the other small German statelets, a truth which however much the latter resented it 'emerged with great force in every political crisis' (Mann, p. 133).

(B) *1858–62: the 'New Era'*

When Frederick William IV's mental illness became too obvious to hide, his brother William took over as Regent, against the prolonged and bitter opposition of the Queen and her Camarilla. Marx wrongly predicted that William would be loath to sack Manteuffel, the 'architect of the counter-revolution' (*NYDT* 27 October 1858, in *MEW* XII, p. 610), but he was justified in his estimate of the superficial nature of the 'New Era'. William had indeed grown disgusted with various corrupt practices over the past decade, but was fundamentally a 'man of honour' and an absolutist, rather than a convinced democrat (see Mann, p. 143 and Holborn, p. 111). Marx shrewdly puts his apparent liberalism down to the necessities of tactical struggle with the Queen and Camarilla: it was in his interest to invoke the constitution, to prove the *necessity* of a regency (*NYDT* 27 October 1858, in *MEW* xii, pp. 605–6). None of this is to deny, however, that, as Marx himself makes clear in his journalism at the time, many deep questions surfaced during the 'New Era', such as the impossibility of the guild restoration, which we have already noted. The other main area where serious questions emerged was that of foreign policy. Marx tended to be overly dismissive of Prussia's record in this area in the 1850s. She had displayed irresolution and lack of purpose since her diplomatic defeat by Austria on the unification issue (see Hamerow, pp. 199–203). Marx however goes too far when he compares Prussia in 1860, after the Franco–Austrian War of 1859, with Austria in the aftermath of the Crimea, on the grounds that each country imagined itself to have gained when in fact defeat loomed around the corner (see *NYDT* 19 May 1860, in *MEW* xv, pp. 46 ff.). Due as much to vacillation as to wisdom, Prussia got more from the Crimean war than did the victors, earning Russia's preference over Austria at a crucial stage (see Mann, p. 130). When war broke out between France and Austria, Marx acutely portrayed the German's dilemma (*NYDT* 13 March 1859, in *MEW* xiii, pp. 280–3), but argued strongly, against Lassalle, that Prussia had a duty to act in Germany's name and defend Austria. He denied that Prussia could gain from the defeat of Austria (*NYDT* 27 May 1859, in *MEW* xiii, pp. 323–7) and was clearly wrong in that. Overall, he exaggerated the ill-effects of Prussia's undoubted moral weakness. He overlooked how her very vices insulated her from the sufferings of more courageous nations, leaving her well situated to exploit their difficulties.

Here, then, we find Prussia, in both economic and political spheres, at the end of the decade having benefitted more by luck than by judgement, and requiring a distinct change of course to capitalise on the advantages so undeservedly acquired. As the two tasks indicated were industrial development and German unification, we might think that the 'normal' deduction would be that the bourgeoisie would come to the helm; in Germany, all that was needed or possible was a change of course. The bourgeoisie had become predominant in strictly municipal government (*NYDT* 3 December 1858, in *MEW* XII, p. 642); at higher levels they quite failed to use the opportunist openings made by William in the fabric of reaction. Marx graphically portrays their political bank-ruptcy by showing how they depended not on their own will or strength, but on the natural event of the King's madness (*NYDT* 28 April 1860, in *MEW* XV, pp. 39–42).

(C) *1862 onwards: Bismarck*

The New Era came to a clear halt with William's plans for reorganisation of the army (see pp. 133ff. above). Marx com-ments on the importance of the Prussian army as a state force, and says that the Prussian ruler's title of '*Kriegsherr*' means much less 'warlord' than 'possessor of the army', that is, ruler of the country because ruler of the army (*NYDT* 8 November 1860, in *MEW* XV, pp. 191–4). There were various pressures for a reor-ganisation. One was the example of Austria's defeat in 1859, and the galling isolation of Prussia in the diplomatic aftermath. In addition was the fact that a great part of Prussia's army was in the *Landwehr*, a citizen reserve which was dominated by the bourgeoisie (see Mann, p. 151). If the army were to be a pillar of the state, this must be cured. The proposed reforms virtually abolished the *Landwehr*, as Marx commented (*NYDT* 19 May 1860, in *MEW* XV, pp. 48–9). The lower house defeated the proposals, but granted interim funds for running the army; the government used these to implement the reforms, thus implicitly abolishing parliamentary authority. Everything seemed set for a classic confrontation of legislature and executive, but nothing happened: the bourgeoisie were afraid to fight when Bismarck was made Prime Minister in 1862 and set up anti-parliamentary policy as a going concern. Marx gives cogent reasons for not expecting a serious fight. The men of 1848 were unlikely to become heroes now, with an unreconciled class enemy above them, the peasants decimated and depressed, and the artisans alienated from indus-trial freedom in every form. William might safely play at Charles I, without even having to sacrifice a Strafford (*NYDT* 8 November 1860, in *MEW* XV, p. 193; see also *NYDT*, 5 May 1856 in *MEW* XI, p. 640).

The alternative to a classic bourgeois reform movement was the

policy of enlightened conservatism which was implemented by
Bismarck. Perhaps Bismarck was a 'great man of history' precisely because his motives are so enigmatic. It is tempting to see
him as for one reason or another an enthusiast for industrial
progress; in fact from the 1870s onwards he felt an increasing
revulsion from the materialistic Germany which he himself had
nurtured. He began as an unrepentant Junker, dancing and
drinking champagne at the fall of Radowitz, who had briefly
introduced some progressive measures before his replacement
by Manteuffel (see Hamerow, p. 203). He eloquently denounced
economic freedom, but his years as Prussia's representative at the
German Confederation at Frankfurt in the 1850s converted him.
He saw that trying to resist economic freedom only produced the
worst of both worlds, as he wrote to a friend (see Hamerow, pp.
250–1). The crucial fact about his conversion is that it extended
only to means, not ends. He retained his principles – the survival
of the monarchy, the prestige of the Junkers, the greatness of
Prussia – but saw that they must be pursued in ways which the
new world would allow. He never embraced the bourgeois
Weltanschauung: but he perceived the inevitability of bourgeois
industry. Even unification was, with him, merely the best way
of preserving Prussia, given the pressures which otherwise might
lend force to the rise of Austria, or even of a popular revolution
(see Mann, p. 162). We need not attribute his success to genius
alone: it happened also because his project meshed with certain
needs which the bourgeoisie keenly felt, but could not fulfil in their
own way. Their dilemma is typified by the 'constitutional
conflicts' over the army reforms. They were defeated within the
status quo, and did not dare go outside it; their inability
constitutionally to gain increased power over the state forces
meant that they could not deprive those forces of the upper hand
in any likely extra-constitutional struggle.

A crucial element in Bismarck's success was the fact that after
their political defeat in 1848 the bourgeoisie turned to industrial
activity (see *NYDT* 15 October 1856, in *MEW* XII, p. 56 and *NYDT*
1 February 1859, in *MEW* XII, pp. 683–7). But what was required
for this to endure was that the reaction should actually 'deliver
the goods', as Bismarck succeeded in doing. The authoritarian
regime registered foreign policy successes, and it not only allowed
industry to develop, but positively encouraged it by Prussia's

promotion of the German *Zollverein* (Customs Union). A crucial turning-point came with Prussia's success in the war with Austria in 1866, despite Marx's earlier disparagement of her hopes in such a conflict (see *NYDT* 27 December 1858, in *MEW* XII, p. 662). The impact on German liberalism was, quite literally, shattering. Where liberalism had managed to maintain some kind of oppositional spirit while the regime thwarted its aims, this was impossible when the regime started *achieving* them. Most liberals broke with the Progressive party, and as National Liberals worked with Bismarck. The Lower house granted an indemnity for the years of 'unparliamentary' government, and accepted a mere facade of authority (see Mann, p. 177). We should not count this just a nationalistic flight of fancy on the liberals' part. While patriotism was undoubtedly a large motive, they equally saw in unification the possibility for their economy to develop with 'all the benefits which the industries of the western powers had long enjoyed and which even the Italian middle classes now began to enjoy' (Mann, p. 149). Only an impossible revolution would give the liberals the power to do this for themselves, and anyway Bismarck did it better. While bewailing the concomitant 'Prussianisation' of Germany, Marx and Engels accepted the fact:

As soon as Bismarck by using the Prussian army carried out the Little-German scheme of the bourgeoisie with such colossal success, the development in Germany has so firmly taken this direction that we, like others, must acknowledge the *fait accompli*, may we like it or not. (Engels to Marx, 25 July 1866, in *MESC*, p. 169).

The fact that unification was a bourgeois 'material interest' is important. It underlines the fact that Bismarck's real success was not achieving unity, for which most social groups had longed for decades, but achieving it 'without the elements associated with it for fifty years: parliamentary rule, democracy and demagogy' (Mann, p. 172). In doing this, Bismarck did not try, and would have been unable, to ignore the bourgeoisie politically. He saw that the constitutional conflict must not endure if progress was to be achieved. Marx makes the important point that all the reactionary revisions since 1848 could not quite wipe out the fact that the principle of a constitution had been granted, and that at least a show of advertence to the bourgeoisie was inescapable (see *NYDT* 3 November 1858, in *MEW* XII, p. 615). Equally astutely, Marx notes the financial advantage to the regime of allowing the bourgeoisie to 'grant' monies, compared with earlier tussles with the Rothschilds (*NYDT* 27 October 1858, in *MEW* xii, p. 606). Long after the triumph of 1870 Bismarck was to say that discontent among the lower orders, though serious, was remediable, but 'discontent among the educated minority leads to a chronic disease whose diagnosis is difficult and cure protracted' (quoted in Hamerow, p. 252). He was careful to maintain the 'show' after he had won on principles, and always to fulfil enough bourgeois demands to keep the show credible and acceptable.

The 'remedies' for discontent among the lower orders were in important respects a continuation of policies initiated under the reaction of the 1850s. The most notable of those had been the measure of 1853 which severely restricted the employment of children in factories. In the late 1870s and 1880s more measures along such lines were passed, but it is significant that they tended to deal with health, rehabilitation, insurance and such topics, as distinct from improving the income or working hours of normal, healthy workers (see Mann, p. 226). While prepared to make certain social concessions to the workers, Bismarck was quite unprepared to grant them any *political* power, and was joined in this attitude by most of the bourgeoisie. An unsuccessful attempt on the Emperor's life by an isolated madman was used as pretext for the Anti-Socialist Law of 1878. This measure did not abolish the socialist party, which in fact gained votes steadily at most elections, but it severely curtailed its organisational freedom. It would take us well outside our scope to determine whether the non-occurrence of revolution before 1918 is attributable more to prosperity, imperialism and astute government than to strategic errors on the socialists' part. We may however conclude this brief survey of developments by noting Marx's awareness of the danger of their being taken in by government blandishments:

The middle-class party in Prussia discredited itself and brought on its present misery chiefly because it seriously believed that with the 'new era' power, by the grace of the Prince Regent, had fallen into its lap. But the workers' party will discredit itself far more if it imagines that in the Bismarck era or any other Prussian era the golden apples will drop into its mouth by the grace of the king. (Marx to Engels, 18 February 1865, in *MESC*, p. 155)

Conclusion: the state of the theory

The lessons of Britain, France and Germany

In all three of these countries Marx was correct in predicting increased industrialisation. This may seem a small success in hindsight, but we must credit Marx, at least for Germany, with a correct prediction which many a powerful and influential man would have scoffed at in the 1840s and early 1850s. But his expectation that this would mean that the bourgeoisie would run the political system was less successful. This leads us to reconsider his claims about the political motivation of the bourgeoisie, and to try to assess the relation between that class and the regime in each country.

The British case is unusual, in that if we define the bourgeoisie widely enough to include landed property, we already have a bourgeois regime at the start of our period. But Marx's interest – quite correctly – was in whether the bourgeoisie in the narrower sense, particularly the manufacturing middle class, would come to the helm. It is probable that they would have become more politically radical if the oligarchy had dug their heels in (although John Vincent warns us against overestimating their political confidence [see Vincent, pp. xxvi–xxx]). Since the oligarchy would have had no counter-constituency to appeal to, and the workers would probably have seen the manufacturers as their champions in such a struggle, we may put the latters' quietism down to prosperity and the oligarchy's wisdom more than to fear of government or of the lower orders. It is then plausible to interpret the oligarchy's retention of political power as a *delegation* from ruling class to governing caste, as does Marx (see p. 176 above). But we must be slow to apply this model in other countries, since delegation is itself a fundamental species of power, implying that the group delegating could assume direct power themselves, but have a good reason not to. The model, for example, does not apply in France, where the bourgeoisie *abdicated* to Bonaparte. During the period of the Empire they gradually regained confidence, although still afraid to reopen the Pandora's box of revolution; prosperity was an adjutant to caution. Bonaparte certainly became less independent as the years wore on, and it is tempting to see him as being reduced to a position of merely delegated authority. It is impossible to decide this conclusively, since although the bourgeoisie did gain power in the Third Republic, this came only after the peculiar circumstances of military defeat and the isolated revolution of their class enemies in the Commune. The German case is clearly one not of delegation or abdication, but of *renunciation:* they were beaten in 1848, and never got over it; prosperity was an aid to self-deception, but it is unlikely that in its absence they would have acquired new courage.

In discussing the function of the state in relation to the needs of the bourgeois economy, we may usefully advert to our earlier typology of servile, pretentious and dominant states (see pp. 13–14 above). The posture of the British regime supports Marx on this part of his predictions: the regime increasingly articulated the interests of the new bourgeoisie, and, while industry was not uniformly victorious in intra-bourgeois conflicts, it was not seriously thwarted. Significantly, even the manufacturers themselves became reconciled to factory legislation as a measure to preserve the work-force. We may then classify the British state as a 'servile' one in terms of our earlier discussion. We have seen that Bonaparte's regime was from the start committed to promoting industry, although it had the ambition of directing the process itself. It is probable that the Second Empire in its early years was a dominant state, but as time went on it was reduced – by Bonaparte's economic dependence on the bourgeoisie – to a *pretentious* role: incapable of dominance, but actively resisting servility. The Prussian regime set out actually to resist industrialisation, but around 1860 it had to change course. There is a trap here for the unwary Marxist, in that the change of course is to be explained not by bourgeois compulsion but by the regime's own prudence. In other words, without any loss of political power, the regime came to see that if it wanted to realise its own ends in the modern world, it would have to tailor them to, and employ, modern means: the bourgeoisie were 'served' because they happened to be the group crucial to the development of the economy, not because they were able to translate this fact into political power. The role imposed by prudence on the Prussian state supports the very wide, weak and general point that the state will have to concern itself with the business of society rather than going its own sweet way; it does not support Marxian contentions on any further point, such as the expectation that the bourgeoisie would themselves acquire political power. On any useful political criteria we must count the state a *dominant* one, which was able to stamp its own character on the economic development which it accommodated (see Engels, *PMQ*, p. 132); if it had decided not to accommodate industry at all, it is very doubtful whether the bourgeoisie would have succeeded in displacing it. The danger of dividing Marx's political claim into two parts – concerning *function* and *personnel* – as we have done is that it might lead us to read too much into the kind of function performed by an authoritarian regime such as Bismarck's.

Thus Marx is justified in his prediction that these countries will all industrialise. He is justified in his claim that the state will have to accommodate this process, although his success in the case of Germany is more trivial than in the other two cases. His claim that the bourgeoisie will acquire political power fared disastrously in Germany, fairly well in a roundabout way in Britain, and fairly well after a long gap and in peculiar circumstances in France.

The theory of the state

In his early years, Marx held to the 'ideal picture' of bourgeois rule which we discussed on pp. 19ff above. In that period, he seems not to have been fully aware of the contradictions involved in regarding the democratic republic as simultaneously the ideal form of bourgeois rule and the political form most conducive to revolution by the workers. In the course of the revolutions of 1848 he comes to believe that, because of these contradictions, the republic 'is generally only the political form for the revolutionizing of bourgeois society, and not its conservative form of existence' (*EBLB*, p. 155). He sees that in times of crisis the bourgeoisie will have to use the state in a repressive manner, rather than as the general 'representative' of society. While this runs counter to his claim that the bourgeoisie exercise their political supremacy 'in the modern representative state' (*CM*, p. 69), it does not falsify his more basic contention that 'the modern state is but a committee for managing the common affairs of the whole bourgeoisie' (*ibid.*). What the experience of the French bourgeoisie taught him, however, is that (as we 'predicted' on pp. 18–23 above) the recourse to repression is dangerous even for the ruling class, and can issue in the triumph of an adventurer like Bonaparte. Shortly after the latter's coup Marx predicted that his regime, by serving the material advancement of the bourgeoisie, would necessarily keep their political power alive (see p. 112 above). As we have seen in this chapter, that prediction was a reasonably successful one, although the bourgeoisie's political power increased incrementally rather than dramatically. It is important to note, however, that in his treatment of the Second Empire in 1871, Marx does not advert to these signs of Bonaparte's being brought to heel. The reasons for this are instructive.

It is difficult to determine his views on Bonaparte in the 1860s, since his journalism decreased sharply in that decade, and he mentions the regime very rarely in his correspondence (see *MEW* XXXI and XXXII). One explanation is his increasing preoccupation with events in Germany (see Rubel, p. 116). But what is more relevant to us is the *nature* of the preoccupation with Germany: Marx's correspondence in this decade is largely taken up with the doings of the General Council and the branches (not only the German branch) of the International, reflecting his 'loss of faith in the bourgeoisie' and turn to the proletariat as the only possible revolutionary class (see pp. 135ff. above). On the occasions when he does dwell on Bonaparte and his fortunes, he tends to emphasise the general chaos in which Bonaparte finds himself, one symptom of which is the need to make concession to the bourgeoisie. That he does not present this more positively as a *progress* for the bourgeoisie reflects his reckoning that they are essentially a spent political force (see e.g., Marx to Engels, 10 and 18 May 1870, in *MEW* XXXII, pp. 504 and 516 respectively). His strategic preoccupations and his tendency to write off the bourgeoisie were intensified, when writing the death-eulogy of the Commune, by the intention of glorifying the proletariat as the sole embodiment of virtue and ultimate political capacity.

It is perhaps for this complex of reasons that, in his work on the Commune, Marx lays such emphasis on the repressive state as the normal form in developed bourgeois society. He retells the story told at the end of the *Eighteenth Brumaire*, of how the various ruling groups in France relied on the state, until the Party of Order's reliance on it after 1848 empowered the state forces to the point of a successful coup (see p. 110 above). There is a subtle difference of emphasis in the later version of this story, however. Marx lays great stress on the essentially repressive nature of bourgeois rule:

At the same pace at which the progress of modern industry developed, widened, intensified the class antagonism between capital and labour, the State power assumed more and more the character of the national power of capital over labour, of a public force organised for social enslavement, of an engine of class despotism. (*CWF*, p. 72; see also *CWF Drafts*, p. 197).

Marx goes on to tell us, in much the same way as twenty years before, how this increasing reliance on repression eventually rebounded on its employers: 'The natural offspring of the "Party-of-Order" Republic was the Second Empire' (*CWF*, p. 72). But where this later account subtly differs from the earlier one is that it has more of a tendency to confuse Bonapartism as an *ultimate means* of bourgeois repression with Bonapartism as an *unfortunate result* thereof. In one of his drafts, Marx goes so far as to say that Bonapartism is 'the state power of modern class rule, at least on the European continent' (*CWF Drafts*, p. 213). While he is slightly more cautious in the final version, he nevertheless tends to blur this vital distinction. From the strategic point of view which he is taking at the time, this is understandable and perhaps even permissible. Insofar as he believes, as he says in 1875, that 'society will not recover its equilibrium until it rotates around the sun of labour' ('Postscript', in *CCT*, p. 133), he is justified in not inquiring too minutely into the relations between the bourgeoisie and the state, both of which are destined to be engulfed by the revolutionary proletariat. But that does not excuse sloppy analysis of the *status quo*, not only because he claims to be able to probe to the truth about politics, but also because probing to that truth is a prerequisite of any revolutionary strategy, however total, which succeeds otherwise than by the merest chance.

When in 1875 Marx comes to write the *Critique of the Gotha Programme* (see pp. 167ff. above), several factors lead him to take a wider and somewhat deeper view of the modern state. He is writing not a public eulogy but a private critique of strategy, and moreover he has before him the examples of Britain and France, both of which were evolving representative bourgeois democracies. He takes the authors of the programme to task severely for speaking vaguely of 'the present state':

The 'present society' is capitalist society, which exists in all civilized countries, freed in varying degrees from the admixture of medievalism, modified in varying degrees by the particular historical development of each country, and developed to a varying degree. In contrast to this, the 'present state' changes with each country's border. It differs between the Prusso-German Empire and Switzerland, between England and the United States. '*The* present state' is thus a fiction. (*CGP*, pp. 354–5).

We should not underestimate the fact that, in his last major statement on the subject, Marx not only mentioned but stressed the *variety* of state forms to be found in modern bourgeois society. But the question arises as to how much of the original claims about politics – or what plausible reformulation of them – can be made consistent with such empirical diversity. Marx's position here is superior to that in *CWF* in that, while singling out one form (the democratic one) as the 'final state form of bourgeois society' (p. 356), it allows of other forms as well. The regimes which Marx considers have a wide range. At one end is the United States, which consistently throughout his career he regarded as a case 'where the state, in contrast to all earlier national formations, was from the beginning subordinate to bourgeois society, to its production, and never could make the pretence [' *die Prätention*'] of being an end-in-itself' (*G*, p. 884, from *Grundrisse* [Berlin, 1953], p. 844). At the other extreme is Bismarck's regime: 'a military despotism and a police state, bureaucratically carpentered, embellished with parliamentary forms and disguised by an admixture of feudalism' (*CGP*, p. 356). But when Marx – most implausibly – tacks onto this description the claim that the Bismarck regime is 'already under the influence of the bourgeoisie' (*ibid*.), we return to the question of how this array of state forms fits in with his theoretical claims about the bourgeoisie's political power. Having stressed the diversity of state forms as we have seen, Marx proceeds to allow that

Nevertheless, the various states of the various civilized countries, despite their motley diversity of form, do have this in common: they all stand on the ground of modern bourgeois society although the degree of capitalist development varies. They thus also share certain essential characteristics. In this sense one can speak of 'present states' in contrast to the future when their present root, bourgeois society, will have died off. (*CGP*, p. 355)

This argument is highly reminiscent of one advanced more than thirty years before:

Property, etc., in brief the entire content of law and the state is, with small modification, the same in North America as in Prussia. There, accordingly, the republic is a mere state form just as the monarchy is here. The content of the state lies outside these constitutions. (*CHPR*, p. 31)

One is tempted to remark, uncharitably, that Marx has not got very far, in the meantime, in actually *relating* the diverse state forms to their common ground in bourgeois society. The *CGP* argument is an impressive-sounding tautology, but nevertheless a mere tautology. The whole question is what 'essential characteristics' are shared by the political regimes of, for example, Britain, Prussia and the United States. The image of the root may be a good one insofar as one is interested in abolishing bourgeois society, but it is otherwise misleading. It is not established that all these state forms, because they 'stand on the ground of modern bourgeois society' therefore spring from it as do trees from a root. Of course if bourgeois society is their root rather than just their ground, then removing it will remove them. But in any case even if we can show that all of them do spring from this root, the argument does nothing to tell us why the one root should yield such various trees. Not clarifying such points exposes Marx to the danger of confusing the very weak Marxist point which can be made about even dominant states in modern conditions with the stronger point which can be made where the bourgeoisie have direct or indirect political control.

Having taken him thus sternly to task, let us see what sense Marx might have made of the variety of state forms, if he had been more precise. He has had to admit in the course of his career that where the bourgeoisie hold exclusive political sway, they are often compelled to exercise it in a repressive rather than representative mode. This admission can safely be turned into a positive *assertion* of the theory, since both of these modes can plausibly be called modes of 'bourgeois rule'. Ironically, the ideal picture of representative rule which he tended to abandon between 1848 and 1871 became *more* relevant as the British and French polities evolved along such lines in Marx's later years. Then there is the fact that bourgeois repression can rebound on the bourgeoisie, leading to something like Bonaparte's regime. Insofar as such a regime gradually loses its independence because of its financial and other needs, Marx is able to 'reabsorb' it into the theory, but insofar as it does not, it has to be treated as an exception or counter-example, where the state can actually dominate rather than serve the bourgeoisie. While such a case falsifies the claims about bourgeois political power, it can be incorporated in a wider and weaker view which explains bourgeois regimes (representative and repressive) *and* dominant ones of the Bonapartist type as all being results of the structure of bourgeois society and the antagonism of classes within it; where Marx is chiefly interested in abolishing bourgeois society root and branch, this is a tenable point of view, though dangerous for strategy. While the 'root' analogy can cover all these cases, though with different degrees of stringency, it is more difficult to apply it to cases where the bourgeoisie fail to acquire political power in the first place. The class antagonisms of bourgeois society perhaps help to explain the survival, but do not explain the provenance, of such regimes. Where such a regime does see the need for accommodating bourgeois industry, we can explain this in terms of its standing on the 'ground' of bourgeois society, but the connection is the weakest one which the Marxian armoury contains. In 1862, while in the thick of composing *Capital*, Marx wrote to Kugelmann that he had arrived at the basic principles at least, from which even others could reconstruct his system, 'with the exception perhaps of the relationship of of different forms of the state to the different economic structures of society' (Marx to Kugelman, 28 December 1862, in *MEW* xxx, p. 639). There is a passage in *Capital* iii where he briefly sketches an approach to this problem, distinguishing social formations as to the degree to which the forms of the their economic and political power coincide with each other or are distinct but related. He raises some interesting correlations here, which could be developed properly only in the context of an examination of his theory of each different kind of mode of production. He tells us that

It is always the direct relationship of the owners of the conditions of production to the direct producers . . . which reveals the innermost secret, the hidden basis of the entire social structure, and with it the political form of the relation of sovereignty and dependence, in short, the corresponding specific form of the state. (*Capital* iii, p. 772)

As regards the general theory of state forms, this remains little more than a research-design. In this chapter, we have seen that Marx does not succeed even in fulfilling it comprehensively for the one social formation – bourgeois society – which chiefly interested him, although his attempt is far from being a total failure.

8. Aspects of the general theory

As the Introduction has already made clear, this is a study not of Marx's 'materialist conception of history' as such, but of his particular treatment of politics. This final chapter, however, will be more concerned with general aspects of Marx's theory than have earlier ones. Its aim is to set the previous treatment in context, and to show the significance of the wider questions which Marx raised, and in many cases left unanswered, particularly in the later period of his life. The first section will look briefly at what Marx meant by calling his overall theory 'materialist', and at the central claim about history and society which that theory embodies. The second section will look at the interest, deepening over the years, which Marx took in the findings of contemporary ethnography on the nature of early society and the emergence of class division. It will also look at how he applies his conclusions from this material to the question of the prospects for communal property in Russia. As usual, our focus is Marx's specific treatment of politics rather than the general theory as such. For this reason, the third section, with the second as background, will examine more closely the distinction which Marx employs between *government*, which is found in all societies, and *politics*, which is found only in class societies. It will make some points about the connection between class societies and politics, which raise problems for Marx's assurance that the abolition of classes in communist society will guarantee that its government will not degenerate into politics.

The nature of Marx's materialism

It is difficult to assign a single clear meaning to the notion of 'materialism' as Marx employs it. No sooner do we decide that it refers to methodological issues, than we find him then speaking of 'material' factors in society, and *vice versa*. The puzzle is illuminating, however, because it shows us that there is a single basic notion of materialism which runs through Marx's assertions in both philosophical and sociological areas (where 'sociological' stands for the broad study of society rather than a particular discipline). I shall distinguish three kinds of materialism. *Ontological Materialism* claims that all reality is matter. *Methodological Materialism* is the rejection of apriorism in scientific inquiry. *Sociological Materialism* rejects the interpretation of society in terms of people's ideas about themselves. There is little evidence that Marx took a materialist stance upon, or even that he cared much about, the ontological issue. Even his early philosophical notebooks, not to mention the *Theses on Feuerbach*, tend to interpret ontological positions as symptomatic of methodological and political ones (see *MECW* I, pp. 403–501, and *TF*). It may be that Marx's methodological and sociological positions imply an ontological materialism, but he presented them without such an underpinning, and I shall follow him in so discussing them.

Nowadays, we would hesitate before calling methodological or sociological positions 'materialist', but Marx meant something important by so calling them. The root of his position is an opposition to what he regarded as 'idealist' distortions in both method and the understanding of society. These distortions arise from what we might call an overestimation of the role of ideas or concepts. In method, a scientist can be lured into constructing neat conceptual universes more and more abstracted from the real subject-matter from which the concepts derived. He can even come to regard his own 'mental production' as a production of the real world. Marx alleges that Hegel in this way 'fell into the illusion of conceiving the real as the product of thought', whereas the method of arguing from abstract to concrete concepts is 'only the way in which thought appropriates the concrete, reproduces the concrete in the mind' (*G*, p. 101). A further defect of this methodological idealism is that it distorts the reality which it works upon, since it starts out from a preconceived totality and *necessarily* ends up with a representation of the world as harmonious, even if it is not so (see *CHPR*, pp. 11, 12, 18). A related error ('sociological idealism') can be made in understanding the role of ideas in society and history. Ordinary people as well as ideologists can assign to ideas an eternal relevance and validity, ignoring the particular circumstances in which they arose and which they reflect. This kind of 'sociological idealism' emerges also in the theories of philosophers who hold that 'the relationships of men, all their doings, their chains and their limitations are products of their consciousness' (*GI*, p. 31).

If both kinds of idealism – the methodological and the sociological – misconstrue the role of the human mind, then both kinds of materialism will have in common the proper estimation of that role. A reader of Marx's early critique of Hegel, with its scornful remarks on Hegel's confusion of abstract logical concepts with reality, might infer that Marx rejects *all* theory as necessarily idealistic. But in fact Marx is arguing only against the *abuse* of theory, and puts forward, in his methodological materialism, what he considers the correct use of it. This approach will use theory, certainly, but rather than presupposing the rationality of the world it will ask *how far* it is rational, and issue in a practice to make it fully so. Marx's notion of the correct method, then, is one which feeds into a praxis to rationalise a merely partially rational world. Its motto is not 'to play *school-master* to the event', but rather 'to discover its specific character' (*KP*, p. 416). There are, as it were, two 'stages' in Marx's sociological materialism. The first is the negative stage of denying to ideas the eternal relevance and validity attributed to them by ideologists. The second is the positive stage of putting forward an alternative substantive theory explaining the *proper* status of ideas in society. Marx and Engels first propose this theory in the *German Ideology*, where they speak of material production as the 'first historical act' which must be daily repeated, and whose exigencies explain the nature of men's social relations and their ideas (see *GI*, pp. 31ff.). As we have already seen in chapter 1, this theory starts out from individuals, certainly, but from individuals 'within their given historical conditions and relationships, not [from] the "pure" individual in the sense of the ideologists' (*GI*, pp. 94–5; see pp. 15–16 above).

There are passages where Marx asserts the central role of the economy in an extremely crude manner. One such is a passage which we have already encountered in chapter 2 (see p. 32 above), dealing with the replacement of feudal by bourgeois social conditions:

The feudal relations of property became no longer compatible with the already developed productive forces; they restricted production, instead of promoting it; they became so many fetters. They had to be burst asunder; they were burst asunder. Into their place stepped free competition, accompanied by a social and political constitution adapted to it, and by the economical and political sway of the bourgeois class. (*CM*, p. 72; omission translated from *MEW* IV, p. 467).

Not only does this argument smack of 'methodological idealism', that is, the assimilation of historical movement to the neat inter-connections of concepts; it also seems to conceive of economic change as necessarily *generating*, or at least preceding, change in the rest of society in a way which seems historically implausible. But there are clear instances in Marx's actual historical explana-tions which make nonsense of the idea that economic change *necessarily* precedes non-economic change in society. When dis-cussing conquest for example, he clearly allows that a crucial political change not only precedes but actually causes an economic change (see *GI*, pp. 91–2, and *G*, pp. 96–8). On the narrower issue of the role of production within the economy itself, Marx similarly allows that what is ultimately dependent can come into being before, and actually be a cause of, what is ultimately dominant (see *Capital* I, pp. 340 and 378, and *Capital* III, pp. 322 and 331). Useful light can be thrown on the sense in which Marx does claim that the economy is central by noting an important debt which he owes to Hegel.

The Hegel whom Marx so scorns in his early Critique for his allegedly exclusive interest in logic (*CHPR*, p. 18), in fact uses his philosophical 'Idea' of the organism in a much more empirical and critical manner than the *Critique* suggests (as Marx at times elsewhere recognises: see *EPM*, p. 385, *HF*, pp. 82–3 and *GI*, p. 354). He uses his notion of the organic state to discriminate, among actual states, between 'mature' and 'immature' ones, saying that a bad state 'is one which merely exists; a sick body exists too, but it has no genuine reality' (Hegel, p. 283, Addition to Para. 270; see also p. 280).

Moreover, Hegel says some things about the application of a philosophical theory which are very relevant to Marx's own mature method. He tells us that in our science we arrive at 'a series of thoughts and a series of shapes of experience', and that the time-order of the latter series is 'other than the logical order'. For instance, he says, although the family pre-exists property, still property must come first in our theoretical treatment. To the question why we do not begin 'at the highest point, i.e., with the concretely true', he gives the answer that 'it is precisely the truth as a result that we are looking for, and for this purpose it is essential to start by grasping the abstract concept itself' (Hegel, p. 233, Addition to Para. 32). There is interesting evidence that, in evolving his own mature method, Marx took over much of this strain in Hegel's thinking; that it is, as Marx would see it, 'what is *rational* in the method which Hegel discovered but at the same time enveloped in mysticism' (Marx to Engels, 14 January 1858, in *MESC*, p. 93). He translates Hegel's 'Idea' into the concept of the social formation, with its economic structure comprising forces and relations of production, on which arise legal and political superstructures and to which forms of consciousness correspond (see *CCPE*, p. 20). At least in intention, Marx does not presuppose such a formation ready made (which would be 'methodological idealism'), but uses it as a guiding idea to ask of any concrete society whether it is a case of the emergence, stable recurrence or decline of such organic structure. As in Hegel's approach, we are not the slaves of historical chronology: Phenomenon 1 may emerge long before, and even help bring about, Phenomenon 2, and yet in the established organism 1 may be subordinated to 2. This is the case with Marx's discussion of merchants' and industrial capital (see *Capital* III, chapter 20). It is significant that in spelling out this method Marx specifically praises Hegel for starting his presentation with property, and says that it would be wrong in our theoretical presentation to let the categories follow one another 'in the same sequence as that in which they were historically decisive' (*G*, p. 107). Their sequence must rather be determined by 'their relation to one another in modern bourgeois society' which Marx goes so far as to say is 'precisely the opposite of that which seems to be their natural order or which corresponds to historical development' (*G*, p. 107). Marx proposes a theory that, whatever the historical order in which social phenomena historically emerge, periods of social change will be replaced by periods of stability when the ideology, the legal and political superstructures, and the economy correspond to one another. But this much would make Marx no more than a complicated equilibrium thinker, since the correspondence posited might equally well be stated as 'economy corresponds with . . .' or ' . . . corresponds with economy'. The further, specific element in Marx's claim must be that, in case of conflict, the other levels of society will fall into line with the economy rather than the reverse. The core-claim of his theory will then be that *irre-spective of whether economic change always, sometimes or never precedes the other social change, societies will become stable and organised when their ideology and their legal and political structures meet the requirements of the economy, rather than the economy meeting the requirements of ideology, law or politics.*

If the theory, formulated in this way, avoids stipulating an implausible priority of time-sequence, it is still not without problematic aspects. The materialist conception of history as such has been the topic of almost endless controversies, some of its critics even claiming that its terms are so logically and conceptually inextricable as to make it untestable and unfalsifiable (see Evans, pp. 61–72 for a recent survey of criticisms and G. A. Cohen for a most fruitful rebuttal of some of them). The theory as such is not my topic in this study, and it would take another full work to do justice both to it and to its critics. My analysis of Marx's treatment of politics, however, would seem to imply that it is not 'inapplicable' at least in that area, since I discuss the evidence for and against his claims. It might be responded that the theory is indeed incoherent as its critics allege, and Marx simply and sensibly ignores it in his empirical writings. I believe however that the discussion in chapters 1, 2 and 7, for example, shows a strong link between what Marx says about politics and his more basic theory, so that it is plausible to see his treatment of politics as an application of the theory, rather than as a (witting or unwitting) abandonment of it. This does not mean that his basic theory does not lead Marx to say some extremely simplistic things about politics, but earlier chapters have shown that he has his successes as well as his failures. I include this brief discussion of the basic theory simply in order to put the treatment of politics in theoretical context, and to set the scene for the broad issues discussed in the remainder of this chapter.

A wider canvas: the fate of communal property

The preceding section has given a brief outline of Marx's materialist theory of society, as it is to be found in his better-known writings. Here we must round out the picture by adverting to something less familiar in the main stream of Marx commentary: his profound and enduring interest in questions of ethnography and anthropology. Even as early as 1845–6, Marx and Engels cast their account of the crystallisation of alien structures in terms of world-history, of the replacement of an original 'tribal communism' by private property which eventually would be replaced by post-capitalist communism (see above chapter 1, pp. 14–18). Soon after his 'retreat into the study', Marx began to take an interest in the fate of pre-conquest structures in India, for journalistic and deeper theoretical purposes. The fruits of his sustained interest in ethnography were to emerge in such works as the *Grundrisse* of 1857–8, the *Contribution to a Critique of Political Economy* of 1859, and volumes I and III of *Capital*. We have recently been provided with editions of even later material: Marx's reading notes on Maxim Kovalevsky (see *VS*) and on Lewis Morgan, J. B. Phear, Henry Sumner Maine and Sir John Lubbock (see *EN*) both from the 1870s. We must however beware of hastily erecting a whole new wing of the Marxian edifice on the basis of this material. In the first place, as Hobsbawm tells us, 'Marx concentrated his energies on the study of capitalism, and he dealt with the rest of history in varying degrees of detail, but mainly insofar as it bore on the origins and development of capitalism' (Hobsbawm, p. 20). Moreover, insofar as Marx did deal with this material in its own right, it is far from clear what he meant to do with it, or what were his precise positions on the issues involved. 'How Marx had intended to present his work, whether as a book on an ethnological subject, or as a part of a work on another subject is unclear; his work cannot be said to have taken a particular form, it was rather in the process of gestation' (Krader, p. 7; see also p. 24). It is true that, the year after Marx's death, Engels used his notes to produce the *Origin of the Family, Private Property and the State*, which account Professor Childe has called, though dated, 'the best attempt of its kind' (Childe, p. 23). The relationship between Marx's and Engels's treatments has been discussed by Harstick (p. liii) and by Krader, who concludes that 'Engels was less deep and less precise than Marx; such was the self-estimation of Engels as well' (p. 82; see pp. 76–82). Without taking him as literally speaking for Marx, I have found Engels's book a useful indication of what Marx was getting at. The final reason for caution in this area is that Marx was working while scientific ethnography was still in its infancy, and many 'findings' of his contemporaries are regarded nowadays as museum-pieces.

For example, Professor Childe tells us that modern research has 'played havoc with the contents of Morgan's scheme'. A definitive discussion would need to be a Marx*ist* rather than a Marx*ian* one, which, using the clues provided by Marx's reading notes, reconciled (or tried to reconcile) his basic historical materialism with the answers which ethnography can now give to the questions raised in his lifetime. The aim of this chapter is far less ambitious: it is to assess the significance of the kind of *question* which Marx clearly regarded as important, and to show what light his interests throw on his attitude to politics.

Communal property as common origin

As time went on, Marx and Engels became increasingly convinced of the truth of the *German Ideology*'s postulate of communal property as the original stage in history. They were much taken with the researches of G. L. Maurer, who studied early forms of communal property (see, e.g., Marx to Engels, 25 March 1868 and Engels to Marx, 15 December 1882, in *MESC*, pp. 188–9 and 334–5 respectively). In 1888 Engels restricted the famous opening sentence of the *Manifesto*, that all history is the history of class struggle, to 'all *written* history', citing the researches of Maurer, Morgan and August von Haxthausen as evidence that 'village communities were found to be, or to have been the primitive form of society everywhere from India to Ireland' (*CM*, p. 67 n. 13). That their interest in the question was more than purely theoretical is shown by Marx's gleeful observation to Engels that, after Maurer, 'the Russians now lose even the last traces of a claim to originality, even in this line' (Marx to Engels, 14 March 1868, in *PCEF*, p. 139). Whether the surviving Russian commune (the *mir* or *obshchina*) was the descendant of a uniquely Russian primitive communism was a bone of contention in Marx's disputes with Bakunin, and also with Alexander Herzen (see Harstick, p. xliii). This is why he attacks the 'absurdly biased view' that

primitive communal property is a specifically Slavonic, or even an exclusively Russian, phenomenon. It is an early form which can be found among Romans, Teutons and Celts, and of which a whole collection of diverse patterns (though sometimes only remnants survive) is still in existence in India. (*CCPE*, p. 33; quoted in *Capital* i, p. 49).

But there is a theoretical motive in the dispute as well. It is not, as might be imagined, the insistence on communal property as a primitive 'ideal' or 'golden age'. As early as 1844 Marx had rejected any regression to the '*unnatural* simplicity of the *poor*, unrefined man who has no needs and who has not even reached the stage of private property, let alone gone beyond it'. (*EPM*, p. 346). Throughout his career, Marx emphasised the inability of original communism to handle the complexity of human development, and he had no nostalgia for it. The theoretical import of communal property was to illustrate the merely historical necessity of all forms of private property, and to back up the abstract theoretical possibility of post-capitalist communism by showing that communal property had once already been the basis of social formations. In this vein, Marx frequently emphasises the 'artificial' nature of private property, and especially of capitalism, in that they involve the historical destruction of quite different prior social systems.

To describe the relation between people and things in such primitive communism, Marx uses a concept of 'possession' or 'possessory rights' rather than 'property'. Under such a system, it is of course necessary for individuals to have the use of certain things, and even to have assured, stable rights to use them, but they have not the right to alter the way in which, or to decide by whom, they will be used, which right inheres in the community. This kind of 'individual possession' (*G*, p. 492) is illustrated by the rule among American Indian tribes that 'persons, removing from one village to another, could not transfer their possessory right to cultivated lands or to a section of a joint-tenement house to a stranger; must leave them to their gentile kindred' (*EN*, p. 147). Amongst certain tribes, not even food was private property (*VS*, p. 1). Marx sees this relation between men and things as being eroded over time by a 'deepening individualisation of relations to goods' ['sich befestigender Individualisation der Vermögensverhältnisse' (VS, p. 36)]. This is relevant to the forcible accumulation of capital which we have discussed in chapter 6 (pp. 147–49 above). We can now see capitalist private property as the result of a long historical process of the intrusion of individual, private property into a previously communal system: 'The positing of the individual as a *worker*, in this nakedness, is itself a product of *history*' (*G*, p. 472).

Forms of dissolution of communal property

Marx's concern with the *end-product* of this development is evident in the title of the famous section of the *Grundrisse* called
'Forms which precede capitalist production' (*G*, pp. 471–514; also
edited separately by Hobsbawm as *PCEF*). It dwells for most of
its length on the question of 'which conditions are necessary so
that [the worker] finds himself up against a *capital*?' (*G*, p. 498).
But in the course of answering this question, Marx does propose
a typology of forms in which communal property evolved into
private property systems, and in the later notebooks he deals in
a similar way with Morgan's discussion of the decline of the
gentile system. A *gens* is a 'group of families with supposed
common origin, sharing name and religious rites; [or a] clan'
(*Concise Oxford Dictionary* Oxford, 1976, p. 443). Several gentes
formed a *phratry*, and several phratries a tribe; in cases such as
that of the Iroquois, the tribes in turn would form a confederacy.
A crucial feature of this gentile constitution is that it had no
politics in the sense which Marx gives to the word, as we shall
see in our final section. What is more relevant here is that it
originated as a system of communal property; Morgan attributes
its decline to the emergence of private property. He traces how
increasing numbers and other pressures began to erode the merely
possessory system which we have mentioned, and there was a
'tendency towards two forms of ownership, namely, through the
state and through individuals' (*EN*, p. 134). He notes how the
gentile organisation became incapable of articulating the new
relationships resulting from individual property. The distinction
between *rich* and *poor*, a consequence of individual ownership,
cut across the gentile system, since within one gens there now
could be rich and poor families (see *EN*, pp. 213, 230, 232). There
also developed a growing number of poor who were not members
of any gens, and would not be accepted into any: 'this class of
persons a *growing element of dangerous discontent*' notes Marx
(*EN*, p. 213; see also pp. 228 and 232).

This discussion puts in perspective the earlier typology of the
Grundrisse. There Marx discusses three main forms of community, each of which embodies a development beyond the simple
communal form. The first is the *Oriental* or *Asiatic* commune,
although the geographical name should not mislead us: Marx saw

it as having occurred in other continents too, as is made clear in the letter to Engels quoted on p. 212 above. It is, on Marx's terms, anomalous in that while its form of property is still communal, there yet exists over and above it a state to which the small communes have to pay tribute as well as performing 'common labour for the exaltation of the unity, partly of the real despot, partly of the imagined clan-being, the god' (*G*, p. 473). Marx explains this state of affairs in a most Hegelian manner, saying that as the inhabitants possess property as mere moments of a unity 'it follows that this unity can appear as a *particular* entity above the many real particular communities' (*ibid.*). But elsewhere he explains it, less philosophically, by the fact that the many small scattered self-contained communes have one general need, for vast schemes of irrigation, which the state fulfils (see *NYDT* 25 June 1853, in *OCM*, p. 90). This case will be important for our discussion of politics, since it combines communal property with what looks suspiciously like political government (see p. 238 below). Marx allows of a variant within this form – the *Slavonic* form – which need not concern us here.

Marx sees the second main form, which he calls the *Ancient* form, as the 'product of more active, historic life, of the fates and modifications of the original clans' (*G*, p. 474). It also presupposes community of property, but unlike the Asiatic form it does not see it as 'the substance of which the individuals are mere accidents' (*ibid.*). As we have already seen from Marx's notes on Morgan, this form combines private and communal property. The distinctive thing about it, Marx says, is that 'the latter appears as posited by the former, so that only the citizen is and must be a private proprietor' (p. 486), and the common land forms an *ager publicus* in which 'his property as citizen has a separate, particular existence at the same time' (*ibid.*). It differs from the third, *Germanic* form, in which the individual families appear as much more self-subsistent, and the community is a mere 'coming-together' of the scattered families for particular common purposes. True, there is here also an *ager publicus*, but it figures not as the crucial property of the community presupposed to its members, but 'only to the extent that it is defended militarily as the common property of one tribe against a hostile tribe. Individual property does not appear mediated by the commune; rather, the existence of the commune and of communal property appear as mediated by, i.e., as a relation of, the independent subjects to one another' (pp. 483–4).

Our interest here is less in the details of this typology than in the story which it tells, of the decline of primitive communism, passing through a series of 'compromises' between communal property and the needs of higher development. Throughout Marx's ethnography there runs the rather Hegelian picture of an original unity of mankind which needs to be sundered for development to take place. All these forms 'necessarily correspond to a development of the forces of production which is only limited, and indeed limited in principle. The development of the forces of production dissolves these forms, and their dissolution is itself a development of the human productive forces' (*G*, p. 496; see *Capital* I, p. 51).

There is a lot of work to be done, on the level of mere clarification, in the relating of this typology to the more famous list of 'Asiatic, ancient, feudal and modern bourgeois' modes of production which Marx was to propose about a year later (*CCPE*, p. 21). Hobsbawm treats the two schemes as relating to slightly different questions, the *Grundrisse* tracing the breakdown of communal property, and the '1859 Preface' tracing the major steps between communal and capitalist production. The two overlap to an extent: the Oriental or Asiatic (including the Slavonic) form of breakdown of communal property is also the first stage of the second schema, and both have the same second stage: the Ancient mode. The Germanic form of the *Grundrisse* schema is connected but not identical with the feudal form of the 'Preface' one, and the *Grundrisse* discussion naturally does not include a stage of bourgeois production (see Hobsbawm, pp. 37–8). This treatment opens up a thicket of problems; for example, some commentators deny that on Marxist criteria there can even *be* an Asiatic mode of production (see Hindess and Hirst, chapter 4, and Mandel 1971, chapter 8). There is also the vexed question of periodisation, in the sense of how we fit concrete societies into typologies. Periodisation also is a problem in the sense of the rigidity or otherwise of the succession of stages as Marx conceives them; that question will arise in the following two sub-sections.

The prospects of the Russian commune

Ever since the emancipation of the serfs in 1861, Marx had taken a keen interest in Russian affairs. 'In order that I might be specially qualified to estimate the economic development in Russia' he later recalled, 'I learnt Russian and for many years studied in official publications and others' (*ML*, p. 292). In February 1881 he received a letter from Vera Zasulich, a Russian revolutionary then living in Geneva. She apprised him of the debates going on amongst revolutionaries in her country, as to whether the Russian commune should be sacrificed as a lost cause to capitalist development, or could be made the basis of a regeneration of communal relations adequate to the needs of the modern world. She informed Marx that the 'Marxists' claimed that Marx believed, or if he had spoken on the issue *would* say, that it was a lost cause. Zasulich, who rejected this view, asked Marx to adjudicate (see Blackstock and Hoselitz, pp. 276–7). Marx wrote her a very brief reply about three weeks later, apologising that a sickness of nerves had delayed him (*ZL*, p. 319). The 'sickness of nerves' had not however prevented him from writing four detailed drafts of a lengthy reply. We shall refer to the short actual reply later; for the moment, what is relevant are Marx's considerations in the drafts.

Marx says that the only serious historical argument against the commune is the analogy with Western experience, where communal property 'has everywhere disappeared with the progress of society' (*ZL Drafts*, p. 222). He in general rejects this argument by analogy, pointing out that the decline of communal property and the establishment of capitalism in Western Europe 'are separated from one another by an immense interval which embraces a whole series of successive revolutions and stages of economic evolution' (*ibid.*). He attaches great weight to the precise *historical context* in which any event or phenomenon is situated. If Russia were isolated from other countries, he allows, she would have to retrace pretty well the same protracted and difficult path. But she has the distinction that her own peculiarly tenacious form of communal property has survived into a world economy dominated by more advanced modes of production. Marx sees a certain hope in this combination of a peculiar type of commune with an advantageous context. We shall examine each in turn.

Marx classifies the Russian commune under a general heading of 'village communities', which he regards as the 'latest', that is the most developed, form of communal property. It has three chief characteristics. (i) It has transcended the emphasis on the 'strong but narrow' bond of blood or adoption, and it has the strength of being 'an association of free men not related to one another by close blood lines'. (ii) Each peasant owns his house and farmyard, whereas in the 'more archaic' type of community there was no private ownership at all. And (iii) the land is periodically divided among the peasants, each of whom then works his plot on his own account and appropriates the fruits thereof, whereas earlier forms of commune controlled both work- and consumption-patterns much more closely.

These three characteristics confer on the village community a 'dualism' (*ZL Drafts*, p. 220) which is easy to understand in terms of our previous discussion: the village community seems more successfully than other forms to have struck a balance between its communal basis and the development of individualism. If it can maintain this balance, it can 'give full scope to an individualism which is incompatible with the structure of more primitive communities' (*ibid.*). But this very strength also contains a negative potential:

> movable property, which is beyond the control of the community, and subject to private exchange in which ruse and accident play a great role, rests more and more heavily on the entire rural economy. This is the decomposing factor of primitive social and economic equality. It introduces heterogeneous elements which provoke conflicts of interests in the bosom of the community, and which call forth passions designed to encroach first upon the communally owned farmlands, then upon the communal property of forests, pastures, wastes, etc., which once converted into *communal annexes* to private property will fall victim to the latter in the long run. (p. 221)

The context will prove crucial in deciding which set of potentialities in the commune will be encouraged, and which repressed. On the positive side, the commune has the theoretical possibility of taking over the technological fruits of capitalism without taking over its production relations, or repeating a path of development as long and arduous as the West underwent. There is a chance that communal property could run as it were 'around the back' of capitalism and become the basis of a new development towards which capitalist production itself is tending. If this is so, then it 'can cast off its old skin without first committing suicide' (p. 222; see also *ML*, p. 354). In the following year, introducing the second Russian edition of the *Manifesto*, Marx and Engels specify a crucial *political* condition for such a benign social development: 'If the Russian Revolution becomes the signal for a proletarian revolution in the West, so that both complement each other, the present Russian common ownership of land may serve as the starting point for a communist development' (Preface to Second Russian Edition of *CM*, in Taylor, A. J. P., Ed., p. 56). If the capitalist world is not thrown into disarray in some such manner, then it is likely that the commune will fall to a 'conspiracy of powerful interests': the state in league with the capitalists, and the large landowners keen to replace the commune partly by mortgaged peasant-proprietors and partly by landless rural wage-labourers. 'And how can the village community resist, if it is stamped under foot by the exactions of the state, pillaged by commerce, exploited by large landowners, internally sapped by usury?' (p. 224).

'*Stages*' *and historical necessity*

Marx concludes that what threatens Russia is this coalition of hostile forces, and 'neither historical necessity, nor a social theory' (*ibid.*). It is on this very same issue that, a few years earlier, he had registered his most explicit disavowal of any claim to have discovered an 'iron law of history'. N. K. Mikhailovsky, a Russian revolutionary of the *Narodnik* group, had written a review of *Capital* in which he claimed that Marx had discovered and propounded just such a law, and that he also concluded from it that Russia must inevitably develop towards capitalism along Western European lines. Marx replied that what he had done in the section on 'Primitive Accumulation' in '*Capital* I (see pp. 147–9 above) was no more than 'trace the path by which, in Western Europe, the capitalist economic system emerged from the womb of the feudal economic system' (*ML*, p. 293). He went on to quote a short passage from the French edition of 1873, where indeed this historical process is specifically assigned to 'the countries of Western Europe' (*ML*, p. 293); he quoted the same passage in the short letter which he actually did send Zasulich (*ZL*, p. 319). Blackstock and Hoselitz refer to the 'problem' that this restriction to Western Europe occurs only in the French edition, and that Marx did not incorporate it in, for example, the Russian edition which Mikhailovsky was reviewing (see Blackstock and Hoselitz, pp. 279–81). The answer is fairly simple: Roy's French translation 'did not come up to Marx's high expectations and he found himself having to rewrite whole sentences and even pages' (McLellan 1973, p. 421). In the course of revising the translation Marx also reworked many details of the argument, so that he declared that the work had 'a scientific value independent of the original' ('Postface to French edition', in *Capital* I, Harmondsworth 1976, p. 105). Marx was not so intimately involved with any other edition of Capital I after the original German one of 1867, complaining that work for the International had kept him from working on the substance of the Russian one as he would have liked (see McLellan 1973, p. 420). Blackstock and Hoselitz are thus well justified in their claim that there is not 'a contradiction or inconsistency in Marx's thought' on this point (p. 280); he was simply employing the one edition in which he had had the opportunity to enter a new qualification to his theory, and its absence from other editions is explicable. He absolutely rejects Mikhailovsky's attempt to metamorphose his

historical sketch of the genesis of capitalism in Western Europe into a historico-philosophical theory of the *marche générale* (general path) imposed by fate upon every people, whatever the historic circumstances in which it finds itself . . . events strikingly analogous but taking place in different historical surroundings [lead] to totally different results. By studying each of these forms of evolution separately and then comparing them one can easily find the clue to this phenomenon, but one will never arrive there by the universal passport of a general historico-philosophical theory, the supreme virtue of which consists in being super-historical. (*ML*, pp. 354, 355).

But dispelling the 'Blackstock and Hoselitz problem' does not settle every issue. In what he says about Russia, Marx certainly observes his early injunction to bring out 'empirically, and without any mystification and speculation, the connection of the social and political structure with production' (*GI*, p. 37; see p. 207 above). The problem is to reconcile this approach with other things which he says. For example, he tells the smug German reader of the analysis of British conditions that '*de te fabula narratur*' (Preface to First Edition, *Capital* I, p. xvii). What his later discussion of Russia shows is that we must add to our reflections on the 'necessity' of capitalist development (see pp.

160ff. above) a further qualification that that kind of necessity operates *within* a given mode of production, and not *between* modes. It is interesting, indeed, that even in 1867 Marx twice refers explicitly to 'Continental Western Europe' when he argues that 'the country that is more developed industrially only shows, to the less developed, the image of its own future.' (see *Capital* I, pp. xvii and xviii). The restrictions introduced in the French edition were, evidently, not absent from his mind even then. Marx seems to believe that a country such as Russia has a kind of freedom, in certain circumstances, to choose which of a range (or perhaps no more than a pair) of modes to adopt. The question arises of reconciling the relative freedom of 'ideology' or 'consciousness' implied by such a choice with the central role of the economy as outlined on p. 210 above. Marx can still argue that the country in question, while having freedom in *that* respect, cannot develop a particular one of these modes without accommodating its ideology, law and politics to that mode's requirements. In the first place, then, he can argue that Russia has 'the finest chance ever offered by history to a nation [not] to undergo all the fatal vicissitudes of the capitalist regime'. In the second place, however, he can also argue that if she does continue along the capitalist path 'she will not succeed without having transformed a good part of her peasants into proletarians; and after that, once taken to the bosom of the capitalist regime, she will experience its pitiless law like other profane peoples' (*ML*, pp. 353, 354). I do not mean to suggest that Marx necessarily turned out to be *right* about Russia; simply, that what he says about her freedom of choice is theoretically compatible with the insistence on the central role of the economy, even while it relaxes some of the constraints which seem to follow from that role.

Politics: its nature, origin and demise

Marx did not produce a general theory of politics, any more than he produced a general theory of human history. But the material which we have discussed on communal property also gives us indications of what he thinks of 'politics as such', and this section will deal with them. This treatment will put the more detailed discussion of modern politics in previous chapters into its wider context, and show us what elements of a Marxist account of politics in general can be gleaned from Marx's own writings. We shall distinguish, as does Marx, between politics and government. *Government* is the running of the general affairs of any collectivity: primitive commune, class-society or mature communism. *Politics* is that specific kind of government which is found in class-societies, and is absent from primitive and mature communism. Sometimes Marx and Engels present this distinction as being between 'government' and 'administration', but I shall maintain the first version of it. There are problems as to whether this is a meaningful distinction, and also as to whether if so it applies to the cases to which Marx applies it, and we shall return to these later. For the moment we are interested in how Marx treats the government of class-society, and why he insists on calling it distinctively political.

Politics and divided society

The decline of the primitive commune which we studied in the preceding section is described by Morgan as the emergence of civilisation. 'Civilisation' denotes the new individuation and complexity which shatter the primitive 'substance' of the commune. Marx picks up Morgan's assertion that politics 'first emerges with civilisation' (*EN*, p. 143). In view of the preceding discussion it will not be surprising that *property* is regarded as a central feature of the transition:

> Greek society comes first under notice about first Olympiad (776 B.C.) and from then until Cleisthenes' legislation (509 B.C.) proceeds transition from gentile to political (civil) organisation...Property was the new element that had been gradually remoulding Grecian institutions to prepare for this change. (*EN*, pp. 196–7; see also p. 207)

The increasing influence of property and the resultant differences between rich and poor made the gentile constitution increasingly irrelevant. Marx traces the various attempts to re-classify people, from which gradually evolved the articulation into *classes* distinguished by amount and type of property (see e.g., pp. 210 and 215). For our discussion we may broadly distinguish an *owning class* who receive, and a *working class* who provide, the goods of the society ('working class' here, of course, being a historically wider category than the modern proletariat). Once there is such a division, the mode of governing the society can no longer be isomorphic with its social organisation, since there is now a social group who, if they had governmental power, would use it to introduce fundamentally new rules. Engels tells us that in this situation:

Only one thing was missing: an institution that would not only safeguard the newly-acquired property of private individuals against the communistic traditions of the gentile order, would not only sanctify private property, formerly held in such light esteem, and pronounce this sanctification the highest purpose of human society, but would also stamp the gradually developing new forms of acquiring property, and consequently, of constantly accelerating increase in wealth, with the seal of general public recognition; an institution that would perpetuate, not only the newly-rising class-division of society, but also the right of the possessing class to exploit the non-possessing classes and the rule of the former over the latter. And this institution arrived. The *state* was invented. (*OFPPS*, p. 528)

This illustrates the important point that the state's functions are more than direct protection/repression, in the physical sense at least. The state also sustains the ideology by which the working class believe that they are getting an adequate share of the society's goods or that their failure to do so is due to ill-luck, personal unworthiness, or some such explanation. This may well be a kind of repression, but only in the sense of keeping certain ideas outside their heads, and it operates without physical compulsion. A similar duality of state functions *vis-à-vis* the working class also emerges from the *German Ideology* account of how the power of the members of the owning class 'is based on conditions of life which as they develop are common to many individuals, and the continuance of which they, as ruling individuals, have to uphold against others and, at the same time, maintain as holding good for all' (*GI*, p. 366; translation amended from *MEW* III, p. 311). From these arguments it is clear that the state is to be conceived as an instrumentality of class rule. But as we have seen throughout this book, there is the problem that states do not always operate in quite this role. It is then open to the Marxist to invoke what in chapter 1 we called the 'chronological succession overview', and attribute the state's non-servility to the fact that we are in an interregnum between social formations and there is thus no single dominant class in society (see pp. 24–7 above). But we have seen in the course of our study that there can be cases of non-servile states which are not so plausibly to be put down to 'delayed succession', arising as they do *within* an established social formation. Such cases are much harder to handle on the view that the state is unproblematically an instrument of class rule: we have to throw up our hands and admit an exception, or else deny the data.

There is however another account which asserts the same connection – between politics and class society – but in a more complex way. I shall refer to the two as the 'simple' and 'complex' accounts for brevity. It is very important to make it clear that the complex account in no way tries to minimise the centrality of class in Marx's analysis, nor does it try to identify political and other alienations with 'the human condition' as Marxists rightly refuse to do. But it differs from the simple account in that rather than using 'mode of production', 'social formation' and 'class' as its ultimate building bricks, so to speak, it sees them as forms given by economic development to a more basic 'material', which is alienated human activity. A vital category in this complex account is that of the *division of labour*. To Marx, this means something much more fundamental than Adam Smith's stages of pin-making. It refers to the way in which, once the 'strong but narrow' bonds of the primitive commune have been transcended, society takes on the form of a complex of unco-ordinated individual activities, where each individual follows the logic of his particular situation, and nobody has an overall plan of the totality. We must guard against a reductionist individualism here. Marx does not believe that post-communal history is a perpetual war of all against all. The whole point of his sociological materialism is to show that it consists of 'a coherent series of forms of intercourse' (*GI*, p. 90). There is a series of forms of intercourse because, in any interregnum, certain individuals acquire resources which compel other individuals either to starve or to work for them: in this way a mode of production and a social formation crystallise. But while these structures, and thus the correlative classes, are real and far from accidental 'emergences', it is still true that they do *emerge*, and are not just to be presupposed. They tyrannise the individuals bound by them because, and only because, 'the individuals, whose forces they are, exist split up and in opposition to one another' (*GI*, p. 83) (see pp. 14–18 above). What is of central importance to us is the fact that 'division of labour' is a general and negative characteristic of *all* post-communal history: it is the reason why there *is* no overall plan in the sense of a conscious regulation, and why the only 'plan' which emerges is the historically transient and partial coherence imposed by the needs of economic production. Having given us an account of the tensions and contradictions of this history, Marx and Engels tell us that 'all these contradictions are implicit' in the division of labour in this broad sense (*GI*, p. 44).

Before discussing the relevance to politics of this complex account, I must answer the obvious objection that my presentation of it is based solely on the *German Ideology*, and that there is no evidence of Marx's having held it later in his life. I believe that it is impossible to sustain this objection in the face of ethnological material which we have already encountered in this chapter. In the *Grundrisse*, the *Ethnological Notebooks* and elsewhere, Marx constantly emphasises the contrast between stable, 'transparent' communal life, and post-communal life, where competition, individual wealth, 'ruse and accident' are the rule. This, and no more than this, is what I mean by stressing the division of labour; in the later as in the earlier works Marx regards structure as something emerging from this flux of unco-ordinated activity, but achieving no lasting city until the communist revolution abolishes history in this sense. Of course he never minimises the role of class, but he does not regard even the dominant, the owning class as being 'in charge' of history: it is no more than a contingent ordering (however pertinacious) of the alienated human activity which is the stuff of history. As well as these clear indications of continuity, there is the supporting evidence of Engels's work, written under the influence of Marx's ethnological notes within a year of Marx's death. Engels, who consulted the *German Ideology* in the course of writing the work (see *OFPPS*, p. 494), tells us that the gentile constitution was 'burst asunder by the division of labour and by *its result, the division of society into classes*' (p. 575; emphasis added).

We may then place Marx's account of politics in general in this broader context, and when we do so some important complexities follow. Firstly there is a general truth which holds for all members of the collectivity. This is, that there is a distinction, and the constant possibility of an opposition, between an individual's interest and that of the collectivity:

the division of labour implies the contradiction between the interest of the separate individual or the individual family and the communal interest of all individuals who have intercourse with one another . . . Just because individuals seek *only* their particular interest, which for them does not coincide with their communal interest (in fact the general is the illusory form of communal life), the latter will be imposed on them as an interest 'alien' to them, and 'independent' of them. (*GI*, pp. 44, 46)

In other words, unlike the pattern of activity within communal society, the rules of post-communal society are rules with which the interests of its members come into conflict. Presumably Marx does not deny that such a conflict is *possible* in the commune; we shall see in the case of the criminal that it in fact emerges. But he could answer that in fact in communal society, in almost all cases, this tension between the general rules necessary for the collectivity's survival and the opportunities open to its individual members has not emerged to the light of day, and that will do for our purposes. It certainly has emerged in post-communal society, and that is why that society needs a separate centre of authority which is able to *impose* the rules on the individuals. It is central that this necessity for imposed rules holds *even of the members of the owning class*. But there is of course a vast difference between their and the working class's relation to that imposition. What the owning class has imposed on it are rules which, if they obey them, will advantage their representative member. The working class have imposed on them rules which, even if they scrupulously obey them, will disadvantage their representative member. Thus the conception of the necessity for a state within post-communal society has a two-fold significance, which Krader brings out well:

The separation of private rights within one and the same social class thus calls for a dual activity of the State: the first is the subordination of all social classes to the organ of control of one, in which the political power is now formed and concentrated; at the same time, the State acts as the organ for the suppression of the opposed private rights and interests within the propertied class. (Krader, p. 67).

This more complex perspective explains some crucial instances of state non-servility towards the owning class, but not quite in the way that might be expected. It would be ridiculous to infer from the fact that the state has a 'ruling-class cohesion' function in relation to the owning class, directly to the conclusion that it therefore can become pretentious towards it. We have already seen Marx's argument that the power of the state over the *individual member* of the owning class is radically distinct from power over the *class as such* (see p. 23 above). What is relevant about the 'ruling-class cohesion' function is that it symptomises the fact that the owning class themselves are part of an 'unplanned', an alienated world. For that reason, they have need of the unwieldy instrument of a state separate from themselves, in order both to ensure their hegemony over the working class and to preserve their own cohesion. The fact that that state even in normal times has authority over individual members of the owning class is a symptom of the general alienation between social class and political power, but in itself could never account for a pretentious or dominant state. The owning class, as it were, own the theatre, but they do not write the script – indeed there *is* no settled script – so that the drama frequently gets out of hand. This is chiefly because there is a section of the chorus who want a completely different production, and are acquiring the power to impose it. There has thus to be a management which is capable in times of crisis of imposing its will on everyone in the enterprise to keep it from disruption, and which in peaceful times can sustain the chorus's illusion of having a real say in what happens. The 'unmanageability' of the overall situation is symptomised, but by no means exhausted, by the fact that the owners' internal squabbles also force them to rely on the management to maintain their own cohesion.

The simple account correlates politics with class, and claims that the state will normally be a servant of the owning class; when this does not happen it either invokes a delayed succession or admits an exception. The complex account can make the same correlation, and can explain the same cases as can the simple one. But it can explain some of the cases which the simple account has to admit as exceptions. Marx conveys a central feature of the complex account in his image of the bourgeois state as 'no more than a reciprocal assurance of the bourgeoisie against its individual members and against the exploited class' (*NRZ-Revue*, April 1850, in *MEW* VII, p. 288) (see p. 23 above). The complex account recognises that precisely because of the 'unplanned' and 'unmanageable' nature of divided society, the owning class can find itself in a situation where the conflict with the working class requires that the state – the 'insurance company' – be given power not only over the individual owning-class members, but over the owning *class* as such, as the only way of meeting the political challenge of the subject class. In the article just quoted, indeed, Marx notes how the insurance company 'must become ever more expensive and apparently ever more independent *vis-à-vis* civil society, as the suppression of the exploited class becomes constantly more difficult' (*ibid.*).

There are at least two important objections to this whole line of argument. The first is that it has rendered the theory unfalsifiable, by expanding it to encompass all conceivable counter-evidence. The 'division of labour' here might look suspiciously like an intellectual 'hold-all', to catch the fragments when the politics/class correlation fails. This is a salutary objection, but not a conclusive one. In the first place, my invocation of the division of labour is intended to do no more than point to a range of factors which should be included in explanations of state postures: those involved in the generally 'unplanned' character of post-communal society. It is not put forward as a simple explanation in its own right. In the second place, while the theory, on the complex account, allows us to expect and explain more cases of non-servile states, it will still exclude, and be falsified by the occurrence of, certain cases. It does not re-interpret Marx along the lines simply that 'the state might be servile, or might not, and either will do', which would be a fairly useless theory. What it does is to retain the central claim that the standard posture of the state will be servile, while understanding more of the factors making for non-servility than does the simple account. Even in the extra cases which it allows for, it does not abandon the central claim about servility. If for example a state to which the owning class had temporarily submitted succeeded in maintaining its independence of the owning class, then even on the complex account Marx's theory would be falsified.

The second objection is that I am saying here not what Marx said but what I think he ought to have said. My study has, I hope, made it quite clear that Marx very often makes claims about politics which reflect the simple rather than the complex account, and often does not allow of the ways in which things can rebound on the owning class. But the study has shown, in the case of the complex account and of the closely related 'structural contradiction overview' (see pp. 24–7 above), that there is in Marx's own writings, although he frequently ignored or was unaware of it, the basis of a wider and more complicated view which manages

both to make some of his central assertions and to take more
cognisance of the contradictions of reality. My treatment has not
sought to do more than to show up the tensions which arise for
the simple account and the 'chronological succession overview',
and to suggest that many of Marx's basic claims can be retained,
and made more plausible, within a more complicated position the
basis of which is in fact discernible within his own writings.

Government and communal society

In this section I shall argue that Marx's distinction between
government in general and politics is fairly plausible for primitive
communal society as he depicts it. I shall argue that it is also more
plausible than is sometimes allowed as regards mature communist
society, but that there are some questions which cast doubt on
the claim that mature communist government will *assuredly* be
non-political, and that Marx does not adequately meet these
questions.

We have already seen that Marx believes that in primitive
communal society there is no built-in antagonism between individual and collective interest. We shall have reason later on to
consider the case of the individual criminal, but we shall grant
Marx the assumption that, short of individual criminals, people
in general do not perceive a distinction nor *a fortiori* a clash
between their own and the collective interest. It must however
be noted, since it will be important later, that the reason for this
state of affairs, as Marx himself notes on a number of occasions,
is to be attributed to the *lack of development* in both individuals
and community. With these qualifications, however, we may grant
him his 'identity of interest' between primitive individual and
commune. It then becomes plausible to distinguish the running of
this kind of society from what we call politics, on the grounds that
it is a case of genuine *self-government*, where the members of
the commune are not subject to a centre of authority outside
themselves. It is of course possible to define a set of questions
which are *general* or *collective* ones, and which can be distinguished from the question of, for example, how long someone may
grow their hair, how clean they keep their hut and the like. What
distinguishes non-political government is that these general
questions are genuinely settled by the agreement of everyone, and
there is nobody on whom a decision is imposed (excepting, as we

shall for the moment, the criminal). It is however difficult to believe that everyone will always agree with every decision in such a society; surely there will at least sometimes be minorities who are defeated on a vote or by some similar procedure. Marx gives little attention to this problem, although he mentions that 'unanimity was a fundamental law' in the Iroquois Council (*EN*, p. 162). Perhaps he feels that where I am overruled simply by a specific temporary majority of my peers after being heard by them, I am not oppressed (for fuller discussion, see Plamenatz 1975, chapter 14). For purposes of argument, we may grant that in communist society, except in the case of the criminal, 'self-government' is attained at least in these terms. Marx notes that the system of such a commune is 'purely social' (*EN*, p. 184). He devotes a lot of attention to Morgan's depiction (in *Ancient Society*) of the gentile system of government:

Where gentile institutions prevailed – and prior to the establishment of political society – we find peoples or nations in gentile societies and nothing beyond. 'The state did not exist' (p. 67). As the *gens*, the unit of organisation, was *essentially democratical*, so necessarily the *phratry* composed of gentes, the *tribe* composed of phratries, and the gentile society formed by the *confederations* or (what is a higher form) coalescing of tribes [were also democratic]. (*EN*, p. 144)

This 'democratical' system did not, it seems, exclude the existence of some distinct holders of governmental offices: there were people whose particular job it was to perform governmental tasks. But there was nobody who was excluded for any reason from holding one of these offices, and they were strictly subject to election and recall: even when, in emergencies, a tribe needed to defend itself from external aggression, and relied temporarily on a 'head chief', this was 'in a *form too feeble* to correspond *to the conception of an executive magistrate*. The *elective tenure of the office of chief*, and the *liability of the person to deposition*, settle the character of the office' (p. 163). It is very significant for this 'purely social' system that the government, in the analytical sense in which it could be distinguished from the people not holding government offices 'dealt with persons through their relations to a gens or tribe...Thereafter comes political organisation, founded upon territory and property; here government deals with persons through their relations to territory, as for example the township, the county, and the state' (p. 143). The government, in communal society, is simply the particular part of the whole social system which deals with general questions, at successive levels of generality.

Ordinary affairs adjusted through the chiefs; those of general interest submitted to the determination of the council, and the council sprang from the gentile organisation...Gens represented by its chiefs. Tribe represented by the council of the chiefs of the gentes. Called together under circumstances known to all, held in the midst of the people, open to their orators, it was certain to act under popular influence...Right of gentes to elect and depose sachems and chiefs, right of the people to be heard in council through orators of their election, and the voluntary system in the military service. In this lower and middle ethnical period democratic principles were the vital element of gentile society. (*EN*, pp. 150, 162, 172).

We are not entitled simply to say that this material represents 'Marx's view of primitive government': it is no more than what interested Marx in *Morgan's* account of the matter. But Marx, never slow to register dissent in these notebooks, does not do so here, and we may take the topics covered as broadly indicating what he thought characteristic of pre-political government. Those who happen to hold government positions are subject to election and recall, the only reason for their holding the positions being that they were chosen for them by people equal to them in every other respect. There is no concept of 'subversion', as no change of governmental personnel would bring about a change in the running of the system.

Our chief interest anyhow is not in these indications for their own sake, but for the light which they throw on Marx's ideas about *post*-political government in communist society. Marx was consistently reluctant to 'paint the future', but we can work out some broad lines of how he thought communist society would work (see McLellan 1971, part two, chapter 8, and Evans, pp. 158–63). Although he warned against it as premature beforehand, and identified himself with it more out of general loyalty than out of theoretical conviction, Marx did see in the *tendencies* of the Paris Commune of 1871 certain of these broad lines, especially in the area of government (see Avineri, pp. 239–49). One of these tendencies is very closely linked to the nature of pre-political government: the tendency to abolish the state, that is, government in the sense in which it exists over against the social order (see *CWF*, pp. 70–3). Not only can the working class not achieve their aims through the *bourgeois* state; even the 'workers' state' which they evolve in making the revolution must be the agent of its own destruction (see pp. 164–7 above).

In his polemic against Bakunin Marx answers the question whether all 40 million Germans will be members of the government with: 'Certainly! (For the whole thing begins with the self-government of the Commune.)' When Bakunin says that then there will be no one to be governed Marx replies 'According to this principle, when a man rules himself, he does not rule himself, since is he not only himself and no one else?' (*NB*, p. 108). We have already noted in the previous chapter that Bakunin makes some very telling points about post-revolutionary government, and we shall return to some of them in the remainder of this chapter. For the moment, however, I want to bring out the fact that Marx's conception of 'everybody's participation in self-government' is less naive than these replies to Bakunin sound, and is in fact in many ways parallel to Morgan's account of pre-political government. We may begin by noting a highly sophisticated argument from the 1843 *Critique* of Hegel. Although the 'truly human society' which Marx envisaged in 1843 may not simply be identi-fied with his later theory of communism, his early argument about the nature of government in the 'ideal' society throws useful light on his later conceptions.

The question of whether civil society should participate in the legislature either by entering it through deputies or by the direct participation of all as individuals is itself a question within the abstraction of the political state or within the abstract political state; it is an abstract political question. (*CHPR*, p. 117)

Marx rejects this separation between 'political state' and concrete society, saying that if people really are members of the state, 'then it is obvious that their social existence is already their actual participation in it' (*ibid.*). But if social existence is directly participation in the affairs of the community – as it will be after the abolition of the state/society distinction – then I am no longer diminished or dominated by the fact that some of my community's members carry out specifically governmental functions: 'if we are talking about definite concerns . . . then it is obvious that not all as individuals accomplish them. Otherwise, the individual would be the true society, and would make society superfluous. The individual would have to do everything at once, while society would have him act for others just as it would have others act for him' (p. 118). I need certain people to look after general governmental matters just as I need dentists, bakers, and shoe-makers. All of these people 'represent' me, but not in the alienated sense of participating instead of me in an alien polity:

For example, the shoemaker is my representative insofar as he fulfills a social need, just as every definite social activity, because it is a species-activity, represents only the species; that is to say, it represents a determination of my own essence the way every man is the represen-tative of the other. Here, he is representative not by virtue of something other than himself which he represents, but by virtue of what he is and does. (pp. 119-20)

In another work of the same period, Marx condemns represen-tation as 'something passive', distinguishing it from the ideal of 'the people's *self-representation*' (*OCEP*, in *MECW* I, p. 306). On either reading of his attitude to representation, what will happen in communist society is that certain people will carry out govern-mental tasks as peers performing a service for me, in the same way as a shoemaker for example 'works for' me now (overlooking the fact that he has in current society little or no choice as to whether or not he shall be a shoemaker). It is in the same spirit, and for the same reasons, that Marx nearly thirty years later praises the tendency of the Paris Commune to turn all govern-mental functions into direct channels of self-government: 'Public functions ceased to be the private property of the tools of the Central Government. Not only municipal administration, but the whole initiative hitherto exercised by the State was laid into the hands of the Commune' (*CWF*, p. 73).

Marx's treatment of the place of public officials in the Commune shows at least an implicit awareness of some of the problems of post-political government. The tendency for the exercise of central and influential functions to lead to pretentiousness on the part of the official is counteracted by the fact that all of them were 'turned into the responsible and at all times revocable agents of the Commune...From the members of the Commune down-wards, the public service had to be done at *workmen's wages*. The vested interests and the representation allowances of the high dignitaries of State disappeared along with the high dignitaries themselves' (*ibid.*).

But Marx's confidence about communist government is

grounded less in the perequisites of public officials, or lack thereof, than in the kind of overall function which they will have to perform in society. They will not dominate society because society will no longer need to be dominated. There will no longer be antagonistic divisions within the social order, and thus there will be no need for an external power to impose society's order on itself. The kind of social order in which people will live – both predictable and co-operative – will not necessitate authoritarian government, and thus there will be no 'niche' for authoritarian pretensions to flourish in. In the language of games theorists, running society will henceforth be a *co-operation* rather than a *competition* problem, in which everyone is committed to finding a generally satisfactory outcome. In this respect, we should note an important although often unnoticed development in Marx's thinking. There is a wildly utopian early version of communism as 'the genuine resolution of the conflict between man and nature, and between man and man . . . [which] is the solution of the riddle of history, and knows itself to be the solution' (*EPM*, p. 348). But by the time he comes to write the Manifesto, Marx's presentation of communism is a less millenarian one. He defines it not as the abolition of all distinctions, but as the abolition of private property in the means of production:

When, therefore, capital is converted into common property, into the property of all members of society, personal property is not thereby transformed into social property. It is only the social character of the property that is changed. It loses its class character . . . Communism deprives no man of the power to appropriate the products of society; all that it does is to deprive him of the power to subjugate the labour of others by means of such appropriation. (*CM*, pp. 81, 82)

This is of course still a fundamental economic revolution – or even an 'abolition of economics' – but the point is that, rather than resolving every tension in history, communism is now conceived as *initiating* a whole new history of variety and diversity, where the individual rather than capital will be 'independent' and have 'individuality' (*CM*, p. 81). It is significant, although it should not be over-emphasised, in this context that in the later '1859 *Preface*' Marx defines communism as the abolition of bourgeois relations of production, which are

the last antagonistic form of the social process of production – antagonistic not in the sense of individual antagonism, but of one arising from the social conditions of life of the individuals . . . This social formation brings, therefore the pre-history of human society to a close. (*CCPE*, pp. 21–2)

It is difficult in capitalist society to take one type of dispute and call it 'social' as distinct from another called 'individual', and this is not what Marx is doing here. What he means is that in post-communist society there may well be antagonisms, but these will be genuinely between the individuals involved, because of personal characteristics, rather than because of the built-in antagonism of socially-imposed roles. In this sense there is a reasonable argument that where the social order itself does not regularly and necessarily throw up antagonisms between groups of individuals, there will be no need for the kind of *authoritarian intervention* without which divided society could not function. In this sense we may argue that the *functions* of government will be less conducive to pretensions on the part of office-holders than they are in divided societies.

But now we must return to the case of the *criminal*. It is interesting that Marx notes in his work on Morgan how the gentile system dealt with cases of murder (*EN*, pp. 154, 204). It is not surprising that in pre-political society there were some individuals who for one reason or another rejected the established ways of doing things. It also follows from the accent on individual diversity, even individual antagonism, in Marx's presentation of post-political communism, that there will probably be such cases there too. The question then arises whether the power which government will need to exercise over criminals in any form of society does not imply *politics* of a kind. The difficulty is to isolate some difference which makes the relation of the state to the owning-class criminal *political*, while leaving that of the commune to its criminal member merely *governmental*. We might say that there is a difference, in that in the latter case the crime is not happening in a divided society, but that begs the question of what the difference is. The difference between the communal criminal and the *working*-class criminal is fairly clear. But do not the communal criminal and the owning-class criminal have imposed on them standards which, if they observe them, will advantage them, and do they not both reject such standards? We might concede that the relation of the state to the owning-class criminal is governmental, and use other features to distinguish politics in divided society from government in communal society.

Or, we could concede that the relation is inherently governmental, but argue that attendant circumstances in divided society – the fact that the government is political *vis-à-vis* the working class, and thus is 'distant' from society as a communal government is not – make the relation as it were 'political by contagion'. Or, finally, we could argue that the relation was in fact inherently political rather than governmental in divided societies because the standards of even the owning class in divided society are significantly less 'internal' to its members than are those of communal society to everybody (see pp. 20ff. and 226ff. above). The answer is probably a combination of the second and third of these lines of argument. The relation is less straight-forward in divided than in communal society. if we make the (irreducibly normative) judgement that there are in principle certain standards which a reasonable man *ought to* accept, and those of communal society are more clearly of such a nature than those of the owning class in divided society. But this peculiarity is not in itself sufficient to make an important difference between the two cases; it is the additional fact of the state's political relation to the working class which as it were 'contextualises' its government of individual owning-class members as politics rather than self-government. I would not claim that the above resolves the question: it is intended to show a problem about the distinction which Marx wants to draw.

A quantitative extension of this case raises a qualitatively new problem: whether there would not emerge in communist society some group anxious to seize control of other people's means of production, and in that way to subject and exploit them. These might be die-hard reactionaries, or else products of that 'innate urge to power' which is sometimes adduced as a criticism of the Marxian doctrine. On the question of an 'innate urge' the Marxist could reasonably answer that we find out about innate factors only by removing environmental ones, and that his experiment is thus still rationally defensible. As to the success of such a group – whatever its provenance – he would presumably argue that since control over economic resources was publicly and universally shared, it would be impossible for it simply to seize them; the numbers and power of the people opposing it would make the project absurd. This empirical argument is a cogent one, although in the nature of things it can hardly be 'knockdown'.

But there is a final and much more important question about communist government. At a number of points in this chapter we have noted that Marx regards primitive communism as *undeveloped*, and attributes much of its harmony to this fact. But the communism which will come with the end of class society will be one built on a sophisticated and complex prior development. It is clear that not all the division and articulation of activity will be abolished by the abolition of ownership of the means of production. Marx cannot believe this, since then communism would be a regression rather than a progress. In other words, it seems likely that aspects of the division of labour are going to survive into communist society. In our discussion of class society, we presented the division of labour as, so to speak, 'parallelling' as well as underlying the existence of classes; but here we would have it continuing on its own after the classes are abolished. It would take more than a full chapter to rehearse the contents and the complexities of the debate on the possibility of alienation in communist society (see Mandel 1971, chapter 11, and Plamenatz 1975, esp. pp. 169–72). Suffice it to say that it is very definitely a matter of argument rather than definition, and the case is far from closed. This raises the possibility that the sheer size and complexity of issues to be resolved in a communist economy, as against the specialised skills and experience of each citizen, could give to government the political character of being alien and authoritarian. On this point, it is interesting that in their account of the original emergence of politics with civilisation, neither Marx nor Engels makes property *alone* responsible. Marx follows Morgan in paying attention to the way in which the need for defence and aggression against other collectivities evolved the office of *basileus* or *rex* which, while not identical with a modern 'king' or 'executive' had a 'tendency to usurp additional powers' (*EN*, p. 207). Engels recounts how the gentile constitution developed from 'an organisation of tribes for the free administration of their own affairs' to 'an organisation for plundering and oppressing their neighbours; and correspondingly its organs were transformed from instruments of the will of the people into independent organs for ruling and oppressing their own people' (*OFPPS*, pp. 571–2). Although Engels says that class-divisions within the gens were a *condition* for this to happen, the two are not identical. In this context the case of oriental despotism is crucial. We have already seen (see p. 215 above) that that social formation is unusual in combining a distinct state-organisation with communal property of a kind which is 'not yet a class society, or if it is a class society, then it is the most primitive form' (Hobsbawm, p. 34). What is significant here is that even if there are no classes at all in this social formation, its way of life necessitates intervention by a distinct state; we are close to a 'politics' based on division of labour (in the broad sense) but not on classes. In this context we may not overlook an argument which occurs in *Anti-Dühring*, written by Engels at Marx's behest, and which Marx had read to him in manuscript form. In this work, Engels tells us that the state, 'which the primitive groups of communities of the same tribe had at first arrived at *only in order to safeguard their common interests* (e.g., irrigation in the East)' (p. 179; emphasis added) and for external protection, *acquired* the function of regulating a class-system; there is a very similar argument on pp. 214–15 of the work. It would be extremely rash to infer that Marx and Engels would therefore allow of a politics based on division of labour but not on classes, but the problems of their conception of mature communism, allied with these indications on the emergence of early politics, raise some fundamental theoretical problems. For the moment, we may conclude by saying that it is probable that the only secure solution to these difficulties will be the extent to which communism, rather than simply recasting the economy in a communal form, will in fact create free time for real individuality, and build the realm of real freedom on its conquest of the problem of necessity (see *Capital* III, pp. 799–800).

Conclusion

This chapter began with a brief discussion of Marx's historical materialism. This did not rebut the charges frequently made against that theory, but briefly indicated an interpretation of it which seems more likely to meet them. The reason for this brief discussion was to situate Marx's treatment of politics within its broader theoretical context. The rest of the chapter looked at what indications of Marx's views about 'politics in general' could be gleaned from the extensive ethnographical material which he produced. The chief theme of that material is the shattering of original communism by the growth of private property and resultant class divisions. Marx sees these divisions as the reason for the emergence of politics, i.e. of alien government. His rather pessimistic estimation of the chances of survival of the contemporary Russian commune is discussed, as well as the relatively flexible approach to historical necessity which that estimation appears to imply. In the context of this ethnographic material, the correlation between a distinct state structure and the dominant class in society – the central theme of the whole of Marx's political theory – is discussed anew. It is argued that as well as the simple correlation, there is also latent in Marx a more complex one which can handle more of reality but at the price of greater flexibility. The chapter closes with an account of Marx's distinction between politics and proper communal self-government, and an indication of some difficulties which arise for his expectations on that score.

Conclusion

In 1863 Marx re-read Engels's *The Condition of the Working-Class in England*, and wrote to him thus:

How freshly and passionately, with what bold anticipations and no learned and scientific doubts, matters are treated here! And the very illusion that the result too will leap into the daylight of history tomorrow or the day after gives the whole thing a warmth and high-spirited humour – compared with which the later 'gray in gray' makes a damned unpleasant contrast. (9 April 1863, in *MESC*, p. 131)

The comment serves as a good epitaph for all the harsh optimism of their early years. We have seen that even in those years, though he may have been unaware of it, Marx's theory contained some buried mines, and that these exploded into history in 1848. We have seen how this led Marx to take a more complex view of the explanation of political action than he had thought necessary before 1848, and that the setbacks of bourgeois politics in that year initiated a 'loss of faith in the bourgeoisie' and a more central insistence that only the proletariat could make sense of history; Marx however did not let this change in perspective tempt him into reactionary anti-bourgeois alliances. We have looked at the role which he assigns to politics within his mature economic theory, and at how that theory grounds his conception of proletarian revolution and his broad principles of strategy.

However much he lost faith in the bourgeoisie, Marx's career coincided only with the beginnings of the organised workers' movement, and if in France he tended to write off the bourgeoisie as a spent force (wrongly, as the Third Republic was to show), in both Britain and Germany he continued to expect that events would force them to become politically radical. This did not happen in either country, as the 'oligarchy' accommodated itself to the needs of Victorian England, and Bismarck rendered an unlikely bourgeois revolution 'unnecessary' by achieving national unification and industrialisation under an authoritarian regime. Marx's claim that the modern state would have to concern itself with the needs of the bourgeois economy is satisfied – although with varying degrees of stringency; his claims about bourgeois control of that state are far less successful.

We have considered the materialist conception of history very briefly, the intention being to characterise it rather than to go into the many criticisms which it has incurred; it serves as the theoretical context of this investigation. A feature of Marx's general ideas which is explored in some detail in the final chapter is his understanding of early societies, and of the communal property and 'democratical government' which he believed to be proper to them. His ideas on the decline of such early communal societies influenced his estimation of the likelihood of Russia's escaping the need for capitalism through the survival of her rural commune. What he said about Russia in both published and unpublished writings suggests that he was prepared to relax some of the 'necessity' of his statements on history and on capitalist development, while maintaining that a nation could not make its social and political development independent of the mode of production (chosen or unchosen) which it was developing.

He often presents the relation between politics and class society in a simple and direct manner which while striking and suggestive cannot handle all the subtleties of the connection between economic and political power. There are in his and Engels' writings the elements of a deeper and more complex approach, emphasising the system of alienation and division of labour of which even the 'ruling class' are a part. That approach can make sense of more phenomena than can the simple one, without becoming so empty and general as to be useless. His distinction between politics and government is plausible although not entirely watertight, and his assurance that communist government will escape all the alienations of politics is open to serious question.

A significant fact about Marx's treatment of politics is the difficulty of summing it up in a few basic general formulae. It says much for his attention to empirical detail that one has to read his actual accounts of events, periods and personalities to catch their full import. Indeed, so far is he from a 'mechanistic' or 'reductionist' approach when he actually deals with concrete problems, that the difficulty is to reconcile what he says about them with the kind of general claim which he wants to maintain. I have presented an interplay between concrete studies and general theory here, although I believe that the modification of the latter did not always keep pace with the ramifications of the former (see Evans, p. 164). While his treatment of politics cannot be spelt out in a few short propositions (for good reasons as well as bad), we are left at least with the following basic elements of the Marxian approach:

(i) a claim about the central role of the economy which, whatever the logical and conceptual problems of the general materialist conception of history, is applicable in the area of politics;

(ii) a set of ideas about revolutionary crisis, the requirements of a successful revolutionary coalition, and the criteria for ‘political foundedness’;

(iii) a claim about modern society, deriving from (i) and (ii), to the effect that industrialisation will impose certain tasks on the political system and give the bourgeoisie control of that system;

(iv) a conception of the place of politics in the genesis, functioning and overthrow of the bourgeois social formation;

(v) an approach to workers’ revolutionary strategy which is informed by (iv); and,

(vi) an understanding of the nature of politics, its relation to class society, and the possibility of overcoming political alienation in communist society which, while leaving important questions unresolved, is suggestive and profound.

Bibliography

This bibliography presents works as they have been referred to in the text – by abbreviated title or author or editor – in alphabetical order. The similarity of so many titles has necessitated a mixture of these two methods in the section on 'Anthologies and Collected Editions' of Marx and Engels.

WORKS OF MARX AND ENGELS

Individual Titles
(unless otherwise specified, by Marx alone)

Anti-Dühring	(Engels) (Moscow, 1975)
ASI	*The Alleged Splits in the International* in *Documents* v, pp. 356–409
BCR	'The Bourgeoisie and the Counter-revolution' in *R1848*, pp. 186–212.
Capital	Volume I (London, 1896) Volume II (Moscow, 1967) Volume III (Moscow, 1962)
CCHPRI	'Contribution to the Critique of Hegel's "Philosophy of Right": Introduction' in *EW*, pp. 243–57
CCPE	*Contribution to the Critique of Political Economy* (London, 1971)
CCT	*The Cologne Communist Trial* Tr. by R. Livingstone (London, 1971)
CFR	'The Constitution of the French Republic Adopted November 4, 1848' in *Notes to the People* Vol. I (London, 1851) pp. 125–30
CGP	'Critique of the Gotha Programme' in *FI*, pp. 339–59
CHPR	*Critique of Hegel's 'Philosophy of Right'* Ed. by J. O'Malley (Cambridge, 1970)
Circular	Circular Letter to Bebel, Liebknecht, Bracke *et al.*, (With Engels) in *FI*, pp. 360–75
CM	*Manifesto of the Communist Party* (with Engels) in *R1848*, pp. 67–98 (Reference is also made to *The Communist Manifesto*, Ed. by A. J. P. Taylor (Harmondsworth, 1967) for the Preface to the Russian Edition.)
CSF	*The Class Struggles in France: 1848 to 1850* in *SE*, pp. 35–142

CWF   *The Civil War in France* in Karl Marx and Friedrich Engels, *Writings on the Paris Commune* Ed. by H. Draper (New York and London, 1971), pp. 51–101

CWF Drafts   First and Second Drafts of *CWF*, in Draper, ed., pp. 103–213

DLTW   'Debates on the Law on Thefts of Wood' in *MECW* I, pp. 224–63

DP   'Draft Plan for a Work on the Modern State' in *GI*, p. 669

D13J   'Der 13. Juni' in *MEW* VI, pp. 527–8

EBLB   *The Eighteenth Brumaire of Louis Bonaparte* in *SE*, pp. 143–249

EN   *The Ethnological Notebooks of Karl Marx* Ed. by L. Krader (Assen, 1974)

EPM   *Economic and Philosphical Manuscripts* in *EW*, pp. 279–400

G   *Grundrisse* Tr. by M. Nicolaus (Harmondsworth, 1973)

Grundrisse   *Grundrisse der Kritik der politischen Okonomie* (Berlin, 1953)

GI   *The German Ideology* (with Engels) (Moscow, 1968)

Herr Vogt   in *MEW* XIV, pp. 385–686

HF   *The Holy Family* (with Engels) Tr. by R. Dixon (Moscow, 1956)

IA   'Inaugural Address of the International Workingmen's Association' in *FI*, pp. 72–81

IDGC   'Instructions to Delegates to the Geneva Congress' in *FI*, pp. 85–94

JA   'June Address to the Communist League' (with Engels) in *R1848*, pp. 331–8

JQ   'The Jewish Question' in *EW*, pp. 211–41

KB   'Konspekt von Bakunins *Staatlichkeit und Anarchie*' in *MEW* XVIII, pp. 599–642 (partially translated as *NB*)

KP   'The King of Prussia and Social Reform' in *EW*, pp. 401–20

KRB   'Der Kommunismus des "Rheinischen Beobachters"' in *MEW* IV, pp. 191–203

LNF   'Louis-Napoleon und Fould' in *MEW* VII, pp. 296–8

MA   'March Address to the Communist League' (with Engels) in *R1848*, pp. 319–30

MCCM   'Moralising Criticism and Critical Morality' in Stenning, pp. 134–70

ML   'Mikhailovsky Letter' in *MESC*, pp. 291–4

MPF   *Manuskripte über die polnische Frage* (The Hague, 1963)

NB   'Marginal Notes on Bakunin' Tr. by H. Mayer in *Etudes de Marxologie* 2 (1959), pp. 91–177 – Cahiers de l'ISEA, 91, Series S, no. 2 (partial translation of *KB*)

NM   'Notes on James Mill', in *EW*, pp. 259–78

NOZ   *Neue Oder-Zeitung*

NRZ   *Neue Rheinische Zeitung*

NYDT   *New York Daily Tribune*

OA   'On Authority' (Engels) in *AAS*, pp. 100–4

OCEP   'On the Commissions of the Estates in Prussia' in *MECW*
            I, pp. 292–306
OFPPS   *The Origin of the Family, Private Property and the State*
            (Engels) in *MESW*, pp. 461–583
PC   *The Principles of Communism* (Engels) (London, 1971)
PCEF   *Pre-capitalist Economic Formations* Ed. by E. Hobs-
            bawm (London, 1964)
PI   'Political Indifferentism' in *Bulletin of the Society for the
            Study of Labour History* No. 20 (Spring 1970), pp. 20–3
PMQ   *The Prussian Military Question* (Engels) in *FI*, pp. 121–46
PP   *The Poverty of Philosophy* (Moscow, 1956)
RCR   *Revolution and Counter-revolution* (Engels) (London,
            1971; misattributed to Marx in this edition)
RG   'Review of Guizot' in *SE*, pp. 250–5
RIPP   'Results of the Immediate Process of Production' in
            Capital, Volume I (Harmondsworth, 1976), pp. 940–1084
RPL   'Rede auf dem Polenmeeting in London am 22. Januar
            1867' in *MEW* XVI, pp. 200–4
SFT   'Speech on the Question of Free Trade', in *PP*, pp. 207–24
SHC   'Speech on the Hague Congress' in *FI*, pp. 323–6
SP   'Speeches on Poland' (two each by Marx and Engels) in
            R1848, pp. 99–108
TF   'Theses on Feuerbach' in *GI*, pp. 659–62
TSV   *Theories of Surplus-Value*
            Vol. I (London, 1969)
            Vol. II (London, 1969)
            Vol. III (London, 1972)
VS   *Vergleichende Studien zur Geschichte des Grundeigentums
            im Nachlaß von Karl Marx* – Marx's notes on Maxim
            Kovalevsky, Ed. by H. P. Harstick (D. Phil. Dissertation,
            Westfälische Wilhelms-Universität zu Münster, 1974)
WI   '*World* Interview' in *FI*, pp. 393–400
WLC   'Wage-labour and Capital' in *MESW*, pp. 70–93
WPP   'Wages, Price and Profit' in *MESW*, pp. 185–226
ZK   'Zirkular gegen Kriege' in *MEW* IV, pp. 3–17
ZL   'Zasulich Letter' in Blackstock and Hoselitz, pp. 278–9
ZL Drafts   Drafts of *ZL*, in Blackstock and Hoselitz, pp. 218–25

                    Anthologies and Collected Editions
AAS   Anarchism and Anarcho-Syndicalism (Moscow, 1972)
AOB   *Articles on Britain* (Moscow, 1971)
            Blackstock, P. W. and Hoselitz B. F., Eds.: *Karl Marx
            and Friedrich Engels – The Russian Menace to Europe*
            (New York, 1952)
            Bottomore, T. B., Ed.: *Karl Marx: Early Writings*
            (London, 1963)
Documents   *Documents of the First International*, 5 Volumes (London,
            n.d.)

EW	*Karl Marx: Early Writings*, Introduction by L. Colletti (Harmondsworth, 1975)
FI	*The First International and After* Ed. by D. Fernbach (Harmondsworth, 1974)
IIQ	*Ireland and the Irish Question* (Moscow, 1971)
IISH	International Institute for Social History (Amsterdam) collection of Marx manuscripts; Series B is of reading notes
MECW	*Marx Engels: Collected Works* (50 Volumes projected; started publication London, 1975)
MESC	*Marx Engels: Selected Correspondence* (Moscow, 1975)
MESW	*Marx Engels: Selected Works* in One Volume (London, 1968)
MEW	*Marx Engels: Werke* 39 Volumes plus 2 supplementary volumes (Berlin, 1956–68)
NRZ	*Articles from the Neue Rheinische Zeitung 1848–9* (Moscow, 1972)
OCM	*On Colonialism and Modernization* Ed. by S. Avineri (New York, 1969)
Oeuvres:	*Économie* Vols. I and II Ed. by M. Rubel (Paris, 1963 and 1968)
R1848	*The Revolutions of 1848* Ed. by D. Fernbach (Harmondsworth, 1973)
RS	*Revolution in Spain* (London, 1939)
SE	*Surveys from Exile* Ed. by D. Fernbach (Harmondsworth, 1973)
Stenning	*K. Marx: Selected Essays* Ed. by H. Stenning (London, 1926)

WORKS BY OTHERS

Avineri, S. *The Social and Political Thought of Karl Marx* (Cambridge, 1968)

Bakunin, M. *Etatisme et Anarchie* in *Archives Bakounine* Vol. III (Leiden, 1967)

Berlin, I. 'Historical Inevitability' in Gardiner, P. (Ed.) *The Philosophy of History* (Oxford, 1974) pp. 161–86

Bindoff, S. T. *Tudor England* (Harmondsworth, 1961)

Bloom, S. F. *The World of Nations* (New York, 1961)

Boon, H. N. 'The Social and Economic Policies of Napoleon III' in Osgood, S. M. (Ed.) *Napoleon III and the Second Empire* (Lexington, and London, 1973)

Chang, S. H. M. *The Marxian Theory of the State* (New York, 1965)

Childe, V. G. *Social Evolution* (London, 1963)

Cobban, A. *A History of Modern France*, 3 Volumes (Harmondsworth, 1965)

    Aspects of the French Revolution (London, 1968)

The Social Interpretation of the French Revolution (Cambridge, 1964)

Cohen, G. A. 'On some Criticisms of Historical Materialism', in *Proceedings of the Aristotelian Society*, Supplementary Volume 44 (1970), pp. 121–42

Cohen, P. S. *Modern Social Theory* (London, 1968)

Collins, H. & Abramsky, C. *Karl Marx and the British Labour Movement* (London, 1965)

De Luna, F. A. *The French Republic under Cavaignac 1848* (Princeton, N.J., 1969)

Duncan, G. *Marx and Mill* (Cambridge, 1973)

Edwards, S. *The Paris Commune 1871* (London, 1971)

Evans, M. *Karl Marx* (London, 1975)

Fernbach, D. Editor's Introductions to *FI, R1848* and *SE*

Fleischer, H. *Marxism and History* (London, 1973)

Giddens, A. *The Class Structure of the Advanced Societies* (London, 1973)

Hamerow, T. S. *Restoration, Revolution, Reaction* (Princeton, N.J., 1958)

Harstick, H. P. *Vergleichende Studien zur Geschichte des Grundeigentums im Nachlaß von Karl Marx* (D. Phil. Dissertation, Münster, 1974)

Hegel, G. W. F. *Hegel's Philosophy of Right* (Oxford, 1967)

Heimann, E. *History of Economic Doctrines* (New York, 1964)

Hindess, B. & Hirst, P. Q. *Pre-Capitalist Modes of Production* (London, 1975)

Hobsbawm, E. Editor's Introduction to *PCEF*

Holborn, H. *A History of Modern Germany 1840–1945* (London, 1969)

Honderich, T. (Ed.) *Essays on Freedom of Action* (London, 1973)

Hunt, R. N. *The Political Ideas of Marx and Engels* (Pittsburgh, Pa., 1974)

Johnson, C. H. 'Economic Change and Artisan Discontent: The Tailors' History, 1800–48' in Price (1975)

Jordan, Z. A. (Ed.) *Karl Marx: Economy, Class and Social Revolution.* (London, 1972)

Kindleberger, C. P. *Economic Growth in France and Britain 1851–1950* (Cambridge, Mass., 1964)

Krader, L. Editor's Introduction to *EN*

Krieger, L. 'Marx and Engels as Historians' in *Journal of the History of Ideas* 14 (1953), pp. 381–403

Kuczynski, J. *The Rise of the Working Class* (London, 1967)

Lefebvre, G. *The Coming of the French Revolution* (New York, 1947)

Levine, N. *The Tragic Deception: Marx Contra Engels* (Oxford and Santa Barbara, Calif., 1975)

Lichtheim, G. *A Short Hisory of Socialism* (London 1975)
Marxism (London, 1961)

Lucas, C. 'Nobles, Bourgeois and the Origins of the French Revolution' in *Past and Present* 60, pp. 84–126

McLellan, D. *Karl Marx: His Life and Thought* (London, 1973)
The Thought of Karl Marx (London, 1971)

Maguire, J. M. *Marx's Paris Writings: An Analysis* (Dublin, 1972)

Mandel, E. *The Formation of the Economic Thought of Karl Marx* (London, 1971)

Mann, G. *The History of Germany Since 1789* (London, 1968)

Martin, N. A. 'Marxism, Nationalism and Russia' in *Journal of the History of Ideas* 29 (1968), pp. 231–52

Mayer, H. 'Marx, Engels and the Politics of the Peasantry' in *Etudes de Marxologie* 3 (1960), pp. 91–152 – Cahiers de l'ISEA, Series S, No. 6

Moore, B. *Social Origins of Dictatorship and Democracy* (Harmondsworth, 1973)

Morgan, L. H. *Ancient Society* (Chicago, 1877)

Moss, B. H. 'Parisian Producers Associations (1830–51): The Socialism of Skilled Workers' in Price (1975) pp. 87–114

Nairn, T. 'The Fateful Meridian', in *New Left Review* 60 (February–March 1970), pp. 3–35

Noyes, P. R. *Organisation and Revolution* (Princeton, N.J., 1966)

Palmade, G. *French Capitalism in the Nineteenth Century* (Newton Abbot, Devon, 1972)

Plamenatz, J. P. *Karl Marx's Philosophy of Man* (Oxford, 1975)
    Man and Society 2 Volumes (London, 1963)

Poulantzas, N. *Political Power and Social Class* (London, 1973)

Price, R. (Ed.) *Revolution and Reaction* (London, 1975)
    The French Second Republic (London, 1972)

Rubel, M. *Karl Marx devant le bonapartisme* (Paris, 1960)

Rubel, M. and Manale, M. *Marx Without Myth* (Oxford, 1975)

Sanderson, J. B. *An Interpretation of the Political Ideas of Marx and Engels* (London, 1969)

Schweinitz, K. de *Industrialisation and Democracy* (New York, 1964)

Shapiro, G. 'The Many Lives of Georges Lefebvre' in *American Historical Review*, January 1967, pp. 503–14

Soboul, A. *The Parisian Sans-culottes and the French Revolution 1793–4* (Oxford, 1964)

Taylor, A. J. P. Ed. *The Communist Manifesto* (Harmondsworth, 1967)

Taylor, C. *Hegel* (Cambridge, 1975)

Taylor, G. V. 'Non-capitalist Wealth and the Origins of the French Revolution' in *American Historical Review* January 1967, pp. 469–96

Tilly, C. and Lees, L. H. 'The People of June, 1848' in Price (1975) pp. 170–209

Vincent, J. *The Formation of the Liberal Party 1857–1868* (London, 1966)

Walter, G. *Histoire des paysans de France* (Paris, 1963)

Webb, R. K. *Modern England* (London, 1969)

Woodward, E. L. *The Age of Reform* (Oxford, 1954)

Zeldin, T. *The Political System of Napoleon III* (London, 1958)

Index

alienation, 15, 20, 26, 142, 144–6, 159, 225, 227, 233
anarchism, 164ff.
army, 61, 63, 64, 84, 96, 103, 110, 112, 119, 127, 133ff., 176, 178, 187–8, 193–4, 202
artisans, 42ff., 51, 52, 55–6, 60, 79ff., 87, 105ff., 133, 179, 181, 190, 193
attitudes (of worker), 150ff.
authoritarianism, 165ff.

Bakunin, M., 164ff., 212, 232
Barrot, O., 79, 80, 92
Berlin, I., 121
Bismarck, Count Otto von, 133ff., 167, 189, 193ff.
Blanc, L., 83
Blanqui, A., 73, 139
Bonaparte, Louis-Napoleon, 8, ch. 4 passim, 115, 116, 121, 124, 130, ch. 7 passim
Bonapartism, 136, 201ff.
bourgeoisie, 17–27, 28–31, 33, 37, 39, 40, 42, 43, 46, 52, 53, 54, 55, 58, 60, 61, 62, 66, 67, 68, 72, 75, 78, 79, 82, 84, 86, 88, 91, 92, 95, 102, 103, 105ff., 108, 109, 110, 111, 114, 115, 119, 124, 126, 127, 131, 132, 133ff., 153, 158, ch. 7 passim
bureaucracy, 6, 7, 43, 57, 61, 63, 66, 81, 110, 112, 119, 190ff., 202

Camphausen, L., 49, 53, 59, 60, 61, 62, 63, 65
capital (capitalism, capitalists), 14, 16, 25, 35ff., 74, 106ff., ch. 6 passim, 209, 219
caste, governing, 176ff., 197ff.
Cavaignac, L.-E., 79, 85, 91, 98
Changarnier, N., 103, 127
Chartism, 154, 178, 180
Childe, V. G., 211–2
civil society, 6, 7, 14ff., 20, 21, 142–4, 232
class, 15ff., 23, 28, 44, 58, 83, 102, 109, 112, 118, 185, 187, 204, 222ff.; middle class, 174, 175, 177ff., 195–6, 197; middle classes (middle estates) 41ff., 99
coalition, 50, 65, 68–9, 83, 94, 99, 176f.
Cobban, A., 33ff., 98, 105, 184, 186
Cohen, P. S., 116
communal property, communal society, ch. 8 passim; Russian commune 212, 217ff.
Commune of Paris (1871), 198, 200, 231, 233
communism, communist society, 16, 88, ch. 8 passim
conquest, 25, 208ff.
consolidation, policy of, 54ff., 82, 92, 131
constitution (foundations), 7, 32, 56ff., 59, 60, 75, 77, 82, 86, 175f.
Corn Law Repeal, 153–4, 174ff.
Crédit Mobilier, 182ff.
Crimean War, 176, 186, 192
criminal, 226, 229, 235

De Luna, F. A., 73, 85, 91, 92, 95, 98
democracy, 51, 67, 81, 90, 95, 122, 135, 195, 201
Disraeli, B., 180
division of labour, 21, 120, 224ff., 237ff.

Economist, The, 104
Edwards, S., 106, 185–6
Empire, Second (French), 80, 172, 181ff., 197ff.
Engels, F., 9, 11, 12, 43, 69ff., 77, 99, 100, 116, 122, 129, 133, 168, 169, 189, 195, 199, ch. 8 passim, 240
enthusiasm, 44–5, 83, 86, 126, 131–2
ethnography, 205, 211ff.
Evans, M., 99, 115, 173, 231, 242
exchange, ch. 6 passim
exploitation, 14, 139ff.

factory legislation, 151ff., 196, 198
fatalism, 121ff.

Fernbach, D., 180f.
Fleischer, H., 117
force, 63, 147ff., 164, 169
Fould, A., 80, 89, 97
Frederick William IV, 8, 10, 48, 49, 67, 190ff.
free action and necessity, 121ff.
Free Trade Treaty, 184
Freiligrath, F., 165

Giddens, A., 28
Gentile system, 214ff., 222ff., 237ff.
Gladstone, W. E., 180
Görres, J., 51
Guizot, F., 173

hallucination, 82, 145
Hamerow, T. S., 49ff., 105, 190ff.
Hansemann, D., 49, 53, 63, 65, 66, 67, 69
Harstick, H.-P., 211
Hegel, G. W. F., 6ff., 27, 59, 145–6, 206ff., 215, 216, 232
Heimann, E., 14–15
Heinzen, K., 24, 25, 43
Henry VII, 178
Henry VIII, 149, 173
Herbert, S., 177
Herzen, A., 212
Hobsbawm, E., 211, 214, 216, 238
Holborn, H., 50, 190ff
Hunt, R. N., 11, 42, 99, 163, 165

idealism, 181, 206ff
ideology, 21ff., 63, 143ff., 161, 221
illusion, 21, 45, 82, 84, 126, 132, 145
individualism, individuals, 15ff., 207, 213ff., 224ff., 232ff.
industry, industrialisation, 78, 105, 107, 108, 112, 136, ch. 7 *passim*
instrumentalism, 109, 116ff., 123
interest, 21, 60, 75, 111, 116, 124ff., 135, 136, 185, 187, 225ff., 238
intermediate groups, 40ff., 74–5, 108–9
International Workingmen's Association ('First International'), 156, 163, 164, 171, 178, 188, 200

Jacobins, 8ff., 14, 51, 80, 139
Johnson, C. H., 106–7
Jones, E., 100, 102, 178
Junkers, 50, 107, 174, 190ff

Krader, L., 211, 226
Kuczynski, J., 50–1, 107

labour-power, 141ff.
Lamartine, A. de, 83
landowners, 31, 50, 55–8, 78, 108, 118, 151–5, 164, 173ff., 190, 219
Lassalle, F., 74, 167, 186, 192
Ledru-Rollin, A., 94, 128
Lefebvre, G., 126
Legitimist Party, 94, 96, 104, 117ff., 182, 189
Lenin, V. I., 99
Lichtheim, G., 10, 164
Louis-Philippe, 92
Lucas, C., 35–6

McLellan, D., 70, 138, 188, 220, 231
Malthus, T. R., 155
Mann, G., 49ff., 67, 167, 190ff.
Manteuffel, O. von, 190f.
Marx-Aveling, E., 116
materialism, 205ff.
Maurer, G. L., 212
Metternich, Prince, 49, 51, 70
Mikhailovsky, N. K., 219
Moore, J. B., 34ff., 173ff., 179
Morgan, L., 211ff., 230ff., 235ff.
Moss, B., 107
motivation, 113ff.

Nairn, T., 178–81
Napoleon, 12, 19, 24, 89, 110, 111
National Group, ch. 4 *passim*
nationalism, 69ff., 165
necessity, 121ff., 130, 160ff., 220–1
Noyes, P. H., 51–2

Oligarchy, 137, 176ff., 197
Ollivier, E., 189
Order, Party of, 80, 88, 94–103, 116, 122, 201
Orleanist Party, 94, 96, 104, 117, 182
overviews, 24ff., 76, 109, 223

Palmade, G., 33ff., 78ff., 182ff.
Palmerston, Lord, 153, 177ff.
peasants, 11, 33, 38, 45, 50–1, 55, 74–5, 79ff., 86, 91–9, 108, 111, 130–4, 177ff., 181ff., 187ff., 190, 193, 218
Peel, Sir R., 176–7
petty bourgeoisie, 41ff., 80, 88–9, 92, 95–6, 99, 108, 115, 127, 130–4, 136

politics, abolition of, 59–60, 166, 215, 221ff.

possession, possessory right, 213ff.

power, 25, 58, 64, 88, 108–12, 119, 125, 133–6, 144, 149–50, 175, 182, 190, 196ff., 226ff., 235; abdication, delegation and renunciation of, 197ff.

Price, R., 78ff., 87, 95, 109

process, 64ff., 77, 80ff., 93–5, 102, 130

Proudhon, P.-J., 33, 156

Raspail, F.-V., 89

'Red' Party, 79–80, 91, 94

Reform Acts (1832 and 1867), 172–4, 180

representation, 22ff., 44, 48, 54, 83, 109, 111, 177, 199ff., 233

repression, 22ff., 53, 55, 98, 112, 143, 182, 187–8, 199ff., 223

republic, republicans, 10, 79ff., 86ff., 91ff., 97, 100ff., 109–10, 124, 132, 172, 189, 199, 201

revolution, 20, 43, 44, 57, 106, 114, 122, 158ff., 178, 181, 197, 219, 232; French (1789), 31–9, 54–5, 59, 61, 73, 74, 126, 131, 173; French (1848) ch. 4 *passim*, 131; German (1848) ch. 3 *passim*, 131

Rothschild family, 184ff., 196

Rubel, M., 133, 183, 188, 189, 200

Ruge, A., 8

Russell, Lord John, 175

Schneider, E., 184ff.

Shapiro, G., 32–3, 36

Smith, A., 15

Soboul, A., 35, 38

state, ch. 1 *passim*, 56, 58, 166–8, ch. 7 *passim*, 214, 219, 223ff.; dominant, 7, 13, 198ff., 223ff.; pretentious, 13, 22ff., 198ff., 223ff.; servile, 7, 8, 12, 13, 22ff., 198ff., 223ff.

Stirner, M. (pseud. J. K. Schmidt) 16–18, 23

strategy, 61, 99, 151, 163ff., 185, 201

structure (system), 14ff., 25ff., 39, 64ff., 80ff., 139ff., 152, 161ff.

surplus value, 141ff.

Taylor, C., 161ff.

Taylor, G. V., 33ff.

Thiers, L.-A., 109

Tilly, C. and Lees, L. H., 87, 106–7

Tories, 119, 135, 173ff.

trades unions, 150ff., 155ff., 163, 179

Vincent, J., 197

wages, 141, 152, 155ff., 164

Wakefield, E. G., 148

Weitling, W., 138

Weston, J., 156–7

Weydemeyer, J., 77

Whigs, 135, 173ff.

William I, 133, 191ff.

workers (proletariat), 20, 27, 40, 42–3, 45–6, 50, 52, 59–61, 79ff., 86–7, 91–9, 105ff., 114–5, 124, 128, 130ff., ch. 6 *passim*, 178ff., 182, 187ff., 196, 219

Zasulich, V., 217ff.

Zeldin, T., 182, 186ff.